AF228760

DEMOCRATIC DEALS

DEMOCRATIC DEALS

A Defense of Political Bargaining

Melissa Schwartzberg and
Jack Knight

Harvard University Press

CAMBRIDGE, MASSACHUSETTS | LONDON, ENGLAND | 2024

Library of Congress Cataloging-in-Publication Data

Names: Schwartzberg, Melissa, 1975– author. | Knight, Jack, 1952– author.

Title: Democratic deals : a defense of political bargaining / Melissa Schwartzberg and Jack Knight.

Description: Cambridge, Massachusetts ; London, England : Harvard University Press, 2024. | Includes bibliographical references and index.

Identifiers: LCCN 2023034806 | ISBN 9780674279322 (cloth)

Subjects: LCSH: Political science—Decision making. | Democracy. | Power (Social sciences) | Deliberative democracy. | Negotiation—Political aspects. | Democracy—United States.

Classification: LCC JF1525.D4 S45 2024 | DDC 321.8—dc23/eng/20231120

LC record available at https://lccn.loc.gov/2023034806

For my dad, Barry Schwartzberg; my father-in-law,
Howard Jones; and my *Doktorvater*, Bernard Manin

—*Melissa Schwartzberg*

For my wife, Margaret Louise Brown

—*Jack Knight*

CONTENTS

DEMOCRATIC DEALS

Introduction

In the aftermath of the 2008 financial crisis, President Barack Obama urged Congress to pass legislation reforming the credit card industry. Developed by consumer protection advocate Elizabeth Warren, and commanding wide popular support, this legislation aimed to prevent companies from engaging in what were widely regarded as unfair practices. These practices included arbitrarily raising interest rates without notice and trapping consumers into paying late fees by changing the payment deadlines each month.

H.R. 627 was introduced by Rep. Carolyn Maloney (D-NY) in January 2009 and passed the House by a vote of 357–70 on April 30. This bill allowed rate increases on existing balances if cardholders were thirty days late in making a minimum payment. The original Senate version of the bill, introduced by Banking Committee Chairman Sen. Christopher Dodd (D-CT), would have banned rate increases on existing balances regardless of missed payments. But once the House had passed the bill, Dodd struck a deal with Sen. Richard Shelby (R-AL), the top Republican on the Banking Committee, to allow credit card companies to raise interest rates if cardholders were sixty days late in making a minimum payment.[1] The Dodd-Shelby amended bill was expected to receive enough Republican votes to pass the Senate. In his weekly address to the nation on May 10, President Obama indicated that he was eager to have the legislation sent to him for signature before Memorial Day.

Enter Sen. Tom Coburn (R-OK). Abundantly aware of President Obama's ambition to sign this into law within days, and of the bill's overwhelming popularity, Senator Coburn proposed on May 12 an amendment to the credit card bill allowing visitors to national parks to carry loaded and concealed guns, a measure he had sought for two years to get through Congress. "Timing is everything in politics," Coburn said to reporters.[2] The bill passed the Senate 90–5.

Some House Democrats balked, refusing to vote for the amended bill. Sam Farr (D-CA) said, "This is a credit card bill. And there's no purpose in the credit card bill to have a gun bill. We talk a lot about pork in this House. I think this is an act of chicken."[3] But a Senate Democratic aide acknowledged the inevitability of the move: "This is something a robust majority is going to have to deal with. This is the only way for the minority to get votes on bills they think are important."[4] The amended bill passed 279–147, and went to the White House for signature.

There is nothing unusual about this example of legislative politics, except perhaps the extent to which the aim of credit card reform had bipartisan and popular support. The law emerged from interparty and intraparty bargaining, from its general contours down to the fine-grained details. Senate rules permitting nongermane amendments enabled Coburn's last-minute maneuvering, the success of which derived in part from the temporary bargaining advantage given to Republicans by President Obama's impatience to sign the bill.

It is a profoundly ordinary piece of legislation.

But is it justified? That is, should democracies enforce laws produced by a bargaining process marked by asymmetrical power?

Despite the ubiquity of bargains in political life, contemporary political theory provides remarkably little guidance as to how we should think about such cases, because it tends to treat the mechanism of bargaining as suspect. Take the influential literature on deliberative democracy. Deliberative democrats argue that to be justified, laws must emerge from the public exchange of reasons among free and equally situated persons. Political decisions should be grounded on principles that everyone can reasonably accept, or that no one could reasonably reject, constraining the arguments that can be offered in the context of deliberation. To be sure, most deliberative theorists recognize that this model serves as a "regulative ideal," and that real-world political decision-making will rarely satisfy it. Yet even as a heuristic, it departs so sharply from the horse-trading under asymmetrical power that characterizes legislative politics that it provides no guidance at all as to how one might distinguish between justified and unjustified political bargains within a democratic community.

In this book, we aim to do just that: to establish the conditions under which political bargaining in democratic communities might be justified. We will argue that democracy, at its core, is about treating members' interests equitably. On that basis, we will defend certain types of power asymmetries, and trade-offs among interests that emerge from them. But we also argue that democratic communities can and should set constraints on the bargains that such inequalities yield, just as they already do on private contracts. We will adapt these doctrines for democratic decision-making, and use them to shed light on the scope of permissible bargaining across and within political institutions, and between private actors and the state.

By taking up the study of democratic bargaining, we return to an older tradition of political theorizing. Postwar pluralists such as Robert Dahl, Charles Lindblom, and David Truman, who shaped political science at the dawn of the behavioral revolution, took bargaining to be the central means by which social groups and parties produced policy, particularly in the United States. Indeed, in his landmark *A Preface to Democratic Theory*, Dahl wrote that in America, "Decisions are made by endless bargaining; perhaps in no other national system in the world is bargaining so basic a component of the political process" (Dahl 2006, 150). The ambition of the pluralists was not merely explanatory, but normative—Dahl, most famously, sought to defend polyarchical regimes on the grounds that even small groups could make their claims heard and make elected officials at least partially responsive.

Other political theorists, notably Sheldon Wolin, rejected pluralism as conservative and conventionalist, failing to challenge preexisting distributions of power. In later years, Dahl acknowledged that they had a point, and that in his earlier work he had been insufficiently attentive to inequalities deriving from race, education, and information, and other socioeconomic conditions (Dahl 2006, xix–xx). But with the turn from pluralism, a wedge emerged between normative political theory and the rest of political science. Political scientists across subfields drew on these early insights to provide theoretical support for empirical research on topics as diverse as legislative coalitions, judicial decision-making, and the origins and termination of war. Yet political theorists mostly migrated away from what Wolin characterized as "scientistic complacency" (Wolin 1969), some turning to the close study of canonical works, others drawn to the hope of participatory democracy and then to deliberative democracy, and still others to the vision of a just society advanced by John Rawls.

Rawls himself recognized the importance of bargaining over legislation. In the initial stages of the four-stage process by which the society creates laws and institutions, bargaining is excluded on the grounds of justice (Rawls 1971, 25). However, in a response to a critique by Jürgen Habermas—who accused him of relegating democratic decision-making to an inferior status beneath liberal rights (Habermas 1995)—Rawls explained that he did not intend to claim that the shape of legislation would be entirely given by the principles of justice. Rather, once agents choose the two principles in the original position (the first stage), and draw up constitutional norms in a constitutional convention in light of those principles (the second stage), they create legislation on that basis in a third stage. (The fourth stage features judicial review to ensure coherence of ordinary law with the constitution through public reason.) In that third stage, citizens and legislators may vote their "comprehensive views" within those bounds and when questions of justice are not at stake; they need not justify these votes by public reason (Rawls 1993, 235). Crucially, in a footnote in the reply to Habermas, Rawls wrote that at this third stage there is an additional, "formidable complication" that he "can only mention here":

> "Namely, that there is an important distinction between legislation dealing with constitutional essentials and basic justice, and legislation dealing with political bargaining between the various interests in civil society which takes place through their representatives. The latter kind of legislation is required to have a framework of

fair bargaining both in the legislature and in civil society. The complication is formidable because it is a difficult task to spell out the criteria needed for drawing this distinction and illustrating it by instructive cases." (Rawls 1995, 152)[5]

Our difficult task is to spell out the criteria for democratic bargaining, and to illustrate them.

Bargaining and the Equitable Treatment of Interests

At its core, bargaining is a process by which multiple actors produce a collective decision over the terms of their joint activity and the distribution of its benefits. The bargaining process can take different forms. Some will be short-term interactions that are characterized by explicit negotiations resulting in a specific agreement. This is the form that most legislative bargains take. Others will involve longer-term interactions in which the actors engage in a sequence of give-and-take strategies that serve to continuously redefine the terms of their ongoing activity. This is the form that interbranch conflicts over the interpretation and implementation of statutes commonly take.

Within the bargaining process, there are a number of strategies available to the actors as they seek to reach a decision. One feature distinguishing bargaining from other methods of decision-making is that the actors may use whatever advantages they may enjoy because of favorable asymmetries in power to influence the choices of the other actors. In any single bargaining interaction, various factors can determine relative bargaining power: the resources that the actors bring to the bargaining process; their previous bargaining experiences; the knowledge of the circumstances surrounding the joint activity; the institutional rules that govern the bargaining process; and their impatience to conclude an agreement, among others. The most important factors are those that affect the resources that are available to the actors in the event that bargaining is either lengthy and costly or ultimately unsuccessful. We can think of these as the existing resources that an actor might retain after the effort to achieve a bargain breaks down. Alternatively, we might think of them as the other options available to the actors if they are left to conclude a bargain with some other party. Commonly, the greater the resources available to the actors if bargaining fails, the greater their bargaining power and, thus, the greater their influence over the collective decision. This highlights the fundamental importance of identifying the sources of bargaining power for assessing the legitimacy of bargains—that is, whether they should be enforceable—as well as for our efforts to define the appropriate institutional constraints on its use.

In this book, we are primarily interested in asymmetric bargaining power, those resources that will typically give some parties a greater share of the benefits of the bargained-for outcome than others. Contemporary democratic theory flags both noninstrumental and instrumental reasons to be concerned about the unequal distribution of political power more generally. A standard worry from the noninstrumental, or "intrinsic," standpoint is that, in a democratic community, the unequal distribution of political power may reflect unequal respect for the members of the community. This disrespect is its own source of harm: it suggests that there are people whose interests matter less than those of others. Rawls characterized this as harm to the "social bases of self-respect" (Rawls 2001, 60). As relational egalitarians maintain, the unequal distribution of power in a community, particularly when such inequality means that comparably important interests are treated unequally, may also inhibit the formation of relationships of social equality crucial to sustaining a democratic society (Anderson 1999; Scheffler 2015; Kolodny 2014). Further, where decision-making power is unequally distributed, the norms generated might conduce to the benefits of some rather than to the good of the whole; the results would be inferior, on instrumental grounds, to those that would have been created under egalitarian distributions of power. Even if the norms did objectively promote the general welfare, if produced through an inegalitarian process, disadvantaged members might have good reason to doubt that their own interests were adequately protected by those norms, meaning that the results would not be publicly accepted as instrumentally superior.[6] At the limit, members who observe themselves to have less power in a political community might doubt that its norms command their obedience; at the limit, those subject to stigmatizing and grave forms of inequalities might reasonably believe that their allegiance is no longer required (Shelby 2016).

We recognize the force of these arguments. But our strategy in this book will be different. First, our aim in this work is not to provide a full philosophical account of the grounds on which democracies might be justified relative to other regimes, nor the conditions under which democratic dictates might be authoritative and legitimate, that is, providing citizens with moral grounds to obey the laws and making it permissible for the state to coercively enforce them. We assume such arguments are available, but this is not our project. Our conception of democracy is simply that it is a regime that secures citizens' interests through enabling citizens to have an equal say over public issues where these interests are at stake, and more specifically, over the representatives who purport to advance these interests. It is possible that another type of regime in certain cases might advance the interests of its members better than a democracy would, but we do not aim to defend democracy against all comers, nor to work out a full justification of how this account trumps others.

In light of that approach, rather than developing an idealized account of egalitarian political relations, we attend to the conditions under which asymmetries of power arise and the restricted circumstances under which they might be justified in a democracy from the standpoint of citizens' interests. It is important that we do not pretend that equality can obtain where it almost surely will not. Specifically, we doubt that equality of bargaining power is achievable, and, even if it were, that it would characterize a normative ideal. In practically any context, characterizing bargaining power as "equal" would occlude other inegalitarian dimensions of power in that domain. The consequence of this neglect may be significant, because it may lead us to believe that the resulting outcomes are perfectly fair, when they in fact derive from unidentified power imbalances. This is a long-standing concern. In *The Power Elite*, C. Wright Mills caustically noted that equality of bargaining power seems "wholly fair and even honorable, but in fact what is one man's honorable balance is often another's unfair imbalance. Ascendant groups of course tend readily to proclaim a just balance of power, a true harmony of interest, for they prefer their domination to be uninterrupted and peaceful" (Mills 1956, 246). The description of an institutional arrangement as securing equality of bargaining power and the balance of interests, he argued, merely smuggled in the evaluation of "the *status quo* as satisfactory or even good; the hopeful ideal of balance often masquerades as a description of fact" (Mills 1956, 246).

Rather than chasing elusive symmetries, we will argue that asymmetries in bargaining power are justified where they serve to protect members' fundamental interests. Specifically, we will use the concept of *equitable treatment of interests* to help us assess when these asymmetries undermine, and when they help to secure, fundamental interests.[7] Throughout this work, we take inequalities of bargaining power to be inescapable and sometimes salutary, and so we accept that political outcomes will reflect these asymmetries. But we take the equitable treatment of interests standard to be primarily a prospective one, designed to guard against efforts on the part of the powerful to entrench their interests and to secure their positions against renegotiation. One strategy we adopt to gain leverage on these issues is to examine the consequences of bargaining for the relative standing of permanent, vulnerable minorities. When we analyze a particular bargained-for piece of legislation, we aim to assess that legislation in terms of its long-term effects on the community's fundamental interests. Although we take this to be a minimal standard, it must suffice to ensure that vulnerable parties will be able to continue to advocate for their interests, and to have their fundamental interests remain immune from ordinary political bargaining.

The equitable treatment of interests plays an important role in this argument, and so requires some close attention. Let us begin by conceptualizing *treatment* (as opposed to concern or consideration), before turning to *equitable* (as opposed to equal), and then to a fuller examination of the concept of interests. As we will see, part of the challenge of democratic lawmaking rests in the inability to directly access "interests"; they are mediated through multiple agents and institutions. Even if democracy rests on individuals' judgment of their interests, these judgments are themselves a mediation; they are then further mediated by individual representatives' conceptualization of the aggregate interests of their constituents, and followed by competition among representatives to satisfy competing interests. As a result, it is likely that many interests will remain unsatisfied. The best we can hope for is that interests will be *treated* equitably by agents in the bargaining process, and so we design political institutions so as to facilitate this aim and to regulate departures, rather than excluding some interests from the democratic process altogether. Broadly speaking, this means that legislative institutions in particular should induce representatives to weigh their constituents' ordinary interests (that is, their policy preferences) equally; as we will discuss in a moment, a majoritarian legislature can accomplish this aim under certain conditions.

The challenge of accessing interests directly is also part of why we use the language of treatment rather than "consideration" or "concern." The appeal of the language of treatment is its specificity and its transparency. The vast case law around disparate and differential treatment, in which similarly situated persons are subject to different behavior or actions, suggests that treatment is often behaviorally observable, meaning that relevant actors can reliably assess whether or not certain interests have been subordinated. Moreover, inequitable treatment need not be rooted in animus, or bad motives. Although in certain legal contexts, to succeed on a claim of disparate treatment, plaintiffs must demonstrate "intent" to discriminate, among the insights from defenders of structural approaches to antidiscrimination law is that even well-intentioned actors may harbor unconscious biases, or operate within the context of workplace structures that inhibit opportunities for members of protected groups without any particular supervisor engaging in intentional discrimination (Bagenstos 2006).[8] This also gives us reason to believe that the broader realization of equal—or, in our language, equitable—treatment should not depend upon altering the dispositions of individual actors, because disparate treatment of interests may arise despite such agents' good intentions. These insights support the view that we might be able to evaluate whether a group's interests have been treated equitably both by scrutinizing the bargaining process and by examining its outcomes, without peering into the hearts and minds of actors. This will prove an important feature of the "structural due process" approach we defend in Chapter 4. By contrast, whether a standard of equal "concern" or "consideration" might have been met is less easy to discern, in part because the answer would need to depend upon the dispositions of the agents.[9] A group alleging disparate *concern* for its interests, absent evidence of disparate impact (that is, with respect to political outcomes), would need to probe the motivations of actors or the actors' subjective views of this group to substantiate these claims, unless concern merely entailed treatment. The language of "consideration" is even more opaque; it is hard to know whether consideration is synonymous with concern, and thus dependent on the motivation of agents, or with "treatment," and thus characterized by the assessment of interests.[10]

Finally, why do we use the language of *equitable* rather than *equal*? The intuition is similar to the familiar one that treating interests equally may not yield fairness, or even substantive equality, when such interests are unequal in importance. Just as we prefer the language of "treatment" to "concern" or "consideration"—in part because we are concerned with the effects of politicians' behavior rather than the exercise of moral duties—we prefer the term "equitable" to "equal." "Equitable" reflects our view that it is appropriate to prioritize some members' fundamental interests over other, more numerous members' ordinary interests.

By using the term "equitable," it may seem that we elide a distinction between *democratic* bargaining and *fair* bargaining. Most previous accounts analyze bargaining in terms of some criterion of justice or fairness, focusing on the substantive outcome of the bargain and asking whether the bargained-for distribution of benefits satisfies the posited normative criterion. Of course, whether a bargain is just or fair is an important question, one that any democratic society would want to take seriously. In fact, we would argue that the democratic process is the best venue available to specify the conditions for a given community about what constitutes a fair bargain. But because we believe democracy and justice are separable, and that democracy can never guarantee the achievement of justice or fairness, we believe we need a different strategy to justify political bargains as such. We must offer criteria by which we can assess the acceptability of bargains that flow directly from democratic commitments. Key among those democratic criteria is that all citizens must have an equal opportunity to select and sanction the agents who will advocate for their interests in the legislative domain.

Finally, let us peer more closely into the concept of interests. Our basic model of political life features actors who are motivated by the pursuit of their interests, though these interests may be self-regarding, oriented toward the partial interest of their own community or group, or, to adopt the Tocquevillian language, "self-interest rightly understood," reflecting the relationship between their own well-being and the common interest. We assume citizens vary in what interests they take to be most significant, although presumably certain interests in their well-being—access to food and shelter and health care and education for their children—will trump other concerns, and so there is a natural distinction between significant and less significant interests from their own vantage point. Indeed, from their subjective perspective, they may place voting in the latter category. However, from the standpoint of democracy, interests in political participation, and in the broader conditions necessary for effective participation (which includes those interests that citizens likely regard as significant), are *fundamental interests*. Within democratic institutions, the primary aim is to facilitate trade-offs among what we will term *ordinary interests*, which include much of what is typically characterized as policy preferences.

The fundamental interest in political participation manifests itself most significantly in equal voting power. Equal voting power, the "equal say," serves as an instrument by which citizens can advance their interests on equal terms (Christiano 2008, 95). We take the ballot to be the primary means by which citizens communicate their interests—ordinary and fundamental alike—to their representatives and the community as a whole. Obviously, today citizens typically vote for representatives rather than for policies directly, so we assume their ballots reflect their judgment of which party in general, or which specific partisan representative, will better advance their interests, however these interests are construed.[11] Note that this account assumes that citizens are best situated to know their own (individual) interests, and that they can express them through the ballot. If we seriously doubt that citizens are capable of judging these interests, we are skeptical that democracy can be justified. We follow a great tradition in this respect, primarily but not exclusively through pragmatism. Dewey, notably, defended the ability of citizens to know best where the "shoe pinches," if he did concede—as we do—that representatives often better know how to fix the shoe (Dewey 1954, 207). Du Bois, similarly, argued that citizens were best situated to know the harms they faced and that the value of the ballot rested in its use to enable citizens to communicate these harms (Du Bois 1999, 83–84). Other traditions—not least utilitarianism—share this conception of citizens as having the fundamental capacity to know their own interests and to communicate them.

Because the ballot constitutes the key means of conveying ordinary interests, equal voting power among citizens is the most important substantive constraint on bargaining within a democracy. To be sure, a set of other liberal rights in freedom of expression and assembly may also constitute such constraints, but democracies vary in their characterization of those rights and their scope; such rights are, appropriately, subject to constitutional bargaining. By contrast, equal voting power is a fundamental interest that cannot be subject to limitations or trade-offs, whether in the domain of ordinary political bargaining or constitutional bargaining.[12] Encroachments on equal voting power—efforts at disenfranchisement, voter suppression, or exclusion—constitute prima facie violations of democracy. Likewise, partisan gerrymandering—which aims to diminish the responsiveness of parties to citizens' interests—and campaign finance systems that distort representatives' behaviors in favor of special interest groups or wealthy donors will undermine the equitable treatment of interests.[13]

Insofar as equitable treatment of interests relies on equal voting power, it also requires majority rule as a default mechanism. The standard justification of majority rule within social-choice theory is provided by May's theorem, which demonstrates that majority rule is the unique voting rule that is decisive, anonymous, neutral, and positively responsive (May 1952). Majority rule treats votes and alternatives equally; it is unbiased in favor of particular voters (anonymity) and unbiased in terms of alternatives (neutrality). A voting rule that would weigh more heavily the preferences of a particular minority group, or offer them a veto, would violate anonymity; a voting rule biased in favor of a particular alternative, such as a supermajority rule that produces a status-quo bias, would violate neutrality. Positive responsiveness entails a "knife-edge" result (McGann 2006, 18), inasmuch as a shift of one vote from one alternative to another can change the outcome. Combined with anonymity, this means that any voter may be decisive; put differently, majority rule gives to voters ex ante an equal probability of having "their way" (Rae 1969). This, of course, is a formalistic way of characterizing equality, one that may obscure deep substantive inequalities of the sort that we hope democracy would seek to redress. But the wider argument on behalf of majority rule—put synoptically, that it weighs the choice of each individual equally—still retains importance. Insofar as individuals' votes reflect what they take to be their interests, majoritarianism constitutes a mechanism to ensure that these ordinary interests in policy outcomes receive equal weight. In a moment, however, we will discuss how the fundamental interests of minorities may outweigh such ordinary interests, and how these fundamental interests might be protected institutionally.

The commitment to equal voting power helps to justify three different forms of asymmetrical bargaining power in a representative system: (1) between majority parties or coalitions and minority parties or coalitions reflecting popular support, (2) between representatives and constituents, and (3) between party leadership and rank-and-file members. First, political power derives (optimally) from the underlying distribution of preferences in the electorate. The value of an aggregative system depends upon the capacity of the ballot to serve as a means by which individuals can advance their interests. In elections, citizens choose among parties that compete to represent their interests. When the allocation of seats to parties in a legislature basically reflects the underlying distribution of votes (understood as the expression of interests), the resulting asymmetries of power are *pro tanto* justifiable: they are a means of weighing interests equally. However, the justification is contingent upon certain constraints both on bargaining strategies and on those outcomes that might harm the fundamental interests of members. Institutions that distort this distribution of votes (for instance, through unequal districting) will be generally unjustified in the legislative context. This is part of what will support, on our account, legislative supremacy; it is the body that most directly reflects citizens' preferences and conceptions of their interest.

Second, representatives qua agents possess more political power than ordinary citizens, but this power is justified by reference to the benefits these asymmetries produce for both the fundamental and ordinary interests of citizens. A large, heterogeneous community will feature plural and competing interests; there will be conflicts over practically every domain, and the question is how to resolve such conflicts from within a democratic standpoint. Negotiation among these interests in the creation of law demands expertise and sophistication in bargaining.[14] We have already argued that we must presume as democratic bedrock that citizens themselves are the best judges of their own interests. But this does not mean that citizens are the best advocates for these interests, particularly when the venue demands expertise and sophistication in bargaining. As such, the basic justification of representation on our approach is that in contemporary democratic communities, citizens better protect their important interests through deputizing representatives to bargain on their behalf than they would were they to advocate for them directly.[15] Further, ensuring that prospective ordinary legislation will survive constitutional scrutiny (to ensure consistency with fundamental interests), and that the law is drafted in such a way to narrow the scope of interpretation and implementation by judges and agencies alike, requires relatively sophisticated lawmakers. But such agents must be constrained by the prospect of electoral sanction to secure the ordinary interests of members.[16]

We rely on a model of representation grounded in a principal-agent framework. Broadly, on this account, principals (voters) select agents (representatives) to advance their interests in a bargaining setting, subject to the sanction of principals (through elections). As in any principal–agent relationship, representatives may have incentives to shirk, and to raise the costs for principals of monitoring their actions. The electoral sanction is necessary but often insufficient for constituents to exert control over their representatives; representatives may promote narrowly partisan or personal interests that do not track their constituents' interests, and may sometimes do so with impunity. In principle, the ability of voters to know their own interests enables them to judge whether their representatives have acted in their benefit, but the opacity and complexity of representatives' behavior may undermine voters' ability to evaluate the representatives' actions and sanction them accordingly. As a result, we will argue for institutional reforms that strengthen the incentives of representatives to promote constituents' interests (partially by rendering their behavior more transparent), and that would distribute more widely the prospective gains from legislation, consistent with the equitable treatment of interests.

In contemporary representative democracies, political parties condition the behavior of representatives. This generates the third form of broadly justified power asymmetries: the role of parties, and specifically party leadership, in securing legislation that is responsive to citizens' interests. In electoral competitions, parties identify and defend certain interests as particularly important; campaigns enable citizens to judge which candidates and parties are more likely to promote their own interests. Parties inform their members of the costs and benefits of prospective legislation; indeed, no less a theorist of deliberation than Habermas noted that voters "can perceive their own interests only in light of pregeneralized interest positions" provided by parties (Bohman and Rehg 1997, 60). Conflict among parties sharpens disagreement, reducing the scope of alternatives and identifying the key points of contestation. Yet the ability of parties to generate benefits consistent with the equitable treatment of interests depends to a large extent upon the role of leadership, and hence upon disparities in power between leaders and rank-and-file members. Although we argue that the use of threats and offers by leaders in intraparty bargaining should be subject to institutional regulation, the significant value of parties cannot be realized absent such asymmetries.

These are the three important sources of power asymmetries that we believe to be consistent with democratic decision-making. The obvious objection is that in any system that empowers a majority over a minority, the preferences of the members of the minority are likely to be neglected, and so no system that yields asymmetrical power over political outcomes can be justifiable. Counterintuitively, we argue that bargaining under broadly majoritarian politics can more reliably secure the fundamental interests of persistent minorities than alternative mechanisms can. Insights from social-choice theory help to bolster this assertion. Specifically, the possibility of majority cycling—that is, the circumstance in which a majority of voters prefer x to y, a majority prefers y to z, but a majority prefers z to x—is often taken as a challenge to democratic decision-making insofar as such decision-making aims to identify a unique popular will (Riker 1982). That is, if outcomes are unstable, generated primarily by the manipulation of agenda-setters, there is no reason to regard any particular majority decision as reflecting such a will. To be sure, many democrats—including us—regard the notion of a popular will as chimerical, and argue that the value of democracy lies elsewhere (for example, in its egalitarianism). But more importantly, cycling can be an affirmative good for the protection of minority groups and their interests (Miller 1983). Such instability reflects the possibility of multiple potential coalitions, a condition that is often advantageous to minorities, including vulnerable minorities. If a defeated minority can form a new coalition and overturn a majority outcome—and if the members of a majority anticipate that the minority will be able to do so—the winning coalition has an incentive both to refrain from abuse and to offer the minority concessions (McGann 2006, 109).[17]

That said, we also believe it is a condition of democracy that minorities will not achieve their preferred outcomes most of the time. The equitable treatment of interests standard prescribes that the preferences of majorities will often prevail, due to the value of equal voting power. Decision rules that empower any minority to veto political decisions are in general inegalitarian and inconsistent with the equitable treatment of interests. However, insofar as they pertain to fundamental interests and particularly to the fundamental interests of vulnerable members, institutions and policies that shift bargaining power to minorities may occasionally be justified.

To illustrate, we begin with an especially challenging case, in which a vulnerable minority sees its interests treated as an object of bargaining. The Māori who live along the Whanganui River, the Whanganui Iwi, have for centuries made the river central to their lives. The 1840 Treaty of Waitangi between the British Crown and Māori chiefs, the founding document of New Zealand, secured for the Māori their claim to the river. Yet a 1903 statute vested the bed of the river in the Crown, depriving the Māori of control over the river; moreover, the river had come to be seen as a public resource, to which all had access. Against the assertion that they had knowingly surrendered their claims, the Māori people spent decades over the last century in litigation over their rights (Palmer 2022; Kingsbury 2002).

The Waitangi Tribunal, set up in 1975 to resolve these claims, emphasized in a 1999 report that the issue was not merely one of access to the river, but a claim to political agency.[18] Specifically, the Whanganui River enabled the formation of a collectivity. The first level was the *hapū*, kinship group or tribe, comprised of *whānau* (extended families). These *hapū* constituted regional groups depending upon their location on the river (upper, middle, or lower). They also collectively identified as a people or nation, *iwi*, which "served to remind the people of their common origins, that they might work together when confronting an outside force" (Waitangi Tribunal 1999, 2.5.1, 30). *The hapū* saw each other "both as separate groups and as a collective whole": the report emphasizes that the social and political structure of the community derived from the river, itself an ancestor, as a unifying agent. Moreover, other decisions, such as the Whanganui River water transfer to Lake Taupo and the Waikato River for a hydroelectricity power scheme, "violated the political harmony between the people of different places." A basic finding of the report is that *rangatiratanga*, control or authority, was not the "sum total of use or ownership rights but as expressive of political autonomy in the management of the total of the people's affairs" (Waitangi Tribunal 1999, 2.8.1, 50).

Most theorists concerned with the status of vulnerable minorities would argue that the aim of equitable treatment is to create conditions in which the chances of predictable injustice are minimized (as in Beitz 1989, 157). They would focus on the importance of the Whanganui River to the cultural practices of the community, and the injustice of the deprivation. But our focus is different, as our aim is to limn the scope of bargains that can be made compatible with democracy, rather than with justice. Although the deprivation of control over the river constituted a harm to Māori interests in many forms, such as property interests in eel weirs, the democratic constraint on bargaining must focus on their fundamental interests in ongoing political agency, their prospective capacity to secure equitable treatment. Insofar as the Whanganui

Iwi's future political agency depends upon their access to the river, legislation impeding their control raises the types of worries our account will aim to address.

From the democratic standpoint we defend here, whether a piece of legislation that might harm the interests of a given community is justified (and thus ought to be enforced by courts) depends upon the nature of these interests. Where these interests are not tied to democratic participation as such, we generally characterize them as available for bargaining, that is, for trading off against other competing ordinary interests, and as subject to the effects of unequal bargaining power within a legislature. This may mean that, for instance, a different community that has traditionally regarded a water source as central to their way of life may end up losing control over its use. This would, to be sure, constitute a harm to their interests, and potentially an unjust deprivation. A constitution might well codify their access to water sources in order to prevent these impediments. Moreover, this community would have reasons on the grounds of justice to protest the decision through democratic procedures. But from the standpoint of democracy as such, so long as the community's political agency is unharmed, matters such as this will not be permanently removed from the bargaining domain.

To see why, contrast this example of a vulnerable minority with a privileged one: the oceanfront homeowners of the Hamptons community of Wainscott, New York.[19] These homeowners greatly value their quiet, private, and unimpeded beach access. In the summers, the Hamptons face an energy shortage, and New York State has made offshore wind power central to its energy plan. The most direct location for a transmission cable, a four-mile journey, is on the Wainscott beach adjacent to the homeowners' property. The waterfront homeowners have begun to engage in collective action, arguing that their distinct way of life is oriented around the natural beauty of the beach, and that burying the cable beneath the stretch of sand next to their multimillion-dollar properties could subject the beach to erosion. They claim that their fundamental interests in their local culture will be harmed, and they propose that an alternate location in a state park in Montauk, requiring a twelve-mile journey for the transmission cable, should be chosen instead.

Our approach helps us to distinguish between the claims of the Whanganui Iwi and those of the Wainscotters. Although both constitute minorities, their respective bargaining power—their resources and their ability to achieve their ends—differs greatly. So not all minority interests should be secured against majority rule. One advantage of the bargaining approach we adopt is its ability to distinguish minority interests that merit protection on democratic grounds from those that do not. The prospective ability of the Whanganui Iwi to act politically depends upon river control; by contrast, the Wainscotters' ability to do so does not depend on their beach. From the democratic standpoint, we would be untroubled by a bargain that sacrificed this part of the Wainscott beach (if the cable did in fact doom it) to the state's interest in promoting clean energy. But now we need to see why we would think bargaining, rather than deliberation or compromise, constitutes a justifiable means of resolving such conflicts.

Bargaining, Deliberation, and Compromise

We defend the asymmetric distribution of power under certain conditions, at odds with the egalitarian commitments of many political theorists. However, many theorists would agree that realizing the value of representation—almost by definition—requires the assignment of a greater share of political power to some than to others. Those supporting democratic reforms to representation often advocate for procedures, typically deliberation or compromise, that seem to mitigate the effects of these asymmetries. But we need not replace bargaining with deliberation or compromise to achieve democratic ends. Instead, the ambition of our book—and what we believe should become a primary research agenda for democratic theory more generally—is the articulation and justification of a set of procedural and substantive constraints on the bargaining process.

It may seem implausible that bargaining can ever secure people's fundamental interests in the long term, even given constraints on both substantive and procedural forms of inequality. If bargaining outcomes derive from power asymmetries, and marginalized populations such as the Māori—by definition—lack power relative to other groups, it seems improbable that they could benefit. And if bargaining occurs within the context of a larger decision-making process, structured by majority voting, it would seem that minorities would be doubly disadvantaged—their interests neglected within the bargaining process, and their losses secured by a majority procedure. Although there is no guarantee that any given minority group will find their interests protected under a majoritarian system marked by bargaining, we will also argue that alternative mechanisms—specifically, deliberation and compromise—are less likely to succeed, in part because they depend to a greater extent on the willingness of groups to forfeit opportunities for advantage.

A key goal of deliberative democracy, at least in the Habermasian vein, is to enable the "unforced force of the better argument" to prevail, rather than allowing those with unequal resources to secure their interests against others.[20] The procedural goals of proponents of deliberative democrats vary. In its initial formulations, scholars such as Joshua Cohen (1989) defended at least as an ideal the search for consensus, marked by thick, reasoned agreement over outcomes. Others, such as Habermas and Bernard Manin (1987), argue that the legitimacy of outcomes, even if ultimately produced by a majority decision, depends primarily on the prior exchange of reasons. This is because, in their view, majority rule without reason-giving constitutes merely a mechanism of sublimated force, of the imposition of one will over another. Reason-giving mitigates power asymmetries: it provides those opposed to a proposal with an opportunity to try to persuade others, rather than merely being obliged to obey results with which they disagree.

But can deliberation effectively reduce power asymmetries?[21] There are standard arguments why we might doubt that deliberation can do so, both outside of and within legislatures. First, reasons do not present themselves; they are proffered by actors who vary in their argumentative skills. Such skills are not equally distributed, and they tend to track the educational and social advantages of their members (Sanders 1997). Second, insofar as deliberative assemblies or town halls constitute a means of conveying to legislators the interests of their constituents, we might worry that the leisure time required to participate in such activities may also be unequally distributed (Elliott 2023). If representatives take information gleaned from town halls to reflect the preferences or expressed interests of their constituents as a whole, this may further exacerbate inequalities among citizens.

Within legislatures, the effects of deliberation (and compromise) are likely to be submerged by the "partisan steamroller" (Sinclair 2006, 344–45); it is unlikely to mitigate asymmetries across the aisle. Of course, even if we doubt that deliberation yields persuasion across party lines, reason-giving practices may enable legislators to publicly signal their disagreement and provide reasons why proposed legislation is flawed. As a result, it may not be otiose; such practices might conduce to the equitable treatment of interests, if it enabled citizens to better understand the impact of such legislation. This could in principle help to mitigate asymmetries between citizens and representatives. But under strong forms of partisanship, any learning that occurs is likely to be among copartisans, who acquire new reasons for supporting their party's own positions and for opposing those of competing parties.

Put synoptically, for deliberation to have the justificatory force touted by its proponents, reason-giving must either improve the quality of outcomes measured in terms of their "epistemic" value, or—at a minimum—it must lead outvoted minority members to feel that their views have had a fair hearing. Both require actors to be properly motivated to seek the truth (or at least to choose the superior alternative based on the strength of reasons), a motivation that may fail to obtain. Even if it did, the strength and consistency of the motivation would be treated skeptically by politicians and voters alike, in part because they would doubt that they could ever distinguish sincere from strategic argumentation. The distributive benefits associated with legislation mean that appeals to truth are likely to be seen as rationalizations, attempts to dress up interests in the guise of correctness. Even a much less demanding standard— that members of the minority believed they had had an opportunity to have their say before the majority voted—may be difficult to satisfy if citizens believe that the outcomes are predetermined, resulting from the number of votes held by the parties predeliberation. So, unless citizens have exceptionally good reason to believe that representatives are sincerely motivated by a search for truth, or are even just open to having their views transformed by legislators from across the political spectrum, deliberation is unlikely to produce justified outcomes.[22] Of course, one might argue that deliberation is merely a regulative ideal. But because its conditions are so demanding, it leads instead to defeatism. If we cannot reorient around deliberation, and we lack criteria by which we could distinguish among justified and unjustified political bargaining, we can only lament our failures.

In part because of these concerns, in recent years some scholars have defended compromise-promoting institutions as a way station between a deliberative approach and an aggregative, majoritarian alternative. The central goal of the compromise-promoting mechanism is unforced concession—optimally, each actor concedes the same amount from their ideal point. Here the motivation of participants in compromise is fairness in the sense of reciprocity; that is, each actor is willing to concede something so long as the other actors do so as well. The aims of compromise advocates vary: they may take the form of helping members to achieve some but not all of their goals. Others promote "integrative solutions," which helps members identify those issues on which they share interests and reach agreement on those matters, while asking all members to sacrifice certain other interests.

Institutions designed to promote compromise, however, cannot effectively ensure that more powerful actors will not hold out to limit their concessions relative to others. As such, it is difficult to draw a stable boundary between compromise and bargaining. Indeed, we would even argue that any result that purportedly emerged from compromise could be redescribed in terms of a bargained-for outcome: a compromise that achieved true parity in terms of concessions could equally well be characterized as a fair bargain. Perhaps as a result, the language of compromise and the language of bargaining have often been used interchangeably.[23] Habermas himself has tended to treat "bargaining" (*Verhandlungen*) and "compromise-formation" (*Kompromißbildung*) as interchangeable terms, uniformly reflecting the circumstances of conflicting interests, the unavailability of rationally motivated consensus, and the exercise of "nonneutralizable" but equally distributed power.

In *The Spirit of Compromise*, Amy Gutmann and Dennis Thompson follow Habermas in treating the two as basically fungible. Compromises often result from "unprincipled bargaining and reinforcements of the prevailing balance of power," though bargaining can both promote and undermine mutual respect. In their words, "Mutual respect is consistent with a wide range of nonviolent means of reaching agreement, which includes bargaining, provided it is in good faith. But mutual respect excludes means—including some other kinds of bargaining—that are intended to degrade, humiliate, or otherwise demean opponents who themselves demonstrate a willingness to negotiate in good faith" (Gutmann and Thompson 2014, 34–35). Such disrespectful bargaining—again, synonymous with "compromising" or "negotiating"—takes the form of entering in bad faith, misrepresenting others' positions, and refusing to cooperate on matters on which agreement is readily available. Their argument, in part, is that a bad bargaining process, one that fails to demonstrate mutual respect, yields a suspect compromise.

We are broadly sympathetic to Gutmann and Thompson's attempt to place normative constraints on the bargaining process. Yet in our view, their focus on actors who operate in bad faith or seek to humiliate is misplaced, because it relies on altering the motivations of agents, rather than on their institutional incentives. To be sure, Gutmann and Thompson identify the pressures of the permanent campaign as a primary cause of the uncompromising mindset; the uncompromising mindset enables candidates to differentiate themselves from rivals and to affirm their commitment to key principles necessary to mobilize the electorate. Yet they insist that institutional reform, while necessary, is bound to be insufficient; citing the Beatles, they suggest, "You tell me it's the institution. Well, you know. You'd better free your mind instead" (Gutmann and Thompson 2014, 203).

The negotiation literature similarly tends to rely on the disposition of actors. Much of this work rests on a distinction between "integrative" and "distributive" agreements. Mary Parker Follett originally developed an integrative account against approaches to capital-labor relations that prioritize collective bargaining and the redistribution of power: although she conceded that, at the present moment, collective bargaining was necessary, and securing equal advantage for labor and capital was appropriate, the ultimate aim was to transcend these divisions through changing motivations. "If we want harmony between labor and capital, we must make labor and capital into one group: we must have an integration of interests and motives, of standards and ideals of justice" (Follett 1998, 117).[24]

In a chapter on "Deliberative Negotiation," Mark Warren and Jane Mansbridge et al. draw on this distinction; they place "deliberative negotiation" between "pure deliberation" and "pure bargaining," and then distinguish between its "integrative" and "distributive" forms (Warren and Mansbridge et al. 2015). In the distributive form of deliberative negotiation—one step away from bargaining, on their schema—parties look for a fair compromise. They do so in a deliberative setting marked by parties' transparency and their mutual commitment to fair dealings, their understanding of which they freely share as a means of producing a legitimate outcome, in which each party sacrifices something of value. Warren and Mansbridge specifically connect this view to Gutmann and Thompson's insistence that parties should adopt a "compromising mindset" to mitigate the effects of polarization (Warren and Mansbridge et al. 2015, 97; Gutmann and Thompson 2014, 16–24). Politicians ought to adopt "principled prudence" (the recognition that an outcome, even if far from ideal, is superior to the status quo) and an attitude of mutual respect, rather than cynicism and distrust.

Again, we are skeptical that changes in mindset would be sufficient to overcome the institutional and personal incentives to hold out when such strategies may be privately beneficial.[25] The adoption of "compromising mindsets" will not eliminate the workings of power. This is because their strategy requires that parties unilaterally adopt a compromising mindset without any assurance that their counterparts will do likewise. Mindsets cannot be discerned by others; parties can only observe behaviors. So even parties who might want to seek a compromise find themselves in a prisoners' dilemma, worrying that if they adopt compromising mindsets whereas their counterparts do not, they may make themselves even more vulnerable. Moreover, motivations are inescapably opaque: we can never know for certain what motivates actions, and people have strategic incentives to misrepresent their motives, even to themselves. In sum, a focus on motivational changes may make actors who are properly motivated prey to those who would seek to misrepresent their motivations, and reliably discerning "motivational types"—particularly when institutions are the parties—is likely impossible. We cannot rely on the unconditioned incentives of actors to change their attitudes or find themselves motivated through principles; rather, their institutional incentives to promote equitable outcomes must change (Schwartzberg 2018). Whatever strategy democratic theorists adopt for the analysis and justification of bargains must rest on institutional design rather than individual or collective dispositions.

Our own institutional account will draw upon influential conceptualizations of private bargaining, while departing from them in key respects. Osborne and Rubinstein (1990, 1) define a *bargaining problem* in the following way: "i) individuals have the possibility of concluding a mutually beneficial agreement; ii) there is a conflict of interest about which agreement to conclude; and iii) no agreement may be imposed on any individual without his approval." They are primarily interested in private bargaining, but it is important to note that this conception is intended to characterize a generic bargain without mention of context. It assumes that the agreement will be mutually beneficial and that it cannot be imposed against any actor's voluntary choice. Condition (i) captures the circumstances of private bargains that are made by rational actors, actors who would not voluntarily agree to any outcome that would make them worse off than rejecting the bargain. What makes it distinctively a bargain is condition (ii), the conflict over the distribution of the benefits of the collective action. It makes no explicit mention of any institutional constraints on the strategies available to the parties. Therefore, it implicitly allows for the possibility that the actors may have unequal bargaining power, an inequality that will presumably influence the ultimate distribution of benefits, so long as the disparity between the power of actors does not become so wide as to place condition (iii) into jeopardy.

As a conceptualization of private bargaining, this appropriately assumes that the actors will enter into agreements only when to do so would make them better off. Yet when it comes to public bargains in the context of democracy, we need to revise the first and third elements somewhat to allow for the constrained institutional context in which the bargaining takes place. In regard to condition (i), while mutually beneficial agreements may often be available, in certain cases the outcome will diminish the welfare of some of the actors. In democracies, the legislative process typically produces winners and losers. In regard to condition (iii), since our account of democracy rests in part on the justifiability of majority decision-making, there will be circumstances in which the final bargain does not reflect certain actors' interests. But since democratic decision-making is not like a market, where if a prospective buyer dislikes the bargain, she can reject it and seek other opportunities, those actors will be forced to accept the terms of the unsatisfactory bargain. To adopt Albert Hirschman's terminology, citizens and their agents generally cannot exit the established structure of democratic institutions; they must rely instead on their "voice," that is, the political power at their disposal (Hirschman 1972). When others' "voices" drown out their own, those citizens abide by the results either because of their loyalty—their belief that the institutions rightly oblige them, or because they believe that these institutions will in the long run secure their interests—or because they are coerced into compliance. Our conception of democratic bargains must account for these possibilities. Moreover, condition (ii)—the prospect of competing interests—still holds in the public bargaining context, highlighting the fact that public bargaining is about the distribution of benefits of public policy.

To identify the constraints on enforceable bargains, we will also draw on contract law. As in the third condition above, courts will decline to enforce agreements that are marked by duress and "imposed" rather than freely entered. But courts are often willing to enforce bargains in which one party is made worse off than they would have been if they had not entered into the agreement; courts do not require a demonstration of full economic rationality to uphold a bargain. The *Restatement (Second) of Contracts* (1981)—the basic treatise of contract law relied upon by courts—is clear on this point. It specifically notes that so long as the requirements of "consideration" (bargained-for performance or returned promise) are met, there is no requirement that the bargain be mutually advantageous (that is, even where there is no "benefit to the promisor" or "detriment to the promisee"), and the contract can be enforced even when the value given in exchange is much less than the promise or the promised performance (§79).

In the public bargaining scenario, which will occupy most of this book, actors will often find themselves made worse off by a specific bargain. Indeed, these bargains may even be, in effect, imposed upon them; that is, they will be obliged to obey outcomes with which they disagree and which may set back their interests, at least their ordinary interests. An ineliminable feature of a democratic society is that people will sometimes lose: they will be disadvantaged, at least temporarily, by some public bargains. With Adam Przeworski (1991), we presume that, to be stable, democracy must enable losers to believe they are better off absorbing the costs of their defeat in the short term than they would be if they chose to revolt. As a result, some short-term bargains, as we conceptualize them, will make players worse off than their initial starting point. However, we will argue that, to be justifiable, these players must also have good reason to believe that their fundamental interests will be protected by political bargains, and that they are more likely to remain protected prospectively under democracy than under any alternative, feasible regime. They must also have reason to think that their ordinary interests will be treated equitably by democratic institutions: that they will have the ability to choose representatives that can advocate for their interests, and that to the extent their representatives' efficacy depends upon partisan politics, these institutions facilitate changes in which of the party holds power.[26]

Our conception of democracy, and democratic procedures, thus departs from most contemporary political theory, as Table 1 demonstrates. Insofar as the democratic theory literature takes up bargaining, it is as a catchall for decision-making in which unequal power plays a significant

Table 1

	Deliberation	Compromise	Bargaining
Parties	Symmetrical	Usually symmetrical	Asymmetrical
Mechanism	Reason-giving	Unforced concession	Exchange
Goal	Reasoned agreement	Integrative solution	Enforceable outcome
Justification	Autonomy (consent/respect)	Fairness	Equitable treatment of interests

role. As we suggested above, theorists are willing to accept that compromise, and perhaps even some form of "fair bargaining," might be defensible, but only as a fallback if deliberative mechanisms are unavailable, or when arguments run out. By contrast, we defend constrained bargaining as the key means by which citizens can have their interests treated equitably in a democracy, and—from that perspective—as justified. To paraphrase Rousseau, our inquiry is into political agents as they are, and institutions as they might be.

Plan of the Book

Since we propose to import certain key concepts from contract law into our analysis of democratic bargaining, we begin in Chapter 1 by identifying those concepts. Recent work emphasizes the value of private contracting as a source of social relationships among the members of a community. We adopt a somewhat different approach. Values underlying private contracting, including the values of choice, self-determination, and exchange, justify both the state interest in facilitating and enforcing bargaining and the ways in which courts might constrain the scope of bargaining. Toward that end, courts examine the capacity of parties to enter into agreements, the strategies employed in the bargaining process, and the substantive content of the agreements, in part to assess the effect of asymmetries of bargaining power between the parties. Public bargaining realizes values analogous to those in private bargaining, and the democratic state in turn has an analogous and even greater interest in ensuring that such public bargains do not enable exploitation, undermining the future political agency of its members. We argue that the "defensive" doctrines that courts use to police bargains in the private law of contracts—including good faith, duress, and unconscionability—can migrate into the public domain, helping to shed light on how we might think about constraining democratic bargaining.

In Chapter 2, we rely on this framework to examine constitutionalism. There is a long, distinguished history of arguments that constitutions, at least metaphorically, derive from contracting. We begin by taking up this literature, demonstrating that these approaches—and the critical responses they have generated—tend to be insensitive to problems of power asymmetries. Our approach addresses head-on such inequalities, arguing that under certain circumstances, constitutional bargaining can provide a legitimate basis for democratic decision-making. The bargaining approach also resolves important challenges for constitutionalism, notably the structure of constitutional dualism and the relationship between constitutionalism and democracy. Drawing insights from the Canadian doctrines of constitutional duties to negotiate (with respect to federalism) and to consult (with respect to Indigenous groups), we turn to the positive defense of constitutional bargaining as a source of democratic value, and then to the "defensive" doctrines to characterize constraints on constitutional bargaining.

Our analysis of democratic bargaining within, and among, those institutions created by the constitution begins in Chapter 3 with legislative bargaining. Here we further develop the equitable treatment of interest standard as the baseline for representative democracy, arguing that our aim should be to have a benchmark against which we can evaluate both intraparty and interparty legislative bargains. This helps us to gain leverage on the types of threats and offers that may be permissible in the legislative setting, shedding light on the scope and strategies of party discipline. The "defensive" doctrines also help us to evaluate the particular institutional rules that structure legislative bargains. We analyze rules that govern the creation of bills in Congress, including closed and structured amendment rules, restricted layover, and self-executing rules, which have only rarely been subject to normative scrutiny. Through a close study of the legislative history of the Patient Protection and Affordable Care Act (the Affordable Care Act, or ACA), we demonstrate that information-restricting rules in particular do raise serious concern about the equitable treatment of interests.

In Chapter 4, we move beyond legislatures to consider bargaining over the interpretation and implementation of law in both an intrabranch and an interbranch framework. In the former, we examine bargaining in collegial courts and among bureaucrats at administrative agencies. In the latter, we consider veto bargaining between the legislature and the executive branch, and, more generally, the strategic interactions among branches as they anticipate each other's responses in the form of enactment, interpretation, and implementation. We argue that the equitable treatment of interests standard clarifies the difference between justifiable and unjustifiable democratic bargains, both in terms of the substance of legislative bargains and the process by which these bargains emerged. We defend in particular a structural due process approach, which enables courts to analyze whether the legislative process was undermined by asymmetrical bargaining power. Because we argue that legislative supremacy best secures citizens' fundamental and ordinary interests, this places a special burden on representatives to be attentive to how the laws they create will be implemented and interpreted. But our framework also supports robust citizen participation under the Federal Advisory Committee Act, with an aim of redistributing bargaining power away from special interests and toward a wider range of citizens, as well as a call for the loosening of standing requirements for lawsuits that enable citizens to challenge the democratic pedigree of legislative bargains. Finally, our argument calls attention to the crucial role of the separation of powers in policing the bargains struck within branches of government, though partisan capture of multiple branches may undermine their ability to serve as effective checks.

In Chapter 5, we turn to what is often a site of gravely asymmetric bargains: bargains in which state actors are active participants in private bargains with citizens. Those state actors include a wide range of street-level bureaucrats who have different forms of discretion and have various degrees of power. Here we focus on one especially powerful type of street-level bureaucrat, the prosecutor. When the state bargains with private citizens, it should not employ strategies that violate the criteria of good faith, duress, and unconscionability. We argue that plea bargaining immediately runs afoul of this injunction. Moreover, given these asymmetries, we doubt that plea bargaining will conduce to the equitable treatment of fundamental interests. As such, we are skeptical that it can be rendered compatible with democracy, though we also suggest certain institutional remedies—including greater transparency for defendants, and restricting the prosecutor's ability to manipulate both charge and sentencing terms—that might reduce the scope of these asymmetries.

In the book's Conclusion we return to the challenges with which we began, the absence of bargaining in contemporary political theory, and highlight some routes forward for scholars who wish to take up this mantle.

1

The Enforcement of Private Bargains

We seek to distinguish between justified and unjustified public bargains, and to do so, we now examine the treatment of other types of bargains in a democratic society. We argue that criteria developed for the bargaining that takes place in everyday life can appropriately translate to the realm of democratic decision-making. To make this case, we turn to the normative framework that has been developed to regulate bargains in private affairs, the law of contracts.

There is a deep analogy between the logic of the private law of contracting and our conception of democratic bargaining. The law of contracts is grounded on a baseline of voluntary exchange between equally situated actors. As we will see, the justification for using the authority of the state to enforce these private agreements is that society benefits from having a system in which such agreements are secured, so long as the baseline conditions are satisfied and are subject to certain constraints on both the bargaining process and outcomes. Key among those constraints will be limits to the unequal distribution of bargaining power. Courts commonly confront agreements that are the product of bargaining between unequal actors, and so judges must decide where to draw the line as to when the inequalities are too great to justifiably enforce the private agreement. How judges make those decisions provides useful insights into the types of political strategies and conditions that might be deemed illegitimate in the course of public bargaining.

Although public bargaining does not require voluntary agreement on the part of individual citizens in order to be justified, the equal participation requirements within democracy mirror this baseline. A formally equal vote is the primary means by which individuals advance their interests in the public domain, and the broader democratic system enables representatives to bargain over the satisfaction of their constituents' interests. The primary reason why the state enables and enforces public bargaining is also because it generates socially valuable outcomes—again, so long as the democratic baseline conditions are satisfied and are subject, as we will see in Chapters 2 through 5, to an analogous set of constraints on both the bargaining process and the outcomes. As in private bargaining, judges will play a role in deciding whether there are bargaining strategies and conditions—including significant power asymmetries—that undermine the probability that a given piece of legislation will promote society's interests in the long run.

Our argument has three parts. First, we justify our reliance on the law of contracts as a criterion for assessing the enforceability of public bargains. We do so by considering how recent justifications on offer for the enforcement of private contracts relate in important ways to public bargaining in democratic decision-making. Next, we analyze the most important constraints that the courts have placed on private bargaining. Finally, we identify those legal constraints that are most relevant for a democratic criterion of justifiable bargains. In thinking about these questions from a legal perspective, we focus on bargains that people enter into by private agreement but subsequently seek to employ the power of the state to either enforce or dissolve. Here we treat judicial grounds for legal action as normative reasons for constraining the private behavior and agreement of the parties.

The Relevance of the Private Law of Contracts for Democratic Bargaining

General theories of the law of contracts perform at least two necessary tasks. First, they offer a general justification for why the state should use its power and authority to enforce the private bargains created by the individual members of society. They do so by positing a widely shared value that is fostered by the social practice of contracting. Second, they set out and explain the constraints that this value places on both the process of bargaining and the substance of the resulting agreements.

Two general approaches have long dominated the literature on the law of contracts, one placing the emphasis on the procedural effects on individual choice and the other on the substantive implications of the bargain. The first approach is deontological, justifying contract law in terms of some basic value that is instantiated in the contracting process. As Charles Fried's famous work has formulated it, the value of contracting is grounded in a conception of autonomy as an individual's capacity to make promises in an unconstrained and independent way (Fried 2015). We enforce private bargains primarily because such agreements enhance our autonomous choices.

The second general approach to justifying the enforcement of contracts is consequentialist, focusing primarily on the substance of the bargain. The dominant consequentialist approach in the contract literature is derived from the field of law and economics and, not surprisingly, grounds the justification of contract enforcement in social efficiency (Posner 2016). A consequentialist judge will enforce contracts when they produce economically efficient allocations of resources. The overall purpose of contract law is to create an incentive structure for parties to enter in socially efficient contracts.[1]

These two approaches have served as the foundation for the evolution of the law of contracts. They highlight the traditional ways in which contract enforcement has been justified as well as how courts have justified limitations on the legitimacy of private bargains. They look to both the process of bargaining and the substantive bargaining outcomes to assess the value to society of enforcing private exchange. With their emphasis on both the autonomy of choice and the collective benefits of bargaining outcomes, they identify important features of private bargains that have their analogues in public bargaining in a democratic society. These analogues have been explicitly developed in more recent additions to the debates about the law of private contracting, contributions that provide insight into the significant role that private contracting can play in the maintenance of a democratic system of government.

These recent works expand the framework for an analysis of the implications of private bargaining as they seek to examine the ways in which private exchange implicates other social institutions in a society. In doing so, their work, like ours, seeks to draw parallels between the values achieved through private contracting and the values realized through democratic decision-making. We see this most clearly in the analyses offered by Seana Shiffrin and Daniel Markovits.

In analyzing the moral and political value of a system of contracts, Shiffrin highlights the egalitarian interpersonal relationships that are created and sustained by private contracting, and the value such relationships hold for the state. In the private domain, promising enables people to "reaffirm their equal moral status and respect for each other." When made public, "the reinforcement of equal status facilitated by promises takes on a political value"(Shiffrin 2007, 751–52). Broadly speaking, she argues that the social institution of contracting serves as a public means of facilitating private commitments that affirm equal political standing.

We agree that contracting may well help to affirm formal relations of equal status among citizens, and we share Shiffrin's intuition that the process of legislation is analogous in important respects to contracting. However, we depart from Shiffrin in a key respect. Whereas for Shiffrin, private contracting and political agency alike entail the affirmation of equal standing (and even coauthorship), our analogy instead rests on the importance of constrained bargaining. To be sure, the private law of contracts does treat parties as if they act on formally equal terms to pursue private ends through bargained-for exchanges. Yet such formal relations of equality may paper over certain asymmetries of power that the state has an interest in regulating. Similarly, even if equal participatory rights constitute a baseline for democratic decision-making, bargained-for legislation may also reflect certain asymmetries of power within the legislature that the state has an interest in regulating. By emphasizing the egalitarian dimensions of contracting, lawmaking, or common-law adjudication, as Shiffrin does, one worry is that it may obscure the asymmetries of power inherent in all these practices (Shiffrin et al. 2021). Admittedly, Shiffrin does acknowledge that there is also public interest in the protection of vulnerable parties in private contracting situations

(Shiffrin 2007, 752). On her account, a system of public contracting in part aims to protect the parties from the harms generated by breaches that result from particular vulnerabilities. But beyond mere breach, many legally enforceable agreements will reflect unequal bargaining power among the parties, and so for our purposes, a key aim of contract law is to ensure that these inequalities are not so significant as to undermine the bargain.

In his perspicuous account of the contractual condition of "good faith" as the core value of private bargaining, Markovits helps to clarify the relationship between formally equal contracting capacity and substantive inequality. "Good faith" in the performance of contracts is a condition imposed on the parties to any private contract. For example, the Uniform Commercial Code §1-304 (2003) imposes a duty to perform one's obligations under a contract in good faith. In this context, "good faith" is defined as "honesty in fact and the observance of reasonable commercial standards of fair dealing" (UCC §1-201).[2] Markovits argues that contracting parties, through their acceptance of the good faith requirement, create reciprocal relationships in which they recognize the formally equal standing of the other parties to the agreement, relationships that have broader implications for society. He emphasizes that "good faith is the very essence of contractual solidarity, and hence of contract's contribution to social solidarity overall. To make a contract with another just is to adopt attitudes of solidarity in favor of the joint project fixed by the contractual intentions" (Markovits 2014, 294). Markovits plausibly characterizes contractual good faith as "thin": it constitutes merely respect for the agreed-upon surplus allocation, and it is flexible with respect to that allocation on which parties have agreed; that is, it need not entail any deeper respect for each other's equal standing (2014, 291). It is also compatible with substantive inequalities, including inequalities of bargaining power: a party advantaged by the contract can continue to perform it in good faith, so long as she respects the terms of the agreement and "declines to exploit additional strategic advantages that arise within the contract (and perhaps even obtained through it) to revise the settlement still further to favor her" (2014, 291). Markovits's "thin" conception of good faith helps to clarify both the spareness of the parties' motivations and its compatibility with certain asymmetries, and so we adopt it in the rest of the book.

This political approach to private contracting shares important concerns with other recent developments in the traditional approaches to justifying state enforcement. By briefly considering two of them, we can get a better sense of what might be involved if courts employed a democratic perspective to questions of private contracting. One recent alternative, developed by Hanoch Dagan and Michael Heller (2017), builds on the autonomy justification endorsed by Fried and others but extends it in ways that blend with consequentialist considerations. Their "choice theory of contracts" argues that states enforce contracts to enhance a conception of autonomy that is broader than that offered by Fried. They criticize Fried and others in this tradition for limiting their conception of autonomy to a focus on personal independence, a move that effectively limits freedom of contract to a negative liberty from external interference.

Dagan and Heller argue, instead, that the appropriate conception of autonomy should be grounded in the value of self-determination: "The shift from personal independence (or negative liberty) to autonomy (or self-determination) should be natural to liberals, who generally reject the thin (libertarian) conception of freedom as independence. Self-determination represents a rich conception of freedom: its value is what makes our independence worthwhile: we are entitled to be free from coercion because this freedom is necessary for each of us if we are to each write by him- or herself the (separate) story of our (separate) lives" (Dagan and Heller 2017, 42). In this way, they extend the work to be done by the value underlying the practice of contracting. Self-determination involves more than simple choice; it involves the creation of a more encompassing life plan that requires the cooperation of others. For Dagan and Heller, the practice of contracting is the private means by which we obligate others to help us accomplish that plan. This has two important implications that distinguish the account from that of the traditional deontological justification.

The first relates to the parties to the contract: "Exercising your power to enter a contract (voluntarily and affirmatively) in the service of your own autonomy justifiably entails some obligations (limited and affirmative) to the other party as well" (Dagan and Heller 2017, 47). Accepting a promise from someone to help you also entails accepting an obligation to help them. Dagan and Heller argue that the obligation follows directly from the value of autonomy itself, once you understand the broader scope of the autonomy value. In doing so, they expand the significance of the guarantees of autonomy. The second implication relates to the role of the state in facilitating and enforcing contracts: "Its single most important and distinctive normative payoff: a state committed to human freedom must be proactive in shaping contract law, including ensuring availability of a diverse body of normatively attractive types" (2017, 4). This expands the potential role of courts, in particular, and the state, in general, in the practice of contracting. The courts may have the authority to do more than merely limit illegitimate private bargains. They may have the additional authority to favor the conditions that might enhance new kinds of private agreements.

For our purposes here, this expansive justification of contracting in terms of self-determination places greater emphasis on the relative capacities of the parties to the agreement. Here we see some overlap with the emphasis on equal relationships and effectiveness that we find in the democratic perspective. Just as a commitment to democracy should be concerned with the implications of inequalities on the actual effectiveness of democratic participation, this justification of private contracting focuses on the implications for the relative effectiveness of achieving individual goals. Dagan and Heller emphasize that contract law should be concerned with substantive as opposed to formal equality: "If contract is to serve people's self-determination, and not only their (Kantian) independence, contract law cannot rely, as it is conventionally portrayed, on a formal conception of equality that seeks to abstract away the particular features distinguishing one person from another" (2017, 86). If judges endorse this emphasis, courts will focus more on issues of relational equality, making sure that the parties to a contract have reasonably equal opportunities to make "meaningful" choices in the bargaining process.[3] They will ask questions of the form, What types of contracts are the product of negotiations characterized by the lack of meaningful choices for any of the parties to the bargain? And what types of conditions enhance the opportunities to create meaningful choices in the creation of contracts?

Another recent approach that expands the traditional understanding of contract law is a consequentialist account that looks beyond efficiency and focuses instead on other effects of the practice of contracting. It focuses on the effects of the practice on the functioning of the market as a whole. Nathan Oman has offered a cogent justification of contract law that is grounded in what he takes to be the morally desirable outcomes produced by a "well-functioning market" (Oman 2016). He rests his argument on three basic effects of such markets. First, markets "inculcate moral habits" that are necessary to sustain a liberal society. Second, they "provide a framework for peaceful and productive cooperation in the face of the pervasive pluralism of contemporary society." And, third, they produce wealth, which Oman argues makes it possible for us to ameliorate a range of social problems (2016, 40). Together, he claims, these market effects are sufficiently beneficial to society that they are morally desirable. And therefore, they justify a system of contract law whose goal is to extend and maintain well-functioning markets.

Oman's justification requires courts to make a broader assessment of the substance of the contract than they would in an efficiency analysis. When courts are confronted by questions of contract law, Oman argues that they should ask, Would the enforcement of this contract further the positive benefits of a well-functioning market? (2016, 184). If it would, then the contract in question should be enforced. To get at that general question, however, courts would have to address more specific questions about the ways in which private bargains either enhance or undermine well-functioning markets. To what extent does the practice of contracting in a specific case undermine the types of liberal moral habits that a society embraces? Or to what extent does the enforcement of contracts like the ones in a specific case undermine the competitiveness of the market, a central feature of its effective functioning? Each of these questions may require the court not only to look more broadly at the various consequences produced by the contract's substantive terms but also to issues related to the bargaining process and to the relationship between the parties.

Summarizing, these various theories justify the use of the power of the state to facilitate and enforce private bargains. As we have emphasized, they are also employed by courts to justify the ways in which they develop limits on such contracting. As the more recent accounts demonstrate, there are important analogies between private and public bargaining. On the one hand, there are significant similarities in the assumptions about the status of the participants in the bargaining process, similarities between the voluntary nature of the exchange in private bargaining and the equal participation requirements in public bargaining. On the other hand, both private and public bargaining are justified in terms of the ways in which they generate socially valuable outcomes. And both of these justifications are grounded in an understanding that bargaining will produce the desired outcomes only when the bargaining process meets certain necessary conditions, conditions that are also quite similar in the two cases.

We believe that these analogies provide sufficient reasons for employing the law of private bargaining as a criterion for assessing the enforceability of public bargaining. Our subsequent arguments seek to justify this reliance and to demonstrate how it supports a justification of constrained bargaining in democratic decision-making.

The Framework of Constraints on Private Bargaining

While these theories sometimes differ in the types of constraints that they justify, together they provide us with a general framework of the possible ways in which courts have constrained the legitimacy and thus the enforceability of private bargains. There are three main areas courts examine to see whether there are reasons why they should constrain such bargains. The first involves some basic characteristics of the parties to the agreement, factors related to their capacity to enter into an agreement and their understanding of the implications of the bargain. The second involves the strategies that they employ in the bargaining process, asking whether the bargaining process satisfies the conditions of free and voluntary promising, meaningful choice, equitable relationships, and mutual assent. The third involves the substantive content of the final bargain, asking whether the resulting contract produces a fair and mutually beneficial outcome. We shall take these up in turn (Farnsworth 2004; Posner 2016).

In doing so, we should note that we focus our discussion here on the law of contracts as it has evolved in the United States, but we want to emphasize that the general thrust of the argument is readily applicable to most modern democracies. While they may differ in some of the details, the overall categories governing normative constraints on private bargaining are similar,[4] and therefore the implications for our analysis of democratic politics are generally applicable.

The first area in which the courts may target constraints on bargaining involves the nature of the parties themselves. Concerns about beliefs and competence focus on straightforward assumptions about what kinds of knowledge and what kinds of ability it would take to make a free and voluntary promise that was worthy of enforcement. Courts generally want to protect parties who are unable to assess the implications of their promises for their own personal welfare (*Restatement [Second] of Contracts* §15 [1981]). Specifically, courts will often dissolve a contract if the other party had reason to know of the first party's incompetence, if the terms of the bargain are deemed unfair to the incompetent party, and if there are legal remedies that would address any issues of detrimental reliance.

Similarly, courts will consider dissolving a contract when there is some issue of misunderstanding or mistake on the part of one or both of the parties. If the mistake is mutual, then the court will try to decide how significant are the implications of the mistake (*Restatement [Second] of Contracts* §152 [1981]). If the implications are deemed too significant for the remaining terms of the bargain to be carried out, the contract will be voided. Otherwise, the court will strive to enforce the bargain in a revised form. If the mistake is unilateral, the court will try to determine if the unmistaken party was aware of the mistake and used it to his advantage in the bargaining process (*Restatement [Second] of Contracts* §153 [1981]). If so, the court will usually try to find a way to remedy the implications of the unfair mistake.

These doctrines related to incompetency, misunderstanding, and mistake reflect a view that private bargains should be grounded initially in a clear and transparent understanding of the circumstances and implications of cooperative behavior. In the absence of clear evidence of one of these problems, the initial presumption is that the private bargain is worthy of enforcement. Although each of these doctrines focuses the court's attention on the process by which the contract is negotiated, evidence of a violation of one of these requirements can be found either explicitly in the negotiating process or implicitly in any gross inequalities in the substantive terms of the contract. In the latter case the inequalities can lead the court to investigate the underlying capacities and resources of the parties. In this way courts have tied these basic limitations to a general concern about relational inequality among the parties. We return to this below.

The second area of concern in contract enforcement cases focuses on the bargaining process itself. The basic question for our purposes here is, What types of bargaining strategies, if any, are deemed illegitimate and, thus, worthy of constraint under the law of contracts? If a party to a contract can demonstrate that her agreement to the contract was ultimately caused by one of these illegitimate strategies, the court may decide to dissolve it.

Consider three such illegitimate strategies: fraud, undue influence, and coercion/duress. The first of these, fraud, is fairly straightforward. If a party intentionally makes a statement that turns out to be false and the other parties rely on it, then courts will commonly refuse to enforce the relevant terms of the bargain and may dissolve the entire contract. If he makes a statement that he believed to be true but turned out to be false and if he could have easily determined that it was false, what courts call negligent misrepresentation, the courts will usually refuse to enforce the relevant aspects of the bargain. Private bargains induced by fraudulent strategies are not the kinds of cooperative agreements that the courts want to enforce (*Restatement [Second] of Contracts* §§162, 164 [1981]).

At first blush, the other two doctrines—undue influence and coercion/duress—seem like similarly promising constraints on bargaining strategies that might produce unfair agreements. Here we have in mind the kind of unfairness that may follow from bargaining between unequal parties. The general theories of contracting offer different perspectives on the implications of such inequalities for the enforcement of private bargains. The theories grounded in either the value of autonomy or the value of equal status in social and political relationships explicitly call the court's attention to questions of inequality. The theories emphasizing autonomy as independence treat inequality as evidence of the potential lack of autonomy for the weaker actor. Equality is derivative of freedom of choice in this case. The theories that emphasize autonomy as self-determination support the independent valuation of equality as a procedural factor, emphasizing that the assessment of inequalities must go beyond formal guarantees of equality to an analysis of the substantive factors that are necessary for meaningful choice. A similar emphasis follows from the theories grounded in the value of relationships of equal status and respect.

The consequentialist theories, on the other hand, recommend at best a more implicit consideration of inequality. Equality is relevant to the efficiency justification only to the extent that inequality may be a condition that causes inefficiency. It is a more significant factor for the well-functioning market justification because systemic inequality is a factor that undermines competition and thus the effectiveness of the market.

For our purposes here, it is enough to acknowledge that from whatever perspective you justify the practice of contracting, the resulting law governing private bargains identifies the potential negative implications of inequality among the parties. The task is to try to understand how courts have tried to develop an approach to mitigate the negative effects of such inequalities.

The doctrine of undue influence was intended to discourage parties from exerting unreasonable pressure on other parties to the bargaining process (*Restatement [Second] of Contracts* §177 [1981]). Posner (2016, 91) suggests that courts interpret the undue influence doctrine much like that of incompetency. The victim is considered to be vulnerable, due to some temporary circumstances, to efforts to unreasonably pressure him. The instigating party is aware of this vulnerability and nonetheless chooses to use it to his advantage. If a party is subject to this kind of unreasonable pressure, courts may be willing to dissolve the contract. But Posner further suggests that the courts tend to invoke the undue influence defense in very specific and idiosyncratic cases. It does not appear that the doctrine has been applied to instances of bargaining pressure that were facilitated by systemic inequalities, like unequal bargaining power.

On the other hand, the doctrine of coercion and duress has been applied to a number of cases involving disparities in bargaining power (*Restatement [Second] of Contracts* §§174–175 [1981]). We can distinguish at least three general cases in which the doctrine of duress has been employed by the courts. The first is the classic "gun to the head" case where actual threats are used to force a party to do something that the party would not otherwise do. It is easily resolved by the court dissolving the contract. The second type involves cases in which one of the parties is the only person with whom you may bargain if you want a particular good or service. These are instances of monopoly, in which the monopolist is the only real choice you have in a particular circumstance. All of the bargaining power, so to speak, rests with the monopolist. This severe case of unequal bargaining forms the basis of what are commonly called "adhesion contracts," contracts that are created by the powerful party and signed without modification by the weaker party. Adhesion contracts are the product of the proverbial "take it or leave it" situation. The third type of case also involves unequal bargaining power, albeit to a lesser degree than the case of the monopolist. These are cases of what the courts often call "local monopoly" in which one party to a contract has already performed her obligation and then the other party seeks to renegotiate the terms to take advantage of the performing party's sunk costs and potential losses if the contract fails.

Duress would look to be a promising way of addressing unequal bargaining power, but the courts have resisted the temptation to extend this doctrine beyond the most obvious "gun to the head" cases. In these last two types of cases, the court can dissolve the contract if after the fact of the bargain the weaker party seeks to get out of the agreement, but it will often resist this option. As an alternative to dissolution, the court may choose to delete certain terms of the contract that it finds especially unfair under the circumstances (Posner 2016, 104–5). These duress cases thus tend to serve as a limiting case of the range of unequal bargaining power scenarios. Rather than relying on the duress doctrine, courts in the less obvious cases have taken one of two different approaches. The first is the doctrine of unconscionability, which we will take up in a moment. The second is to look to other areas of the law that have developed to address social concerns in a more systematic way. Examples of other such remedies include consumer protection laws and antitrust laws. We will return to these alternative legal remedies in our summary discussion below.

The third area of potential constraint developed by the courts involves a general criterion of unconscionability. The doctrine of unconscionability developed out of a broad concern that there are certain types of contracts that just violate our sense of fairness. Questions of unconscionability generally emerge from an initial assessment of the substantive terms of the bargain. However, in applying this doctrine courts will commonly assess both the procedural and the substantive aspects of the bargain. Courts differ as to whether unconscionability must be found in both aspects of the bargain or whether it is sufficient to find it in only one aspect to determine if the doctrine applies (Wertheimer 1992).

The doctrine of unconscionability has evolved, as in most areas of contract law, through a synthesis of judicial decisions and statutory enactments. The most prominent recent statement of the doctrine can be found in the Uniform Commercial Code. UCC §2-302 defines the authority of a court to constrain private bargains on the grounds of unconscionability: "(1) If the court as a matter of law finds the contract or any clause of the contract to have been unconscionable at the time it was made the court may refuse to enforce the contract, or it may enforce the remainder of the contract without the unconscionable clause, or it may so limit the application of any unconscionable clause as to avoid any unconscionable result."

As stated, the statute does little in the way of defining exactly what unconscionability is. The official commentary provided with the UCC seems at one point to suggest that the test for unconscionability rests on the unequal nature of the bargain: "The basic test is whether, in the light of the general commercial background and the commercial needs of the particular trade or case, the clauses involved are so one-sided as to be unconscionable under the circumstances existing at the time of the making of the contract." But, as Wertheimer (1992, 481) points out in his analysis of the provision, the commentary goes on to limit the range of the constraint: "The principle is one of the prevention of oppression and unfair surprise and not of disturbance of allocation of risks because of superior bargaining power."

Unfortunately, the case law on unconscionability is as unclear as the statutes and commentaries are vague. In a recent review of the case law on unconscionability, Posner (2016, 93) highlights two basic ideas that have been employed in applying the doctrine: lack of sophistication and unequal bargaining power. The problem of lack of sophistication commonly arises when the buyer of a product knows much less about the exchange than the seller. The task of the court is to determine (1) how much information we should expect the seller to provide the buyer in the course of the negotiations, and did the seller provide it; and (2) if the seller did not provide it, was the information differential a material factor in determining the substantive content of the final bargain. The complexity of these informational questions and the difficulty for the courts in answering them are two important reasons why questions of lack of sophistication are no longer considered primarily under the purview of the law of contracts and are rather governed by consumer protection legislation.

Courts have also found it difficult to define exactly what we mean by unequal bargaining power. This difficulty is understandable. Consider the problem in the context of a market exchange. In assessing the implications of asymmetries in bargaining power, a court needs to be able to (1) establish a reasonable and manageable conception of market power, (2) assess the magnitude of the asymmetry in power between the parties, and (3) distinguish which forms of market power are normatively acceptable from those that are not. This last point follows from the fact that the principle of unconscionability is not intended to guarantee strict equality among the parties. It is intended, rather, to prohibit unfair bargains that are the product of illegitimate asymmetries of power. This is to say that not all power asymmetries will be deemed unacceptable and thus unconscionable under the law.

So, it would be reasonable for a court to assess the ways in which the parties to the bargain had accumulated their relative market power at the time of the negotiations of the contract. In principle, economic actors may acquire power in a particular market by producing the best products that appeal to consumers. If they continue to maintain their advantage merely through the quality of their products, then there may be no good reason to limit their influence in a bargaining process. On the other hand, if they acquire their power merely by adopting strategies intended to stifle competition, there may be very good reasons for limiting the enjoyment of the influence brought about by these anticompetitive actions.

In subsequent chapters, we will show that this concern with a distinction between legitimate and illegitimate bargaining power is also relevant for the analysis of public bargaining. This is especially true in a democracy, where the bargaining advantage derived from asymmetries in political power can be a function of both legitimate (for example, the distribution of political preferences among the electorate) and potentially illegitimate (for example, disproportionate resources) factors.

In lieu of clear standards of bargaining power and illegitimate asymmetries in the treatment of private bargains, we can at best provide analysis of how the courts have struggled with an array of cases that vary in their degrees of asymmetry. What this analysis can do is call our attention to the types of factors that the law has identified as relevant to considerations of unfairness and inequality. The most straightforward cases of unequal bargaining power are those in which one party takes advantage of an obvious weakness of the other party. Wertheimer (1992, 481), in his discussion of unconscionability, points out that the early equity courts sought to prevent egregious abuses of bargaining power due to emergency circumstances. He offers the early English case of *The Port Caledonia and the Anna* (1903) as such a clear example (*Reports of Cases Relating to Maritime Law*, Vol. 9, 479–80).

The ship *Port Caledonia* was caught in a storm and was unable to stop its movement in the direction of a second ship *Anna*. Fearing a collision, the captain of the *Port Caledonia* put up signals requesting assistance from any tugboats in the harbor area. A tugboat named *Sarah Jolliffe* responded to the signal. When the captain of the *Port Caledonia* asked the *Sarah Jolliffe* to tow her back to her former location, the master of the *Sarah Jolliffe* said that he would only help if the *Port Caledonia* would pay him 1,000 pounds sterling. After a brief argument in which the master of the *Sarah Jolliffe* refused to budge, the captain of the *Port Caledonia* agreed to the terms. Then the *Sarah*

Jolliffe proceeded to tow the *Port Caledonia* back to safety. When the owner of the *Port Caledonia* subsequently refused to pay the 1,000 pounds, the owner of the *Sarah Jolliffe* sued for the money.

At the trial, the *Port Caledonia* owner admitted that the captain had in fact agreed to the terms but argued that they were nonetheless "exorbitant and inequitable" and thus should be set aside. The court agreed with the defendant, concluding that the agreement was "inequitable, extortionate, and unreasonable." Instead of the 1,000 pounds, the court determined that 200 pounds was a more reasonable payment for the service of the tugboat.

In such emergency cases, the judicial assessment is similar to those treated under the duress doctrine. However, the assessments differ to the extent that the powerful party is, like the *Sarah Jolliffe*, compensated for whatever costs that party actually incurred in carrying out their part of the bargain. A similar type of case in terms of the major discrepancy in bargaining power, but where the discrepancy is a product of differences in market position and not due to emergency circumstances, is the case of monopoly power. Consider the classic case of *Henningsen v. Bloomfield Motors, Inc.* (161 A.2d 69 [N.J. 1960]). In this case, the plaintiff had purchased a car from Bloomfield Motors. The dealer used a standard form sales contract that had been drafted by the Automobile Manufacturers Association. It was the same basic form contract that was being used at the time by almost all of the car manufacturers in the United States. Among the terms of the contract was a limitation on the manufacturer's warranty under the sale, a limitation under which the manufacturer's only duty was to replace any defective parts that the buyer returned to the factory. While using the car, the plaintiff's wife was injured, and the injury was deemed to be caused by a defect in the car. When the plaintiff sued for damages related to the injury, the car dealership offered as a defense that the plaintiff had agreed to the terms of the standard form contract and thus the dealership's liability was limited to an amount equal to the cost of the defective part.

The court ruled in favor of the plaintiff and struck down the warranty provisions for being contrary to good public policy. The court's reasoning relied on what it took to be the "grossly unequal" bargaining position of the parties. To justify this assessment, the court noted that, given the fact that the standard form contract was being used by almost all of the dealerships in the country, the plaintiff really did not have an opportunity to bargain for better warranty terms. The coordinated use of such a one-sided contract served to create a functioning monopoly over contract terms and thus undermined whatever power the consumer might have had in negotiating the terms of the bargain.

In the *Henningsen* case, as in the *Port Caledonia* case, the assessment of the power asymmetry was fairly clear and straightforward even if the cause of the asymmetry was quite different. In such cases the courts were comfortable in ruling that the asymmetries were substantial and thus undermined the legitimacy of the contracts. As the magnitude of the asymmetry becomes less obvious, the courts have had more difficulty offering a clear standard for resolving claims of unconscionability. But they tend to focus on factors that adversely affect the meaningful choices of the parties. This was stated explicitly in the famous case of *Williams v. Walker-Thomas Furniture Co.* (350 F. 2d 445 [D.C. Cir. 1965]). Over many years, Williams purchased several pieces of furniture from Walker-Thomas. She did so under an installment agreement that allowed the furniture store to credit payments on one piece of furniture pro rata to all of the outstanding bills from prior purchases. The upshot of the agreement was that Walker-Thomas reserved the right to repossess older items of furniture until the most recent purchases were completed. In the spring of 1962 Williams bought a stereo for \$514.95. At the time of the purchase, she still owed \$164 on prior purchases. A few months later she defaulted on the stereo purchase and Walker-Thomas sued to repossess all of the items that she had purchased since 1957. The trial court rejected Williams's defense that the contract's term allowing repossession of all previously purchased furniture made the contract unconscionable and thus unenforceable.

Subsequently, the District of Columbia Court of Appeals affirmed the trial court's decision to reject the unconscionability claim. When the US Court of Appeals for the DC Circuit heard the appeal of the case, it held that "where the element of unconscionability is present at the time a contract is made, the contract should not be enforced." The court went on to identify an unconscionable contract as one that includes "an absence of meaningful choice on the part of one of the parties together with contract terms which are unreasonably favorable to the other party" (480). It also posited two factors that might undermine meaningful choice. The first was "gross inequality of bargaining power," which would diminish the meaningful choices available to the weaker party. The second was lack of clarity in the installment contract, which would make it difficult for the purchaser to form an adequate understanding of the choices before her.

Barnhizer (2005, 199–200), in an extensive review of the case law on unconscionability, notes this about the evolution of this area of the law post-Williams: "Although Williams primarily discussed bargaining power disparities in the context of meaningfulness of choice, later courts and commentators have generally reformulated this inquiry as requiring both procedural unconscionability and substantive unconscionability. . . . The absence of meaningful choice standard has come to be understood as procedural unconscionability, while Williams' inquiry into the reasonableness or fairness of the contract terms themselves parallels the substantive element of the unconscionability test."

The basic questions remain: How much inequality is enough to satisfy the unconscionability doctrine? How much is necessary to undermine meaningful choice? And how much must be instantiated in the substance of the agreement itself? In terms of procedural unconscionability, Barnhizer (2005, 199–200) suggests that the courts have developed "two rough categories" of factors that have been used by the courts to make an assessment of inequality and thus unenforceability. The first involves features of the bargaining process itself: "lack of meaningful alternatives, necessity, the nature of the good or service, or inability to negotiate terms." The second set of factors identifies characteristics of the parties themselves that would suggest the existence of inequality: "wealth, business sophistication, education or knowledge, race, gender, "size" of the parties, monopoly power, and consumer status."

In terms of substantive unconscionability, courts have dissolved contracts when they are characterized by a substantially disproportionate division of benefits. Here, unfairness is associated with substantial disproportionality. A number of approaches to substantive disproportionality have been proposed. Consider two prominent ones. One approach that has often been employed is to compare the terms of the bargain in question to what the terms would have been in a perfectly competitive market (Eisenberg 2009). To the extent that one party has successfully bargained for a larger share of the surplus of the exchange than she would have achieved in a perfectly competitive market, that is seen as evidence of an advantage in bargaining power.

This approach has the benefit of capturing one factor that is relevant to the relative measure of bargaining power. In locating the bargain in the more general context of market exchange, it takes account of an important feature of bargaining power: the other options that a bargainer has if she chooses to exit the negotiations. The more outside options a party has, the more bargaining power the party has in any particular transaction. So, it provides us with a way of thinking about unequal bargaining power. And yet it fails to offer a complete answer to the question of how much inequality is unfair in any individual case.

As an alternative to the perfectly competitive market approach to disproportionality, Wertheimer (1992) argues that the comparative referent should be a measure of what a fair division would be. In this context, however, what should we take as a fair division? Wertheimer suggests that "it is commonly thought that an agreement is exploitative or unconscionable when A gets much more value from the exchange than B," and that a fair transaction is "one in which the surplus is divided (approximately) equally." Unlike the market mimicking alternative, this approach is somewhat easier to calculate, but perhaps is more contingent on particular justifications of the practice of contracting.

In concluding this discussion of the legal framework for constraining private bargains, we want to reemphasize the point made earlier that it is unclear whether courts will limit unenforceability to those cases in which they find both procedural and substantive unconscionability. Eisenberg (2009, 1418) notes that, when using this doctrine, courts have recently tended to require more than evidence of disproportionality. They also require evidence of "moral fault"—an intentional action on the part of the more powerful party to use its advantage to exploit the weaker party. Eisenberg further notes that common law courts have been less willing than civil law courts, where the law is more clearly defined by statute, to find "moral fault." Because of the difficulty in adequately applying the doctrine, unconscionability remains a controversial idea for some, and a number of courts have shied away from employing it as a way of addressing issues of unequal bargaining power.

Implications for Public Bargaining

So, what might we draw from the law of contracts, from the rules defining legitimate private bargains, that might be relevant for an analysis of the public bargains that characterize democratic politics? Three features stand out. The first is the duty to act in "good faith" in the performance of one's obligations under a contract. The concept of good faith establishes constraints on how the parties act *after* they have agreed on the terms of a bargain. It sets out broad standards of honesty, fairness, and reasonableness that should govern subsequent behavior in relation to enforceable bargains.

In regard to public bargaining, the concept of good faith can have important implications for the creation and maintenance of a democratic system of governance. First, when it comes to public bargains over policy, to act in good faith would require parties to respect the substantive terms of democratic bargains, lending a certain degree of stability of expectations as to the role of the state in future social and economic affairs. And it would limit efforts to change those policies to the institutional mechanisms made available by the democratic process. Second, when it comes to public bargains over institutional rules and practices, it would create a good faith obligation to respect the bargained-for rules and procedures. The most important implication of this is that it would require all government officials to perform the institutional obligations required of them under the rules, obligations of performance that are necessary for the democratic institutions to work effectively.

As we argue in Chapter 4, good faith, in concert with the requirement of legislative supremacy, requires that political actors who dislike the substance of a democratically enacted statute are constrained to one strategy, changing the substance of the law by a new legislative enactment, as opposed to seeking to change the law by judicial interpretation or administrative regulation. And, similarly, judges and administrators are constrained from attempting to use their institutional authority to change the substantive content of the law.

At the same time, it is also important to note here that our conception of good faith in the democratic decision-making process is a rather thin one. It requires us to follow the rules and practices that structure democratic institutions and to abide by justifiable democratic bargains. The only evidence necessary to assess whether a politician is acting in good faith is the behavioral and readily observable evidence that political actors are following the rules. Therefore, this criterion does not fall prey to the analytical problems that characterize normative requirements that political actors are motivated by an appropriate mindset, like that of compromise.

Although good faith on our account is thin in terms of motivations, it is also robust, as Markovits persuasively argued. He emphasized that good faith "remains possible even under conditions of substantive inequality. Nothing in the patterns of recognition and respect immanent in the contract relations depends on the substantive fairness of the division of contractual surplus" (2014, 291). Principles of good faith constrain future actions even when we don't get the deal that we wanted, as long as we ultimately agreed to it.

The second feature of the law of private contracting that is relevant to public bargains involves the doctrines of coercion and duress. Coercion, in both its explicit and implicit forms, is deemed a reason to deny the judicial enforcement of private bargains. Courts have placed clear limitations on private bargains when any of the parties have intentionally attempted to violate the ability of other parties to make free and voluntary choices. This serves as a constraint on the strategies employed by the actors. The related doctrine of duress targets such bargaining strategies but also identifies, as in the case of adhesion contracts, structural conditions that seriously limit the choices available to the parties. Similarly, concerns about coercion and duress would seem to apply to public bargaining in the context of democratic decision-making. They serve as the limiting case of public bargaining, excluding those political bargains that are unduly influenced by coercion or duress.

The third feature, and the primary one for our purposes, is the doctrine of unconscionability. Unconscionability directly addresses the question of how to deal with unequal bargaining power. The main problem for the courts has been an inability to determine an effective metric for what would be an unfair distribution of power among the parties to an individual bargain. There has been nothing in the different approaches to the normative justification of contracting that has led the courts to such a clear metric. Nonetheless, the courts have identified an array of factors that regularly call into question the fairness, and thus the legitimacy, of the private bargain. While there is no agreed-upon formula for how to weigh the various factors, we can see the variety of conditions under which courts have raised significant concerns about the asymmetries that bedevil private bargaining. The fact that the courts have not arrived at a clearly defined conception merely suggests to us how pervasive the problem of inequality has been and continues to be. The difficulty in arriving at such a standard does not diminish the normative significance of the problem of unequal bargaining power.

As we will see in subsequent chapters, unconscionability and its treatment of unequal bargaining power serve as an important justification for constraining public bargains as well. While the courts fail to offer a clear and precise method for employing the doctrine, they clearly identify a primary normative concern for bargaining in a democratic society. And they offer a variety of factors that come into play when we set out to analyze the normative legitimacy of such bargaining. Here we want to set out the framework for how duress and unconscionability identify and justify normative constraints on democratic bargaining.

In this book's Introduction we offered an argument for how political bargaining, under the appropriate conditions, benefits democratic decision-making. Our account emphasizes the fundamental importance of political participation, of the ability of citizens to assert their own interests in the democratic process. Through various political strategies, democratic citizens, among themselves and then through their representatives, use opportunities for argumentation to champion their various partial and particular interests and to formulate together trade-offs among them. We identify the ways in which asymmetric bargaining can influence this process. Basically, we conclude that public bargaining serves to specify the terms and boundaries of feasible bargains, within both the political domain and the private domain. We further argued that this kind of political exchange, even under conditions of some relative inequality, is more likely than alternative mechanisms to secure citizens' fundamental interests in the long run. But this claim is conditional on a set of institutional constraints on permissible inequalities.

A commitment to democracy requires us to protect every citizen's opportunity to effectively assert their own interests. This does not guarantee that they will get the specific substantive outcomes that they would prefer, but it does require that we, as a democratic society, establish and maintain the procedural and substantive preconditions for that opportunity. These conditions are necessary for the protection of a citizen's fundamental interests. And, through the maintenance of the opportunity for all citizens to effectively participate in the democratic process, the conditions serve as a self-sustaining mechanism for democracy itself.

The criteria of duress and unconscionability provide us with guidance in achieving these protections. They do not establish a bright-line answer to every question about the acceptability of an asymmetric bargain, but they do provide a framework for thinking about the problem. To see this, let's think for a moment about a continuum of relative inequality among bargainers. On one end of the dimension, we have pure equality of bargaining power, exchange among symmetrically situated parties. This is the kind of formal equality that underlies most of the common normative justifications of democracy. At the other end of the dimension is total dominance by one party over the other. This is a degree of inequality that would obviously be unacceptable according to any criterion of democracy. In between are the various configurations of relative bargaining power available to the parties. The farther we move from the end point of pure equality, the greater the asymmetry in the relative bargaining power of the parties.

We assume at least two things about the implications of the location of any bargaining process on this dimension. First, the greater the asymmetry in bargaining power, the more likely it is that some parties experience significant forms of bargaining pressure to acquiesce to the interests of more powerful actors. This raises procedural questions about the voluntariness of their participation. Second, the greater the asymmetry in bargaining power, the more likely it is that the substantive bargaining outcome will distributively favor the interests of the more powerful actors. And it is likely that the inequality in the distribution of benefits of the democratic outcome will at the very least mirror the inequality in the distribution of bargaining power. This obviously raises substantive questions about the acceptability of the democratic bargain.

The basic question is, Where do we draw the line of acceptability on the relative bargaining power dimension? We flesh out the specific implications of this question in the rest of the book. But we close this part of the discussion with a few general implications. First, the criterion of duress establishes a clear procedural constraint on the most egregious kinds of asymmetric political bargains. If a political actor lacks any other meaningful alternative than acceptance of the more powerful actor's offer, then the exchange has the form of a monopoly relationship and should be deemed unacceptable as a democratic bargain. However, in assessing duress, it is important to distinguish between cases in which there are no feasible options due to either systemic factors (for example, institutional rules that exclude people from the bargaining process) or intentional strategies of coercion from those cases in which the less powerful actors are merely unable to persuade others to join them in a successful bargain, leaving acquiescence as the only available option. The former are clear instances of duress, while the latter may merely be the result of the distribution of preferences in the society.

Second, the greater the relative inequality in bargaining power, the more likely the unconscionability of the bargain. The actual determination of unconscionability involves a balancing of procedural and substantive concerns. On the one hand, we must assess the sources of the bargaining power differential, seeking to determine if they are acceptable (for example, the distribution of preferences in the electorate) or unacceptable (for example, unequal economic resources). As we noted above, courts have identified a number of factors that may be considered in assessing the acceptability of asymmetric power in the area of private bargaining. Many of these same factors will be relevant to public bargaining. Some relate to the bargainers themselves and their available resources, factors like race, gender, social status, and wealth that might suggest the possible existence of inequality. Others relate to the nature of the bargaining process itself, the rules of the game so to speak. Given that our focus involves an analysis of democracy as a system of governance, we place special emphasis, in making these assessments, on the rules governing political decision-making throughout the democratic system, identifying ways in which institutional factors may create these inequalities. Once the relevant factors influencing a bargain are identified, if the sources of the unequal bargaining power are determined to be unacceptable, then problems of procedural unconscionability are raised.

But, given the fact that assessments of unconscionability involve a balance of procedural and substantive factors, we must also assess the substantive terms of the bargain. There are some categories of bargaining outcomes that violate the criterion of substantive unconscionability in a democracy. The clearest case is a bargain that harms a citizen's fundamental interests, as identified by the political process and reflected in the constitution, as we will defend in Chapter 2. Such bargains would be deemed unacceptable in a democracy, regardless of the acceptability of the sources of the power inequality.

A second, and related, category of unacceptability follows directly from the commitment to democracy. Effective political participation, one of our fundamental interests, is a foundation of the democratic process. Most of the basic justifications of democracy are grounded, at least in part, on claims about the necessity of effective political participation of all citizens for the achievement of the socially valuable benefits of democratic decision-making (Pettit 1997, 6). It is also important to note that the guarantee of such participation to every citizen in a democratic society serves as a self-sustaining mechanism for the system of governance. And, significantly for our argument here, such a guarantee recommends a prospective viewpoint for assessing the implications of substantively unequal bargains.

Therefore, substantive bargains that harm this interest warrant special scrutiny. And this applies to substantive bargains that might have only an indirect effect on such participation. Policy bargains that exacerbate existing inequalities in society (either social or material) may have a secondary effect of negatively influencing a group's future capacity to participate effectively in the political process. We offer examples of these indirect effects in Chapters 4 and 5.

To the extent that such substantive bargains have these indirect effects on the fundamental interest in political participation, they are problematic on grounds of substantive unconscionability and thus will be deemed an unacceptable political bargain. But note that, from the perspective of the democratic commitment, unequal bargains that diminish existing inequalities, and thus potentially enhance the future political participation of previously weaker political actors, are not subject to the same substantive unconscionability constraint. Thus, bargains that explicitly seek to diminish the relative differences in political bargaining power are acceptable.

Finally, disproportionate bargains that neither infringe on fundamental interests nor diminish the future political prospects of citizens will satisfy the standards of acceptability as defined by substantive unconscionability. Therefore, we acknowledge that bargains characterized by extremely disproportionate distributions of benefits may be democratically acceptable. However, given the requirements of a balancing test involving both procedural and substantive unconscionability, the final determination of acceptability for this category of bargains depends on the process by which the bargain was established. If the bargain was the product of asymmetric bargaining power that is considered procedurally acceptable, then the bargain is also acceptable. Otherwise, the bargain fails the democratic test.

And this leads to one final point about the lessons of private bargaining. For our purposes, there may be some additional insights to be drawn from the other ways, not directly derived from the logic of contracting, that have been used by courts to constrain the unfairness of contracts. These alternatives focus more directly on the effects of systemic inequalities in the society. One such constraint is fairly straightforward. Here we have in mind laws that are enacted to make certain kinds of contracts illegal because they violate public policy. A standard example would be a contract that commits someone to a life of slavery. There is a longstanding tenet of the law that individuals should not be allowed to enter into a contract in which they freely agree to give up their freedom and become the slave of another.

Satz (2010) offers a compelling account of why this and a number of other aspects of social life have been or should be excluded from the possible subjects of private exchange. Here she takes up, in addition to slavery, such issues as prostitution, child labor, women's reproduction, and sale of human organs. Some of her primary arguments justify exclusion in terms of the inequalities in bargaining power characterizing the markets in which these private exchanges take place. In this sense Satz is pursuing the same concerns that motivate us in this study. In addition, she offers other justifications, building on the early work in political economy by Adam Smith and David Ricardo, that highlight the negative effects on individuals as well as social life writ large of allowing private markets for these excluded goods. And this second set of concerns is often the main reason that courts and legislatures have chosen to generally exclude the subject of the exchange from the practice of private contracting.

In the context of public bargaining, the type of legal constraint that Satz identifies as a solution to some of the problems of private bargaining would commonly be treated as a constitutional question. Does the constitution exclude the subject matter of the bargain from the agenda of the democratic decision-making process? This seems like a reasonable question to ask of many of the substantially unequal bargains that would be deemed acceptable on our account. For, while such bargains may offend our commitments to justice and fairness, they will not be prohibited merely by the standard of unconscionability in a democracy. Unless appropriate substantive criteria of justice and fairness are instantiated in a society's constitution, a commitment to democracy alone cannot prevent the perpetuation of existing inequalities in a society.

A second kind of constraint, not derived from the law of contracts but used by courts to constrain private bargains, that might have intriguing implications for the assessment of the acceptability of public bargains is found in the law of antitrust. With the enactment of the antitrust laws, courts have had an additional way of addressing issues of unequal bargaining power in contract enforcement cases. They have tended to use it only in instances of serious disparities of bargaining power, the threat of monopoly power, but it does serve as an explicit and legitimate constraint on the effects of unequal bargaining power on private bargains.

Here it is important to reflect on the appropriate justification of this kind of constraint. Antitrust law can be justified on grounds similar to that of consumer protection legislation, as a means of protecting contracting parties from the unfair features of their individual transactions.

This is the way that it is commonly justified in the literature on contracts (Posner 2016, 102), and it does highlight an important benefit of the law. However, there is an alternative justification of antitrust law that is more relevant for our purposes. Rather than conceiving of antitrust constraints as a protection against unfairness in individual exchanges, we might envision them as a mechanism for guaranteeing the effectiveness of market institutions.[5] The effectiveness of markets is, in large part, a function of the conditions necessary to achieve the collective benefits of competition among economic actors. When these conditions do not apply, the benefits that are used to justify markets are not realized. One of the most important of these conditions is the equality of bargaining power that characterizes perfectly competitive markets. The greater the disparities in bargaining power in a market, the less effective the market will be in producing socially beneficial outcomes.

From this perspective, the justification for constraining private bargains generated by asymmetries in bargaining power follows from our collective interest in the institutional effectiveness of markets. This argument is similar to Oman's justification of contract law in terms of well-functioning markets, and it captures some of the broader concerns about both relational equality and the general context in which contracts are made that are at the heart of Dagan and Heller's account of autonomy. While the focus of antitrust laws is on the overall competitiveness of the markets, the ways in which these laws are applied by the courts puts the focus primarily on the strategies by which market power is acquired. This puts the focus not so much on the exercise of the power advantage in the specific bargain but rather on the relative power asymmetries in the market as a whole. So, in assessing the effects of unequal bargaining power on private bargains, courts will look to the sources of their relative bargaining power. Some sources are deemed legitimate, others not.

A similar justification for constraining political bargains may follow from our concern with the effectiveness of political institutions. As we have emphasized, theoretical claims about the benefits of democratic institutions commonly rest on the assumption of the equality of political actors. Whatever the justification (epistemological goals, diminishing domination goals, guaranteeing egalitarian relations, alternating power and authority goals, etc.) for democratic political institutions, they will not operate effectively and thus will not achieve their desired ends if they are characterized by significant asymmetries in power. Therefore, just as this concern with institutional effectiveness can serve as the basis for constraints on certain classes of asymmetric private bargains, it may serve as a similar basis for public ones as well. Think of it as the democratic political equivalent of economic antitrust laws. We return to this last idea in our concluding chapter.

Conclusion

Both private and public bargaining, at their core, are about the production of collective endeavors that have prospective benefits, over which there is likely to be distributive conflict. Our examination of the private law of contracts has sought to demonstrate the ways in which the values underlying the state interest in facilitating and constraining private bargaining may parallel those in public bargaining. We take the most important values to be egalitarian ones, as well as the effective operation of institutions. Courts' willingness to decline to enforce private bargains on the grounds that they emerge from serious inequalities of bargaining power, on the one hand, or would hamper the attainment of other social benefits, on the other hand, helps us to characterize the scope of justifiable public bargains. Public bargains—over constitutional laws and statutes, and over the enforcement and interpretation of such norms—condition the lives of citizens in ways that are often even more significant than the private agreements that citizens reach among themselves. As a result, it is crucial to consider the justification and constraints on public bargaining, and the conditions under which courts in particular may decline to enforce certain outcomes. This is the focus of the chapters that follow.

2

Constitutionalism and Democratic Bargaining

LAWMAKING IN A democratic community typically relies on bargaining. We have argued already that this is no embarrassment for democracy; bargaining is a central means by which competing interests and claims in a community may be resolved, if provisionally. Yet the worry persists that power asymmetries may contaminate decision-making. Because constitutional rules condition the ordinary political procedures and policy outcomes that emerge, if constitution-making takes the form of asymmetrical bargaining, it is difficult to see how the resulting constitution could secure the equitable treatment of interests that is at the heart of democratic decision-making. As a result, deliberative, inclusive constitution-making would seem to be a more attractive strategy from the standpoint of democracy.

To respond to these challenges, we draw on insights from the private law of contracting that we sketched in Chapter 1. In the conclusion to Chapter 1, we emphasized that the primary aims of private and public contracts alike are about the production of collective endeavors that have prospective benefits, over which there is likely to be distributive conflict. The US Constitution exemplifies such a collective endeavor, distributing bargaining power among institutions. It identifies those fundamental interests that may not be exchanged for ordinary interests; and it generates the institutional context for the satisfaction of ordinary interests, while constraining bargaining within those institutions. The primary aim of constitutional bargaining should be to secure the procedural and substantive factors that are likely to promote the equitable treatment of interests. More specifically, the constitutive and regulative roles played by the constitution primarily pertain to the structure and limitations of political bargaining. If the constitution exacerbates inequalities of bargaining power among institutions, or if it fails to secure the fundamental interests of its members, especially including its most vulnerable members, it falls short of the democratic baseline.

We have two main aims in this chapter. First, we argue that a bargaining theory of constitutionalism better explains how constitutions in fact operate, and clarifies "constitutional dualism" and the hierarchy of norms between constitutional and ordinary legislation. Here we contrast our account to other approaches in the literature that rely on analogies to contract, as well as to the wider literature on constitution-making. Obviously, there is a long history of analogies to contracts to explain and justify constitutions, as well as significant theoretical arguments rejecting such approaches on the grounds that contracts require third-party enforcement, unavailable at the moment of contracting. We criticize both of these approaches, arguing that their failure to take seriously the problem of coercion of vulnerable minorities prevents them from providing meaningful guidance in terms of the normative validity of actually existing institutions, virtually all of which will have emerged from asymmetric bargains. A bargaining theory of constitutionalism better explains both how constitutions emerge and the conditions under which they may be democratically legitimate, that is, when the constitution distributes power in such a way as to prospectively enable the equitable treatment of interests.

Second, we argue that ongoing bargaining is necessary for constitutional norms to be democratically justified, because a constitution cannot dictate terms to parties and reliably satisfy the equitable treatment of interests in a prospective fashion. To illuminate these claims, we analyze Canadian jurisprudence concerning the constitutional duty to negotiate and to consult both in the context of debates over federalism and with respect to treaty and other claims of Indigenous groups. We turn to the "defensive doctrines" to characterize the conditions that undermine the constitution's ability to be justified democratically: that is, where the distribution of power is so unequal that vulnerable minorities cannot reliably secure their interests through political bargaining, or where the conditions that obtain in constitutional negotiations undermine bargaining so severely as to be tantamount to duress.

To foreground the significance of the bargaining approach, note that our strategy departs from recent work in democratic theory, which tends to promote community engagement and robust deliberation at moments of constitutional choice. Two decades ago, in an influential report, Vivienne Hart of the United States Institute of Peace argued that the public had a moral right to participate in democratic constitution-making. Whereas older scholarship characterized constitution-making as a "contract, negotiated by appropriate representatives"—that is, by elites who possess the expertise and technical skills, and rational incentives to compromise—the "constitution of new constitutionalism is, in contrast, a conversation" (Hart 2003, 3). Scholarship after Hart often recommends random selection, with the aim of selecting a cross-section of the community for participation in constitution-making and/or a role for direct community involvement, through mechanisms such as deliberative polling (for example, Fishkin 2009). Indeed, although an attempt at constitutional reform in Iceland in 2010–2013 failed, scholars such as Hélène Landemore have heralded its participatory process, including through crowdsourcing, as a vanguard (Landemore 2020, 178). Yet inclusion is likely to be otiose if it is insensitive to the interests of powerful actors. Thorvaldur Gylfason, who served on the constitutional council, suggested that the constitutional reform process was undermined by Iceland's largest political party, who successfully litigated the popular election of the constituent assembly, and then by additional parties who had a vested interest in the status quo. Among those, he singled out important allies of special interest groups, such as fishing vessel owners, and politicians who resisted a scheme designed to improve the equality of representation.[1]

Our argument is not that wider inclusivity is unnecessary or normatively undesirable. By contrast, it is important for democratic bargaining because it helps to identify fundamental interests that require constitutional protection. But since most contemporary constitution-making processes feature preexisting parties and organized interest groups, it is crucial for the protection of vulnerable minorities that they have representation designed to secure their interests in the constitutional arena.

But this opportunity need not take the form of direct participation in the constitutional drafting process; it can occur through public deliberations (formal and informal) outside of the process. Significant interests can be communicated to representatives, who are in a superior position to bargain on behalf of those interests. As such, throughout this chapter, we treat inclusion as being instrumentally valuable insofar as it may help to redistribute bargaining power in a way that can conduce to the equitable treatment of interests, but not—against the participatory grain—as being of such great intrinsic significance that other processes lack legitimacy (Hart 2003).[2]

Again, the bargaining theory of constitutionalism draws on certain elements of the private law of contracting. It does so advisedly, in part because our argument is not that a constitution reflects the strong element of voluntarism inherent in ordinary contracting, nor that the reasons why a state might not want to enforce contracts made under duress (for example) in private law are identical to those in public law. Rather, courts have developed a set of doctrines for how to assess the benefits and risks of bargaining within a democratic context that we find broadly applicable in both the private context and the public context, even if the scope and nature of these benefits and risks differ. Our main orientation is prospective, designed to ensure that a constitution distributes power in a way that will allow subsidiary bargaining processes—within and among legislatures, courts, and administrative agencies—to operate in an effective and equitable fashion. However, because we are obviously not the first to explain constitutionalism through appeal to contracting, it is worth clarifying how the bargaining approach departs from other accounts that adopt and reject the contract metaphor.

Contracting and Coordination

Some political philosophers, across the ideological spectrum, argue that the justification of norms—particularly constitutional norms—requires us to satisfy demanding conditions of voluntary agreement, if only hypothetically, and so an idealized contracting situation can clarify what norms *ought* to be adopted. This contractarianism imagines a set of persons who sought to determine the conditions of social interaction, and it asks which norms each of these persons could rationally and reasonably agree to adopt. For instance, the veil of ignorance in the Rawlsian "original position" seeks to eliminate the effects of unequal power in the establishment of fundamental norms, such as principles of justice. The veil specifically shields the representatives of free and equal citizens from knowledge of their social position and endowments; they are symmetrically situated *ex hypothesi*, and the principles that result from their agreement are therefore fair. Choice in the original position does not emerge from a bargaining process; indeed, Rawls identified bargaining as such with the use of threat and holdout power (Rawls 1971, 139–41).[3] Rather, it is an "agreement," which the parties accept as obligatory, and which constitutes the basis upon which they will stably order their political community. Again, the agreement itself is purely hypothetical. The authority of this hypothetical agreement—its normative force— derives from the fact that these principles *would* have been adopted by free and equal, reasonable and rational, persons, who aimed to establish fair terms of social cooperation.

Although Rawls did characterize constitution-making as a crucial second stage, in which the parties craft norms in light of the two principles of justice and the wider political culture of their community, the Rawlsian project was never intended to *explain* constitutional emergence, or even to justify actually existing constitutions as such. So its project is quite different from ours. Further, the basic approach to contracting in the selection of principles specifically occludes power asymmetries, including those generated by social standing, and especially with respect to race and gender. Here too we would depart. As Charles Mills has argued, abstraction itself is unproblematic, but abstractions that "obfuscate" the specific social realities that require mapping should be rejected: when we appeal to contracting, we still need to recognize that "race and gender position people differently, in complex asymmetrical interrelations, rather than pretending that we are featureless atomic individuals in egalitarian contractual relationships with each other" (Pateman and Mills 2007, 176). Our account of constitutional bargaining is consistent with this general approach, in which our aim will be to focus on particular power asymmetries in a given community; it is different from a "Rawlsian" (if, again, not exactly Rawls's own) approach, in which one might identify a set of fair principles in the abstract and see whether prospective rules cohere with them, perhaps through the method of reflective equilibrium.

Unlike Rawls's contractarianism, the public choice approach to constitutionalism, associated most famously with the work of James Buchanan and Gordon Tullock, is intended to be both explanatory and prescriptive. Although certain features of Buchanan and Tullock's approach might be characterized as idealized—notably their basic assumption that only unanimous agreement can justly govern constitutional choice for a free society—they do not characterize their project in such a way. Their work famously begins by assuming that net benefits would be maximized under a rule of unanimity, because voluntary agreement among rational agents would remove all relevant externalities. However, because of the costs of decision-making, a qualified-majority threshold weaker than unanimity may be adopted for some collective action: this pragmatic concession alone indicates that their account is not intended to be purely heuristic, but action-guiding. In their words,

> It seems futile to discuss a "theory" of constitutions for free societies on any other assumptions than this. Unless the parties agree to participate in this way in the ultimate constitutional debate and to search for the required compromises needed to attain general agreement, no real constitution can be made. An imposed constitution that embodies the coerced agreement of some members of the social group is a wholly different institution from that which we propose to examine in this book. (Buchanan and Tullock 1962, 23)

At the stage of constitutional choice, a rational individual recognizes a trade-off between securing protection against adverse decisions (voting rules approaching unanimity) and the costs of decision-making (voting rules approaching a simple majority). Buchanan and Tullock suggested that a rational individual would seek the most strenuous protections for "individual human or property rights" anticipating that "property rights especially can never be defined once and for all, and there will always exist an area of quasi property rights subject to change by the action of the collective unity" (Buchanan and Tullock 1962, 62–63). As such, a rational individual would be willing to incur substantial decision-making costs to secure protection against "confiscation."

The account of political bargaining we defend throughout shares features with public choice theory, notably in its emphasis on the maximization of interests, which James Buchanan characterized as "politics without romance." But we depart from the public choice approach in its conceptualization of coercion, particularly its normative preoccupation with majoritarianism as a main source of unfreedom. That approach takes unanimous agreement to serve as the fundamental source of normative validity, assigning excessive weight to the value of individual freedom at the expense of making it far more difficult to depart from the status quo. It also yields serious normative concerns about the status of fundamental interests that do not reduce to property rights, which Buchanan and his coauthors treat as akin to human rights in their inviolability.

To see how Buchanan and Tullock's approach differs from our own, consider how they treat the problem of holdouts to the proposed constitution. At the moment of constitutional choice, no member can be obliged to accept decisions with which she disagrees; a constitution cannot be imposed upon her, and so she must be compensated for what she takes to be the prospective costs associated with collective decision-making until she is willing to agree. Duress constitutes, in essence, a failure to adequately compensate for negative externalities. Indeed, Buchanan and Tullock acknowledge as much, suggesting that "the unanimity test is, in fact, identical to the compensation test if compensation is interpreted as that payment, negative or positive, which is required to secure agreement" (1962, 75). Those who least require constitutional protection, by dint of their existing resources and power, have an incentive to hold out; the most vulnerable, those who both would gain from redistribution and who have the least capacity to withstand pressure, are likely to find their disadvantages entrenched.

In work with Geoffrey Brennan, Buchanan argued that the higher-level abstraction in the creation of constitutional-level rules would inhibit people from knowing their future positions, effectively nullifying these worries about relative positions (Buchanan and Brennan 1985). Insofar as the aim of the project is quasi-Rawlsian—that is, to determine the hypothetical outcomes of constitutional contracting under the veil of ignorance—such an assumption might be warranted. But in most constitution-making contexts, such uncertainty is likely to be constrained: constitution-making will entail bargaining among preexisting parties and groups with interests and expectations of their share of the benefits from contracting. Indeed, Brennan and Buchanan implicitly admit as much: in the final chapter of *Reason of Rules*, Brennan and Buchanan take up the question of constitutional reform in existing democracies to argue that the working out of agreements will in practice likely require a "complex network that includes various compromises, side payments, compensations, bribes, exchanges, trade-offs," to pay off those who stand to lose under structural change (Buchanan and Brennan 1985, 156).

Although we are sympathetic to their basic intuition—that constitutionalism entails bargaining and negotiation, including payoffs and trade-offs—we doubt that such bargaining will immediately yield democratic norms consistent with the equitable treatment of interests. Because the public choice approach valorizes the protection of property rights over other types of interest, and focuses on takings, its adherents tend to neglect those fundamental interests for which there can be no acceptable compensation. In a searing critique of public choice approaches to constitutionalism, Don Herzog provides these examples: (1) a community pays gay people for prohibitions on their conduct, and (2) neighbors who are disturbed by a Rastafarian's dreadlocks (following Dennis C. Mueller's example of a person forbidden to comb her hair) offer to make the woman's next twelve mortgage payments if she will shave her head. Mueller writes, "*R* could be compelled to comb her hair only if she willingly agreed to do so, as she might if she were convinced by the rest of the community that their suffering was severe enough, or she were offered a sufficiently large bribe" (Mueller 1996, 214; Herzog 2000, 920). Herzog notes the oxymoronic language of "willing agreement" and "compelled," highlighting the inability of public choice to make sense of the social psychology of voluntary agreement by marginalized members.

For our purposes, the important insight is that the public choice approach to constitutionalism cannot provide vulnerable members of a community any reason to believe that their fundamental interests will be secure. Insofar as they are disadvantaged under the status quo—and so their outside option is at least as poor as the constitutional contract they are offered—their compliance may be bought cheaply, even when it means the loss of their dignity and potentially their capacity for political agency. Although it is true that many constitutions neglect the interests of marginalized groups yet receive wide compliance with their terms, as a guide to normatively justifiable contracting for a political community, it surely fails. Against the public choice approach, a main advantage of our theory will be that it seeks to specify limits not merely on the outcomes but on the process of bargaining. It acknowledges the inescapability of power asymmetries and thus the risks of unconscionability and duress during constitution-making, and it takes as a condition of democratic legitimacy the protection of the fundamental interests of vulnerable minorities—including recognizing that there can be no compensation for the loss of dignity and political standing.

Given the deficiencies of existing approaches, one might instead argue that there are good reasons to reject contract-based constitutionalism, as "coordination" accounts do. Coordination approaches to constitutionalism tend to focus on the analytical problem of enforcing a constitutional contract absent a third-party agent, and the strategic quandary of why parties might comply with constitutional contracts when it is in their short-term interest to renege. Such concerns have drawn many scholars, including Hardin (1989), Ordeshook (1992), and Weingast (1997), to the coordination account. There is much to say for the coordination view: it seems to explain the conditions under which people generate constitutions (dire), the terms to which they agree (minimally sufficient to produce the wages of peace), why they might continue to abide by the contract when defection might be advantageous (the costs of recontracting), and why nonparties might continue to acquiesce to the constitution when they did not participate in its creation (all of the above, as well as adaptive preferences). Moreover, it seems to provide a more empirically robust account of how constitutions acquire force.

But the coordination account faces significant challenges, both explanatory and normative. First, like the public choice account of constitutional contracting, it is basically insensitive to the role of power in determining the outcome; the apparent social fact of coordination masks, or sanitizes, the process by which the outcome emerged as the focal point. Indeed, a leading theoretical account of constitution as coordination actually begins by presuming the absence of coercion (Hadfield and Weingast 2012, 127). Again, one problem that coordination accounts seek to solve is how compliance with a constitution may be sustained absent a third-party enforcer; for a constitution to be an equilibrium, citizens from divergent perspectives must have incentives to coordinate their behavior to uphold those norms and to punish violators of the provisions. The basic logic of the self-enforcing constitution is that there is an "agreement" or a "pact" among agents to create a new focal point and set of "bright-line constitutional restrictions," and to punish violators thereof.

Although it may well be that a constitution endures only if it does in fact establish such expectations and incentivize actors to participate in decentralized enforcement of its strictures, these accounts tend to describe the resulting outcome in terms of these effects. This approach courts functionalism, so in part to avoid this objection, coordination accounts also usually acknowledge that agreement will emerge from negotiation among the parties (in Weingast's example, the Tories and Whigs in the Glorious Revolution) (Weingast 1997). However, they further presume that if these agreements were entirely one-sided, favoring one set of agents over others, they would not be stable nor incentivize the weaker agents to participate in enforcement. This too depends upon a specific distribution of power. So long as the weaker party to the "coordination" believes the threat posed by defection (for example, to collude with the king) exceeds the threat posed by continued compliance with the "coordination" outcome (the costs of defection are greater than the costs of compliance), the outcome will remain stable. Although Weingast characterizes such a result as social consensus on the legitimate boundaries of the state, one might just as easily describe it as a coercive bargain struck among asymmetrical parties.

Coordination accounts derive their normative force largely from the voluntary compliance of members, as measured behaviorally by their willingness to engage in decentralized enforcement; they are described as "incentive-compatible." From an external standpoint, though, the behavioral fact of individual compliance (including under, and with, a decentralized system of enforcement) may reflect asymmetrical forms of social power: the obedience of marginalized members may be voluntary only in the most attenuated sense of that term. If a minority is sufficiently powerful that its defection would undermine the constitutional order, then it can secure its interests. Yet if the minority is vulnerable, it is hard to see why that minority would expect its interests to be durably protected under such conditions. Its compliance is not necessary for constitutional settlement; it can be coerced. The minority would reasonably worry about the consequences for its members if consensus on the significance of their interests began to flag, or if some agents found it in their interest to dominate.

The coordination strategy, more generally, faces a challenge insofar as it tends to infer from the fact of compliance the voluntary nature of the agreement, and then to justify enforcement on the basis of such an inference. But inferring consent from the absence of exit—particularly given the exorbitant costs of unilateral exit—poses its own problems, a famous Humean difficulty. That is, acquiescence to a constitution cannot justify the coordinated-upon set of norms to those who may be disadvantaged by the outcomes except through reference to the costs associated with the outside option. It sidesteps, rather than confronts, the normative grounds of contracting.

If one begins with the assumption—as one should—that power is unequally distributed, then the coordination theorist has two alternatives. The first is to accept that the agreement of the weaker party may derive from coercion, which the self-enforcing equilibrium approach seeks to avoid both on analytical grounds and for normative reasons. Again, its raison d'être is to explain how norms, including constitutional norms, can be upheld absent centralized coercive force, and how such an account can realize greater liberty through private ordering. But since more powerful agents may be able to coerce weaker members while themselves remaining immune from sanctions, there is little normative reason for vulnerable members to prefer decentralized, and potentially arbitrary, enforcement of unequal norms to state enforcement. Because vulnerable members are all too aware that their compliance is unnecessary for the coordination to hold, they will be unlikely to take seriously the more powerful agents' promises to respect their interests. Put in the language of contract law, there will be no "consideration"; it will be an illusory promise made by the powerful to the vulnerable.

This generates the second alternative—we coordinate on a convention that will enable us to protect the interests of vulnerable minorities, and then, in Hardin's words, we "*arrange* to have it stick" (Hardin 1989, 135). To do so, we may create institutions that function as a third-party enforcer, such as a constitutional court, or complicated amendment provisions. But if this is the case, then the distinction between a coordination-based account and a contract-based account is basically moot. It may well be true that an initial state cannot emerge without the most powerful parties recognizing that it is in their interest to agree, and that defection would make them far worse off. In this narrow respect, the appropriate characterization of original agreement is a coordination game, rather than a prisoners' dilemma. But again, because the gains from coordination may be unequally distributed—as in what used to be called a "Battle of the Sexes" game—farsighted actors will seek institutions that will enforce such agreements against competitors' efforts to enhance their power at their expense. Insofar as the most powerful members have little incentive to treat the interests of vulnerable groups as central to their agreement—because they would doubt that these groups will ever have a chance to dominate—the fact of coordination itself provides scant normative grounds for democratic legitimacy.[4] But there is also no reason to believe that a constitution resting on an asymmetric "coordination" solution, in which the relatively powerful members agree on unequal terms, will realize equality, or generate compliance, to any greater extent than would a constitution resting on a contract that reflects unequal bargaining power. To do so, both will require third-party enforcement to secure the interests of vulnerable members against efforts at encroachment, and even to prevent those actors who are empowered under the constitution from expanding their gains when they believe they could do so without producing a response that would yield the collapse of the regime.

Like coordination models, the bargaining theory of constitutionalism we offer rests on the logic of mutual advantage, but it acknowledges that in most contexts, only the powerful groups or actors need to agree in order for the constitution to acquire force. As a result, it takes seriously the risk that vulnerable minorities will not have their interests protected, and so it does not infer democratic legitimacy from the social fact of apparent agreement. Further, it also takes little reassurance from the mere presence of norms, particularly rights provisions, that seem to afford minority protection. Instead, to be democratically legitimate, a constitution must prospectively secure the conditions of the equitable treatment of interests: specifically, it must create institutions that distribute power in such a way that vulnerable minorities have a meaningful opportunity to renegotiate terms in an ongoing fashion.

Constitutional Dualism and Democracy

The bargaining theory of constitutionalism, focusing as it does on the equitable treatment of interests, also helps to clarify the nature of constitutional dualism, the distinction between constitutional politics and ordinary politics. Bruce Ackerman is perhaps the most famous proponent of such an approach. Ackerman distinguishes between periods of "higher lawmaking," or "constitutional moments," in which the general public is deeply engaged in a deliberative search for the common good, and "normal politics," in which individuals and interest groups largely seek to promote parochial concerns, and legislation emerges from factional competition among representatives of private citizens (Ackerman 1993). But a difference between constitutional and ordinary politics runs deep in normative political theory (for example, Dworkin 1996).[5]

Some scholars argue that the legitimacy of all legal norms requires public reason. Gerald Gaus complained that, in Rawls's work, the point of normal political activity was "obscure" (Gaus 1996, 232). Gaus argued that constitutional politics is concerned with what is "conclusively justified" through the achievement of rational consensus, and thereby set the agenda of normal politics. Yet even if consensus is not to be expected in normal politics, it remains an arena of "inconsistent public justifications" over fundamental matters: it is the "confrontation of undefeated, unvictorious judgments about the demands of basic principles." Gaus approvingly cited Gutmann and Thompson here, highlighting their observation that we should "be reaching conclusions . . . through moral reasoning rather than self-interested bargaining," not through the competition or compromise of interests, and that we ought to embrace lawmaking institutions that "induce legislators to 'act more like judges' by providing principled justifications for their judgments" (Gaus 1996, 232–33; Gutmann and Thompson 1990, 85).

Our own dualist strategy is different. Like Gaus, we do not think that the mechanisms by which constitutions and ordinary legislation are created do, or should, differ in kind. But unlike Gaus, we characterize both constituent assemblies and legislatures as primarily loci of bargaining over interests. To be sure, deliberation may play a role in both constitutional and ordinary politics, but more often deliberation serves to clarify and reduce the dimensions of conflict than to yield consensus (Knight and Johnson 1994). Policing arguments for sincerity, rather than hypocrisy, is a dead end. Even when normative reasons are proffered in either the constitutional or legislative context, actors often have strategic reasons to treat them as epiphenomenal unless they are backed up by a willingness to trade on their behalf. Moreover, constitutional consensus is often unachievable, or where it exists, unidentifiable: that is, even if it did emerge, it is nearly impossible to specify voting rules that might reliably secure it (Schwartzberg 2014). A majority threshold may not produce the breadth of support that consensus is supposed to pick out, but likewise, supermajority rules may enable a recalcitrant minority to block what we might otherwise recognize as a provision with widespread support.

Dualism emerges not from the mechanisms that generate constitutional and legislative norms, but by the significance of the interests and the institutions they protect. Constitutions identify fundamental interests— ones that cannot become a bargaining chip in negotiations over less important interests—and regulate the terms of bargaining for the other institutions that they create. However, this does not mean that constitutional politics is immune from bargaining: as we discuss shortly, bargaining frequently occurs even over the appropriate formulation of rights provisions. Constitutions are bargains writ large, though ones that also condition bargains over legislation, and that regulate interbranch bargaining and bargaining among private individuals and the state. To characterize constitutions as bargains does not shield them from normative scrutiny.

As a dualist system designed to enable lower-level bargains, it might seem that this approach is close to a "precommitment" logic of constitutionalism. Precommitment entails the view that at t_1 an agent rationally chooses to bind himself against some action, lest he be passionately driven at t_2 to undertake it. Elster provides the most famous example of precommitment: Ulysses binding himself to the mast so as not to be tempted by the Sirens (Elster 1979). The analogy is that a democracy precommits itself, through constitutional binding, to protect the rights of minorities against its temptation to engage in majority tyranny.[6] Stephen Holmes characterizes precommitment somewhat differently, offering an enabling model that emphasizes the "constitutive" work that constitutions do, akin to rules of grammar or chess. It enables democratic decision-making rather than limiting it (Holmes 1997).

Our normative strategy differs from these approaches. Of course, we share the view that a constitution enables new political actions; no one could doubt that. But its ability to secure *democratic* decision-making depends crucially on its ability to secure the equitable treatment of interests. Our theory holds that the constitutive and regulative roles played by the constitution primarily pertain to the structure and limitations of political bargaining: it creates new institutions that constitute loci of bargaining, and it regulates and limits the bargaining activities of those institutions.[7] Its constitutive role also entails a distributive function, differentially allocating power across institutions. A constitutional system of separation of powers, with checks and balances, does not require that the legislative, judicial, and executive branches each possess equal power. In Chapters 3 and 4, we argue that a democratic system of bargaining in fact requires legislative supremacy, that is, that the legislature possesses greater bargaining power than the other branches. This is because the legislature is representative; its function is to enable bargaining among representatives to satisfy their constituents' interests, subject to the electoral sanction. Its connection to citizens' interests, as identified by the citizens themselves and transmitted to the representatives, is closer than that of the executive or the judiciary, and so its bargaining power ought to exceed those of the other branches. But the exercise of the legislative power—and the power of the other branches—is also regulated by reference to the equitable treatment of interests standard.

Constitution-making itself is characterized by bargaining, rendering precommitment an inapt description: it is difficult to explain constitution-making in terms of self-binding where plural actors seek to gain advantages over each other both in the short term and in the long term. Better to describe it as a process of contracting, albeit usually an asymmetrical one. Its ability to enable democratic decision-making rests crucially on whether it prospectively secures the equitable treatment of interests. This itself is a broadly flexible concept, though; the argument that only through the deep entrenchment of norms can we secure such decision-making is mistaken, particularly when we recognize that all laws, protecting fundamental and ordinary interests alike, will emerge from asymmetric bargaining. Although the constitution must secure the important interests of citizens (notably in equal voting power), and distinguish fundamental interests from ordinary ones, insofar as only the latter can be traded off in bargains, any given constitution need not be, and cannot be, a permanent resolution. Identifying these interests that should be removed from the legislative bargaining table will require ongoing participation from agents representing the range of parties in the community. The core normative aim of a democratic constitution is to ensure that parties have good reason to believe their interests will be treated equitably in future political bargaining. We now turn to the conditions under which this may be realized.

The Constitutional Duty to Bargain

We do not offer a formal model specifying the necessary and sufficient conditions for democracy to emerge under asymmetrical bargaining. Rather, we primarily aim to provide normative guidance regarding the democratic justification of constitutional norms, both in light of the fact that such norms are very likely to emerge through bargaining, and—even more crucially—to structure future political bargains. To vindicate the claim that constitutional bargaining is able to yield norms that prospectively satisfy the equitable treatment of interests standard, and in particular to protect vulnerable minorities, we turn to examples from Canadian constitutional jurisprudence. With the Supreme Court of Canada, we deny that whatever agreement parties reach and are willing to enforce can satisfy the democratic standard: the bargains that representatives strike may fail to secure the equitable treatment of interests and may require revision in order to be consistent with democracy, particularly once constitutional provisions gain force and meaning through interpretation. Broadly speaking, the democratic justification of the constitution depends on *how* the constitution distributes power both among institutions and among individuals. A constitution-making process in which representatives identify and bargain on behalf of the interests of different groups plays a key role, because it gives minority groups some reason to believe that future bargains will also take their interests into account.

Pivotally, though, these reasons are rooted not in the *motivations* of contemporary agents or future ones but in an institutional framework that distributes power among groups and is designed to facilitate ongoing bargaining. The only way in which minority groups can have any confidence that their fundamental interests will be protected is through the presence of institutions designed to facilitate bargaining on behalf of these interests. As such, the primary aim of the democratic constitution must be to facilitate ongoing, "thin" good-faith bargaining, among all groups in the community, notably including the most vulnerable. Beyond norms of free expression and association, this will require a constitutional framework in which threats to their interests can be contested: through legislative action, in consultation with executive agencies, and via the courts as a matter of last resort. As we will discuss, a relatively flexible constitution, one that allows for constitutional challenges to be addressed through amendment rather than through the courts, may also serve to empower groups to secure their evolving interests.

In what follows, we do not sharply distinguish initial constitution-making processes from other significant moments of constitutional reform. That is because, from our standpoint, all moments of important constitutional change entail bargaining, and are subject to the same normative conditions and constraint. Duties to negotiate and consult, and to mitigate grave power asymmetries, govern *de novo* constitution-making and amendments alike. To be sure, constitution-making typically involves a much more complex set of bargains than constitutional revision does. But constitutions rarely emerge from *tabula rasa*; more often constitution-making involves "rebuilding the ship at sea," to adapt the metaphor of an important book on postcommunist constitutionalism (Elster, Offe, and Preuss, 1998). Certain distinctive problems arise when new constitutions are imposed by external forces, and we will take up those problems shortly, in our discussion of duress. But even there, the duress created by occupying forces may not be that dissimilar from the coercion exerted by victors over losers in civil wars, with similar consequences for the treatment of interests down the line.

We now turn to contemporary Canadian constitutional jurisprudence, which sheds light on the conditions under which minority interests can be treated equitably through bargaining, despite power asymmetries. The Supreme Court of Canada has developed doctrines with respect to constitutional bargaining over minority interests in two significant domains: federalism and Indigenous rights. In the former, interests are relatively well defined and the territory is concentrated in such a way as to make secession a feasible alternative. As such, the primary challenge the court has addressed there is how to accommodate Quebecers' interests without enabling a veto over the wider terms of political community for the Canadian federation. The court's treatment of interests of Indigenous groups is necessarily more complicated. This is in part because of the long history of unjust treatment of Indigenous communities, and also because the many Indigenous peoples in Canada (and alliances and confederations among peoples) possess varying interests, some of which may be in tension with each other. As such, many members of Indigenous groups in Canada (and, of course, around the globe) do not have their fundamental interests protected. The Canadian constitutional doctrine of the "duty to consult" is flawed, and may be criticized as merely performative. Yet it nonetheless provides some guidance concerning how vulnerable minorities might have a prospect of equitable treatment under well-designed democratic bargaining processes.

In what follows, we take up both how minority groups, including Indigenous peoples, might have their fundamental interests protected both in the initial constitution-making process and throughout subsequent interpretive and amendment procedures. We emphasize that bargaining is not a one-shot game in the constitutional setting; rather, a democratic constitution needs to attend to the distribution of bargaining power over time. That requires that institutional design attends carefully to both the specification of substantive interests, particularly in the form of rights provisions, and to the mechanisms by which parties can renegotiate on behalf of fundamental interests, through legislatures, courts, and the amendment process.

Duty to Negotiate

Quebec has long sought greater autonomy within the Canadian federal system, and referendums for sovereignty and debates over the possibility of secession roiled the country in the late twentieth century. Constitutional jurisprudence on the question of Quebec secession focused on the conditions under which it could be both legal and legitimate, insisting that a unilateral decision on the part of Quebec would fall afoul of these conditions. In a famous ruling, the Supreme Court of Canada held that even after a referendum indicated clear majority support within Quebec for secession, the right of self-determination did not enable them to dictate terms to the other Canadian parties, since "that would not be a negotiation at all."[8] The interests of Quebecers in self-determination could not immediately trump "the principles of federalism and the rule of law, the rights of individuals and minorities, or the operation of democracy in the other provinces or Canada as a whole."

Instead, the court recognized a "constitutional duty to negotiate," a duty to engage in constitutional bargaining over the interests of the key parties: the two "legitimate majorities" of the respective populations of Canada and Quebec, and minority groups, including Indigenous populations. Moreover, the court argued that such bargaining over interests had to occur in the political, rather than the judicial, realm. All Canadians—not merely Quebecers—possessed the right to participate in decision-making over Quebec's secession through a referendum authorizing the government to appoint representatives to advocate for their interests, including representatives from other provinces and Indigenous peoples. If a positive vote of a referendum could not legally oblige the federal government to accept secession, the court also did not permit the government to ignore it: rather, the referendum placed the parties to confederation under a duty to negotiate, and to do so in good faith. Negotiation following such a vote would "need to address the interests of the other provinces, the federal government, Quebec and indeed the rights of all Canadians both within and outside Quebec, and specifically the rights of minorities." The court held that it would not control the resulting political bargains, in part because the "methods appropriate for the search for truth in a court of law are ill-suited to getting to the bottom of constitutional negotiations." Only insofar as the bargains seemed to threaten legal rights and obligations under the Canadian Constitution—that is, the fundamental interests of its members—would such questions be justiciable.

Two features of this decision are important for the bargaining theory of constitutionalism. First, the court's decision emphasizes the constitutional significance of the distribution of power in a federalist system. In enumerating its four fundamental and organizing principles of the Constitution, the court began with federalism, followed by democracy, constitutionalism and the rule of law, and minority protections. It provided a lengthy historical discussion of the importance of federalism as "the political mechanism by which diversity could be reconciled with unity." It also linked federalism to democratic participation, "by distributing power to the government thought to be most suited to achieving the particular societal objective having regard to this diversity." In characterizing democracy, the court affirmed that federalism meant that there would be competing majorities, and that the federal system would enable different provinces to pursue policies responsive to the particular interests of people in that province. Democracy also depended upon the construction of majorities through "compromise, negotiation, and deliberation."

But *negotiation* is the key concept in the context of constitutionalism upon which the court relied, and specifically negotiation over the distribution of political power: the court argued that the very logic of constitutionalism in Canada required binding norms defining the balance of political power, and that any amendment required "a process of negotiation which ensures that there is an opportunity for the constitutionally defined rights of all the parties to be respected and reconciled." In characterizing constitutionalism, the court argued (inter alia) that it was a means of "allocat[ing] political power amongst different levels of government," which would be defeated if one of those levels could usurp the powers of others through legislative means.

It was in this context that the court recognized the "constitutional duty to negotiate," a duty to engage in constitutional bargaining over the interests of the key parties. Although the duty to negotiate binds not merely Quebec but the other provinces and the federal government—they cannot reject out of hand the Quebecers' attempt to secede or to renegotiate their terms of federation—the Supreme Court specifically cautions the Quebecers against "dictating terms," acknowledging that they may well have the power to do so. Although the court did argue, again, that the bargain itself would be nonjusticiable, "a Quebec that had negotiated in conformity with constitutional principles and values in the face of unreasonable intransigence on the part of other participants at the federal or provincial level would be more likely to be recognized than a Quebec which did not itself act according to constitutional principles in the negotiation process." In this way, the court in fact opened the door to regulating the bargaining process, as David Haljan recognized (Haljan 1999). Consistent with the structural due process approach we defend in Chapter 4, courts may also be called upon to determine whether key actors have bargained in bad faith, or failed to bargain at all.

Confronted with these challenges, the bargaining theory of constitutionalism invites the following key institutional design question: whether the right of secession helps to distribute bargaining power in a way that promotes the equitable treatment of interests—particularly the interests of vulnerable minorities—or whether it instead empowers minorities to wield threat power over majorities in a way that is tantamount to extortion.[9] The court itself recognized this as a central question, noting that a function of constitutionalism was to ensure that *"vulnerable minority groups* are endowed with the institutions and rights necessary to maintain and promote their interests against the assimilative pressures of the majority" (italics added) while, again, affirming that federalism meant that no province could dictate terms.

A quarter century ago, political theorists engaged in a sustained debate about how to enhance the bargaining power of permanent minorities through institutional design, a question displaced in recent years by focus on inclusive deliberation. In the late 1990s, Will Kymlicka argued that one advantage to extending self-government rights both to Indigenous groups and to Quebec is that it would equalize bargaining power between the majority and a national minority. In his view, characterizing Indigenous and Quebecois populations as minorities within a larger community, in which the presumption of majority rule holds, would always leave them disadvantaged. Giving such groups self-government rights—or even enabling secession, in the case of Quebec—would instead give them coequal status as partners (Kymlicka 1998, 18).

By contrast, in an earlier, influential law review paper published on the eve of Eastern European constitution-making, Cass Sunstein argued against enshrining a constitutional right to secession, in part because it would unduly strengthen the bargaining power of such groups: it would "reduce the prospects for compromise and deliberation in government," and "create dangers of blackmail, strategic behavior, and exploitation" (Sunstein 1991, 634). Were such a right recognized by the constitution, subunits could at any time threaten to secede; the threat of exit would loom as a factor for every important decision, empowering the subunit to hold out rather than to compromise. The right to secede would encourage subunits to seek their own gain via threats that are strategically useful "and based on power over matters technically unrelated to the particular question at issue" (Sunstein 1991, 648). These threats would raise the stakes in ordinary political decision-making, preventing the nation from fair dealing by allowing the subunit to veto otherwise justified policies. These threats would be especially credible if the subunit is capable of existing on its own and might in fact prefer to do so—as in the case of Quebec—and, if the subunit possessed indispensable resources, it would be in an "extraordinary position to obtain benefits or to diminish burden on matters formally unrelated to its comparative advantage."[10]

Allen Buchanan concurred with Sunstein, arguing that a right of secession would enable a territorially concentrated minority to use the threat as a strategic bargaining tool. But Buchanan's worries ran deeper, resisting the appeal to bargaining power entirely.[11] Following the logic of Albert Hirschman, Buchanan argued that the recourse to exit will reduce the inclination to use "voice." He worried that secession will make it less rational for individuals "to invest themselves in the practice of principled debate and dialogue." In his view, healthy democracy rests upon citizens who are committed to "agree to disagree rationally, to appeal to reasons backed by principles, rather than indulging in strategic behavior that is designed to achieve their ends without the hard work of achieving principled, rational consensus" (Buchanan 1998, 22).

We have already expressed skepticism that principled, rational consensus constitutes even a regulative ideal in any constitutional democracy, much less in a fledgling democracy. But note here that the aim of consensus provides no traction at all in cases of deep disagreement and unequal political power; instead, it distracts from the pressing question of how to distribute power in a way that will conduce to the equitable treatment of interests. A vulnerable minority that is forced to appeal to the majority's commitment to deliberation to secure its interests is likely to find its interests neglected entirely, particularly in postconflict settings. Such settings are rarely marked by reflective deliberation with an aim of rational consensus.[12] Note that this is a point often made by scholars with hands-on constitution-making expertise. For instance, where there are dominant majorities and persistent minorities, Brendan O'Leary argued that constitutional framers should seek to induce the powerful to accommodate the interests of the minority, "if necessary drawing out proceedings to make their case, and threatening rebellion as future 'spoilers,' or indeed threatening exit—in the form of secession. If smart they will seek to make the rules for making and ratifying the constitution as super-majoritarian as possible, or, at least, to make their clients potentially pivotal" (O'Leary 2019, 201).

There is an obvious bind here. On the one hand, a vulnerable minority is unlikely to be able to secede, to rebel, or to threaten to veto political decisions. Even in the presence of the formal power to do so, their threat is simply to revert to the nonagreement point (Barry 1991). Depending upon how vulnerable the existing populations are under the status quo, veto power may be worth relatively little. Such is often the case with respect to Indigenous groups, insofar as their fundamental interests may be insecure both under the status quo and under a proposed constitutional scheme that imperfectly secures their interests and that they would prefer to reject. By contrast, there are good reasons to worry that a powerful minority may deploy the threat of secession as a veto over majority decisions, including in contexts in which their important interests are not at stake. Daniel Weinstock characterized this as a "blackmail threat"—"accede to our demands on this policy issue completely unrelated to our group-interests, or we will secede!" (Weinstock 2001, 195). As a result, Weinstock argued that in the creation of the right to secede, a set of procedures might regulate the framework for secession and distribute bargaining power accordingly. He defended the use of supermajority rules to govern secession, and/or a sequence of referendums marked by waiting periods between them, which he argues could diminish the credibility of the threat and reduce the effectiveness of the device as a tactical threat, as few policy disagreements would generate the required support for secession.[13]

The question of secession would then turn into an institutional design question requiring phronesis: the selection of a threshold that shifts bargaining power to the minority in cases in which their important interests are at stake, without generating a blanket veto or even equal power with majorities when they are not (Schwartzberg 2014). Under certain circumstances, this may well be an attractive approach to the constitutional distribution of bargaining power. But in other cases, it may be insufficient, and finer-grained procedural mechanisms designed to secure the interests of vulnerable minority groups, such as Indigenous populations, may be necessary. This is where the constitutional "duty to consult" intersects with the duty to negotiate.

Duty to Consult

The recent history of Indigenous inclusion in the Canadian Constitution illuminates the challenges and possibilities of bargaining as a means of securing fundamental interests.[14] Briefly, in the late 1970s and early 1980s, constitutional reform emerged as a priority in Canada, particularly with respect to the question of the mechanism of constitutional amendments. Specifically, the question of "patriating" Canadian sovereignty came to the fore; since the 1931 Statute of Westminster, the British Parliament had held the power to amend the Canadian Constitution. Many Indigenous groups took the British Crown to be their ally against the Canadian state (Borrows 2016, 114); others saw an opportunity to secure their treaty rights and political standing. In 1978, the National Indian Brotherhood (NIB) sought to entrench Indigenous and treaty rights in the constitution, and to participate in the process of constitutional reform. The federal government invited three national

Indigenous organizations—the NIB, as well as the Native Council of Canada (NCC) and the Inuit Committee on National Issues (ICNI)—to attend negotiations as observers. Their joint rejection of observer status strengthened the ties among these Indigenous organizations and enhanced their bargaining leverage, enabling them to petition the Queen and Parliament and threatening the success of the constitutional reform effort. Throughout the constitutional process that led to Canada's Constitutional Act, Indigenous groups engaged in direct action: large public demonstrations designed to call attention both within Canada and in the international community. Indigenous groups continued to disagree among themselves about the value of constitutional entrenchment of treaty rights at all: some, like the Union of British Columbia Indians, sought full and independent national status. But in part because of the strategic difficulties posed by Quebec, the federal government and other provinces needed support from Indigenous groups (Borrows 2016, 118). After further rounds of negotiation (and litigation both before English courts and the Supreme Court of Canada), the resulting Constitution ultimately included Indigenous and treaty rights and a right for representatives of the Indigenous peoples to participate in future constitutional conferences.[15]

The first two sections of Section 35 in Part II of the Constitution Act read as follows:

1. The existing Aboriginal and Treaty Rights of the Aboriginal Peoples of Canada are hereby recognized and affirmed.
2. In this Act, "aboriginal peoples of Canada" includes the Indian, Inuit, and Métis people of Canada.

Although Section 35 was amended slightly through ongoing constitutional negotiations,[16] subsequent rounds of major constitutional reform—the Meech Lake Accord and the Charlottetown Accord—met with failure. Indigenous peoples played a prominent role in the latter, which would have secured an Indian, Inuit, and Métis right of self-government within Canada. The Charlottetown negotiations in particular were taken to exemplify the benefits of integrative bargaining, marked by "the willingness of all political leaders to accept partial gains and mutual compromises in what was generally viewed by them as a 'win-win' rather than a 'win-lose' situation" (Stein 1997, 333). Nonetheless, a ratification referendum resulted in defeat on October 28, 1992.[17]

Yet in the years since constitutional processes stalled, the courts have developed a jurisprudence for the negotiation of Indigenous rights, one that is attentive to the relative bargaining power of the parties.[18] Here the duty to consult is central, elaborated in the landmark *Haida Nation v. British Columbia (Minister of Forests)* [2004 SCC 73] case. For over 100 years, the Haida Nation had claimed title to the lands of Haida Gwaii and the waters surrounding it, though that claim had not been finally resolved through a negotiated settlement. The cedar trees in the forests of Haida Gwaii were of special importance to the Haida Nation: they were central to the lives and identity of the Haida people, the basis for its economy and culture. In 1961, the Province of British Columbia in Canada issued a license for a tree farm to MacMillan Bloedel Limited, a large forestry firm, permitting it to harvest trees in an area of Haida Gwaii (Block 6); in 1981, 1995, and 2000 the Minister replaced the license, and in 1999 the Minister approved a transfer of this license to Weyerhaeuser Company Limited. The Haida people challenged these replacements and the transfer, arguing that these actions had occurred absent consultation and accommodation, and that while the Haida sought to vindicate their claims to title, the forests and their heritage would be destroyed. The government responded that until the Haida people had proven their claim, they had no legal right to consultation or to have their interests accommodated (2004 SCC 73, at para. 8).

In the *Haida Nation* case, the Supreme Court of Canada found that the government had a legal duty to consult with the Haida people and to accommodate their interests, rooted in the "honour of the Crown." This duty to consult and accommodate entails the "balancing of Aboriginal and other interests" in rendering decisions that would affect Indigenous claims, even when these claims have not been proven. The court stated, "It must respect these potential, but yet unproven, interests." Moreover, the way in which the Crown discharges these duties to consult and accommodate also matters. In their dealings with Indigenous peoples, the Crown must avoid "even the appearance of 'sharp dealing'" (*R v. Badger* [1996], 1 S.C.R. 771, at para. 41). Although good faith is required on both sides, "hard bargaining" on the part of Indigenous peoples would not hamper their right to be consulted.

This is an important feature of how the duty to consult has developed after *Haida Nation*. A legal duty to negotiate flows from the "honour of the Crown," explained in recent opinions as deriving from the Crown's assertion of sovereignty over sovereign Indigenous peoples and requiring reconciliation between Crown and Indigenous interests (*Mikisew Cree First Nation v. Canada* [2018 SCC 40]) (Hoehn 2020). The "honour of the Crown" principle emerged in *R v. Sparrow* (1990, 1 SCR 1075), which held that Section 35(1) secures the "constitutional base upon which subsequent negotiations can take place and affords aboriginal peoples constitutional protection against provincial legislative power." It required justification for the infringement of Aboriginal rights and affirmed that the Crown must be held to a "high standard of honourable dealing"— also citing a prior finding that there should be no appearance of "sharp dealing."

Beginning with *Haida Nation*, the courts have emphasized that negotiation rather than litigation is preferable, in part for informational reasons pertaining to Indigenous interests, and have developed an approach that is sensitive to the significance of the interests at stake. *Haida Nation* characterizes these interests and the strength of the claims as lying on a spectrum; drawing on *Delgamuukw v. British Columbia* ([1997] 3 SCR 2010), the court suggested that some cases "may even require the full consent of an aboriginal nation, particularly when provinces enact hunting and fishing regulations in relation to aboriginal lands." This "spectrum"-based approach helps demonstrate how a constitutional duty to negotiate can help vulnerable groups to secure their fundamental interests through bargaining, without providing a veto over all matters whatever their significance. Where these interests pertain to the rights from which their agency as a community flows—their fundamental interests—they may receive veto power. For less significant matters, their bargaining power will be attenuated, though these "ordinary" interests will still receive some protection through the duty of consultation and accommodation.

Again, it is important to emphasize that recognizing the conceptual merits of the duty to negotiate in this domain does not mean that

Canadian jurisprudence is a wholly satisfactory guide from either the standpoint of justice or the standpoint of democracy. Residual elements of the doctrine of "discovery" and *terra nullius* ("land belonging to no one") lurk in the assertion that the Crown acquired underlying title by asserting sovereignty (Borrows 2016, 142), and the fundamental interests of Indigenous people in meaningful political agency have not been fully realized.[19] Scholars have also objected to how the Supreme Court has often, if somewhat inconsistently, characterized Crown obligations to Indigenous communities as fiduciary in nature, arguing that this rests on paternalistic premises and affirms a hierarchical relationship between the Crown and Indigenous populations that supports, rather than undermines, dependency (Dickson 2019, 9).[20] Moreover, the duty to consult is insufficiently robust and too easily satisfied, criticisms often leveled against cases such as *Taku River Tlingit First Nation v. British Columbia* (2004 SCC 74) and *Chippewas of the Thames First Nation v. Enbridge Pipelines, Inc.* (2017 SCC 41). Yet, if imperfect, contemporary Canadian jurisprudence concerning the duties to negotiate and consult demonstrates that attention to bargaining power, and to the bargaining process itself, may help vulnerable members to secure their fundamental interests.[21]

Good Faith

One of these resources is the focus on the reciprocal legal duty to negotiate in good faith. In Chapter 1, we defended a "thin" conception of good faith. We argued that although we cannot rely on contracting parties' motivations more generally, a good-faith bargaining process is marked by an aim of durable agreement, which also requires that parties agree prospectively to respect the terms of the agreement and to decline to undermine it in light of new advantages. Through the doctrine of good faith in the secession case, the Supreme Court of Canada effectively sought to reduce the threat power that each province otherwise would have possessed—to secede without negotiation—and thereby to reallocate bargaining power. (It also did so in part by raising the specter of international recognition, suggesting that failures to negotiate in good faith would diminish the legitimacy of the outcome in the eyes of the international community.)

With respect to Indigenous populations, the "honour of the Crown" drives the legal duty to negotiate in good faith (*Chemainus First Nation v. British Columbia Assets and Lands Corporation* [1999] 3 CNLR 8 [BCSC], at para. 26; *Gitanyow First Nation v. Canada* 3 CNLR 89 [BCSD], at para. 7). We have already seen that it prohibits sharp dealing on the part of the more powerful actor (the government), but recent cases have provided further guidance as to the duty of good faith. For instance, in *Mohawks of the Bay of Quinte v. Canada* (2013 FC 669), the Mohawks argued that the Minister of Aboriginal Affairs had breached his obligation to negotiate in good faith by mischaracterizing the options available under Canada's Specific Claims Policy, which included the possibility of a land-based settlement. Specifically, the Mohawks argued that the Minister had breached the duty of good faith by engaging in "surface bargaining," characterized as "pretending to want to reach an agreement but in reality having no intention to do so" (para. 49). The court signaled its willingness to examine the settlement record, even when it contained privileged discussions, where the Crown was alleged to have breached its duty to negotiate in good faith (para. 35): the honour of the Crown is a justiciable issue, and the court can clarify the content of that duty.[22]

In a 2005 case, *Mikisew Cree First Nation v. Canada (Minister of Canadian Heritage)* (3 SCR 388), which concerned consultation with respect to the placement of a road, the court found that the Crown did not demonstrate a "genuine intention of allowing Mikisew's concerns to be integrated in the solution," and that it had acted in a way inconsistent with the honour of the Crown. However, the court also noted that had the consultation process occurred, "it would not have given the Mikisew a veto over the alignment of the road. As emphasized in *Haida Nation*, consultation will not always lead to accommodation, and accommodation may or may not result in an agreement." Although it obviously does not flow from the honour of the Crown, nor is it perfectly symmetrical; there is a "reciprocal" duty of good faith on the side of Indigenous groups characterized as a reasonableness standard. Courts have also found that First Nations beneficiaries "cannot frustrate the consultation process by refusing to meet or participate, or by imposing unreasonable conditions" (*Halfway River First Nation v. British Columbia [Ministry of Forests]*, 1999 BCCA 470).

Thin good faith undergirds the prospective quality of the equitable treatment of interests standard, particularly in the constitutional context. Specifically, thin good faith secures the expectation on the part of all members that the constitution will enable ordinary political bargaining on the specified terms, and that powerful actors will not seek to consolidate or entrench advantages that undermine the political standing of weaker parties. The suggestion, then, is that by providing what the court itself termed an underlying "democratic baseline," we will be able to identify when the regime has fallen short. That is, the equitable treatment of interests standard helps us to identify not merely whether a given constitution is democratic but also where bargaining power has been distributed inequitably and requires remedy.

Unconscionability: The Value of Representation and Revisability

As we saw in Chapter 1, courts have had difficulty identifying a bright line for unconscionability. But examining constitutionalism through the lens of the inequalities of power that the doctrine of unconscionability seeks to police can help us identify bargains that might be unjustifiable from the democratic standpoint. A constitution produced under starkly unequal power relations raises worries about the effect of these asymmetries on resulting institutions and legislation, akin to those concerns raised by gravely asymmetric power in the contracting framework. But the democratic vantage point we provide helps to show where these asymmetries will have the greatest bite. In particular, during constitutional negotiations under conditions of inequality, it is especially important to ensure that the fundamental interests of all citizens, and especially marginalized citizens, are protected. Further, it will be crucial to ensure that even if certain allocations of resources are inequitable, these inequalities do not prospectively hamper citizens' prospects for equal participation in political life. We believe our bargaining approach, in which such interests are openly the object of negotiation at the constitutional level, makes better sense than competitor accounts of how constitutions can enable democratic decision-making.

In Chapter 1, we argued that the principle of unconscionability is designed not to guarantee strict equality among the parties but to prohibit unfair bargains from being produced under grave asymmetries of power. Recall that courts distinguish between procedural and substantive unconscionability. Procedural unconscionability arises under two conditions: (1) characteristics of the parties in terms of capacity, sophistication, social standing, or wealth or other resources, that would suggest significant inequality; and (2) lack of meaningful alternatives or inability to negotiate terms. Substantive unconscionability pertains to a substantially disproportionate division of benefits. The greater the inequality in bargaining power, the more likely the bargain is characterized by procedural unconscionability; we deem substantively unconscionable those outcomes that harm a citizen's fundamental interests or diminish the future political power of citizens.

How does this migrate into the constitutional domain? We have already investigated the constitutional duty to negotiate as a means of ensuring equitable treatment of interests. Let us begin with the first condition of procedural unconscionability: significant disparity in status or capacity. At first blush, it might seem inapt to raise unconscionability when the parties to a constitution-making process are elites. To be sure, the sort of inequalities of bargaining power that usually concern contract lawyers (for example, the plaintiff in *Williams v. Walker-Thomas Furniture Co.*, 350 F.2d 445 [D.C. Cir. 1965]) will generally not obtain. But even if the participants are all relatively high-status or powerful in comparison to most citizens, their power both individually and as members of interest groups or parties will vary, affecting their ability to shape the distribution of benefits and burdens for the wider population through the constitution-making process. A reason why the Supreme Court of Canada held that constitutional negotiations would be nonjusticiable had to do with the competence of the actors, measured in terms of their information and expertise in constitutional negotiations. But a worry about procedural unconscionability does arise with respect to the inclusion of Indigenous groups, both because of pluralism and disagreement within such communities and because they may lack resources relative to other groups. This is a point that Canadian constitutional jurisprudence has appropriately stressed in considering the "duty to consult" with Indigenous communities.

There is a four-part test, derived from civil procedure (in *Western Canadian Shopping Centres Inc. v. Dutton* SCC 46, [2001] 2 SCR 534), to assess a petitioner's ability to stand as a representative:

1. The class of plaintiffs must be capable of clear definition;
2. There must be issues of fact or law common to all class members;
3. Success for one class member on the common issues must mean success for all; and
4. The class representative must adequately represent the class. In assessing whether the proposed representative is adequate ... the proposed representative need not be "typical" of the class, nor the "best" possible representative. The court should be satisfied, however, that the proposed representative will vigorously and capably prosecute the interests of the class.

In many cases (for example, *Campbell v. British Columbia [Forest and Range]* ([2012], 323 B.C.A.C. 157 [CA])) pertaining to Indigenous groups, the first question is a significant one: Does the group itself have standing to advance a claim under Section 35 of the Constitution Act, 1982 (which, recall, recognizes and affirms the existing Aboriginal and treaty rights of the Indigenous peoples of Canada). But even when this is uncontested, the authority of the representative to speak for a group, particularly when the group consists of plural communities, may be difficult to establish. Even more crucially, if these technical features are satisfied, the "capacity" of representatives may be limited, in part because of the financial and logistical burdens of negotiation and litigation for their interests, imposed upon them by external requests for consultations about potential infringements upon their rights. As such, satisfying the duty to negotiate may depend upon the provision of resources to vulnerable agents to ensure that they can secure adequate representation. In this light, note that an inclusive, deliberative approach to constitutionalism here might undermine the ability of vulnerable groups to secure their interests: if Indigenous groups are under-resourced compared to others seeking to advantage themselves, dispensing with representatives in favor of participatory constitutionalism might further harm their status.

The lens of unconscionability also enables us to think about a role for the courts in attending to asymmetries in bargaining power throughout the political process as a means of ensuring the equitable treatment of interests, akin in key respects to the "structural due process" of law we defend in Chapter 4. For instance, in a recent, controversial case also involving the Mikisew Cree, *Mikisew Cree First Nation v. Canada (Governor General in Council)* (2018 SCC 40), the Supreme Court of Canada found that the duty to consult pertains to the conduct of the Crown in the context of executive action, or action taken on behalf of the executive. That is, the duty to consult doctrine does not govern legislative action. In 2012, two pieces of omnibus legislation pertaining to environmental protection were introduced in Parliament. The Mikisew Cree First Nation was not consulted at any stage in development or prior to the granting of royal assent. The Mikisew sought judicial review of the legislation, arguing that the Crown had breached its duty to consult because it had a potentially adverse impact on its treaty rights to hunt, trap, and fish. The court unanimously held that the federal court lacked jurisdiction to consider the Mikisew's application for judicial review, but beyond that, the majority internally disagreed. The opinion consisted of four distinct answers to the question of whether the duty to consult governed enactment of legislation with the potential to adversely affect rights protected under Section 35. (The court also found that although the legislature had no duty to consult, the court might be willing to grant declaratory relief in cases in which legislation might adversely affect Aboriginal or treaty rights.)

In a concurring opinion, Justice Abella compellingly argued that the honour of the Crown was still at stake in legislative action, meaning that the duty to consult still applied. Abella's concurrence held that the duty to consult does not depend upon the type or form of government action but is triggered based on the potential for adverse effects on Section 35 rights, which may equally result from legislation or from executive action. It is a constitutional imperative, part of a "generative constitutional order" [citing Slattery (2005)] that mandates the Crown negotiate with Indigenous peoples as a means of reconciling their interests with those of non-Indigenous groups. Further, the constitutional force of the honour of the Crown could potentially be used as a means of reviewing the legislative process; at a minimum, it should be used to strike a balance between the honour of the Crown and parliamentary sovereignty (90 and 92). The opinion draws on cases in collective bargaining to demonstrate that it is possible to challenge existing legislation on procedural grounds but that the general aim should be to achieve reconciliation, if through declaratory relief rather than through invalidating legislation.

This is consistent with our account of structural due process review, in which courts may play a role in ensuring that legislative and executive-legislative bargaining does not violate the equitable treatment of interests. To be democratic, the constitution must distribute bargaining power across parties, and across institutions, in a way that conduces prospectively to equitable treatment. It ensures that the fundamental interests of members of the community cannot be sacrificed for ordinary interests, and that bargaining, both constitutional and ordinary, does not exacerbate existing inequalities. It is both a critical standard, designed to help us assess whether a given bargain comports with equitable treatment, and a prospective standard, in the sense that it aims to capture the effects of a bargain on the future distribution of power among the relevant parties. The constitution needs to not just provide for contestation among parties but to readily facilitate the reallocation of power through regularized channels. Particularly crucial here would be the design of electoral institutions, as well as procedures for reopening consideration through relatively flexible mechanisms for constitutional change.

We have argued that a crucial function of the constitution is to define the scope of citizens' fundamental interests to preclude those interests from becoming the subject of ordinary political bargaining. Yet although the prospective standard of equitable treatment of interests requires the protection of fundamental interests, it does not demand that such interests be identified and secured against all future change. Fundamental interests too must be open for negotiation at some later point, even if constitutional change is more procedurally complicated than other types of legislative change. Although, as we have argued, parties are bound by a good-faith duty not to undermine fragile agreements, there is no duty to refrain from attempting to amend the constitution through whatever procedure is prescribed by the constitution. Indeed, the prospect of future amendments may enable parties to accept bargains that fall short of their ideal points, particularly if they anticipate changes in their relative power, or in the distribution of preferences in the long run. Unamendable laws pose extreme challenges in this regard, but even strenuous constitutional amendment procedures can generate problems from the perspective of unconscionability broadly understood, and for the account of structural due process we develop in Chapter 4.

Briefly, entrenchment means that constitutional framers may be able to lock in power asymmetries, posing a challenge to the equitable treatment of interests from inception. Yet even if, at the time of the framing, constitutional norms do seem to protect the fundamental interests of majorities and vulnerable minorities alike, such norms will be subject to interpretation over time, both by legislatures and by judges. When constitutional norms are not subject to amendment, an important check on whoever possesses final interpretive authority is disabled: typically, that means that only a future constitutional court can revise the interpretation, potentially changing the substance of "open-textured" norms in ways unintended by the framers and/or at odds with majority preferences. That is, even if entrenchment may serve to protect rights as a fallible bulwark against substantive unconscionability, it may in fact operate so as to raise the specter of procedural unconscionability by disabling the ability to negotiate terms. The more extensive and entrenched the set of constitutional rights, the more power a constitutional court possesses to enforce their interpretation against what it takes to be legislative encroachment, affecting the distribution of bargaining power among the branches.

In Chapter 1, we discussed the problems of boilerplate or adhesion contracts, which while improving efficiency may exacerbate problems of inequality of bargaining power: the adhering party typically does not manifest assent to all the terms. Courts decline to enforce adhesion contracts when they feature "unfair surprise" or where the bargaining power is so unequal as to constitute "absence of meaningful choice";

they may also do so because the contract is itself substantively unconscionable, yielding profoundly unequal or oppressive results. Constitutional "boilerplate" often takes the form of rights provisions. Such provisions will rarely manifest unfair surprise, and it is similarly unlikely that
such provisions will be substantively unconscionable. As Tom Ginsburg
has observed, however, constitutional provisions do "migrate" across
documents, "sometimes with only minor amounts of local tailoring"
(Ginsburg 2013, 197). Although importation reduces transaction costs
and may constitute a beneficial form of social learning across states,
these provisions may also be incorporated without careful attention
being paid to their meaning or to their implications in a particular local
circumstance. For instance, constitution framers in transitional regimes
may be encouraged to adopt "boilerplate" rights to "human dignity" or
"bodily integrity." Yet given the open-textured character of such norms,
they may require further specification to ensure that they do not restrict
the agency of those parties they are ostensibly empowering. It is important for constitution framers to bargain over the formulation of rights
provisions (rather than assuming that generic wording will adequately
secure the fundamental interests of its members) and for them to ensure that such provisions are not secured against any further negotiation whatsoever.[23]

Abortion rights provide a salient example of the effect that judicial
interpretation can have on constitutional norms that might seem initially to protect the equitable treatment of interests. For instance, the
German Basic Law famously features an "eternity clause" that renders
unamendable Article 1's proclamation that "Human dignity shall be
inviolable." In striking down liberalized abortion laws, the German
Constitutional Court found that fetuses possessed such dignity (Abortion II, 88 BVerfGE, at 252), a decision that was not subject to challenge
either through legislative means or through constitutional amendment
(Schwartzberg 2007). More recently, given the difficulty of amending
the US Constitution, the Supreme Court's holding in *Dobbs v. Jackson
Women's Health Organization* (597 U.S. __ [2022]) that the Fourteenth
Amendment does not guarantee the right of privacy on which a constitutional right to abortion previously depended (itself determined via
judicial interpretation) is similarly not subject to challenge. That is

because it is effectively impossible to pass a constitutional amendment securing a right to abortion, or to modify the Fourteenth Amendment to explicitly recognize a right of privacy, due to the strenuous supermajoritarian procedure enshrined in Article V of the US Constitution.

Largely as a result of the high barriers to constitutional change, the ultimate power to determine abortion policy in the United States rests not with elected legislatures (or citizens themselves), but with an unaccountable judiciary. More generally, if rights are effectively immune from legislative or constitutional change, the main agents of interpretive change will be the judiciary (Schwartzberg 2007). The absence of accountability constitutes a general reason to resist judicial supremacy in constitutional systems, as we argue in Chapter 4. Because courts are not accountable to citizens, by design, they are less well situated to determine citizens' interests, both fundamental and ordinary. (Recall this is in part why the Supreme Court of Canada has encouraged bargaining among parties rather than litigation, and has generally treated bargaining strategies and outcomes as nonjusticiable.) That means that even though abortion access plausibly constitutes a fundamental interest, since reproductive rights meaningfully affect women's political agency, the specification of rights to abortion ought to emerge from constitutional and/or legislative bargaining, and remain subject to subsequent revision.

Finally, constitutional change often occurs postconflict, when tensions are high and there is a risk of renewed violence. These contexts are rarely conducive to the equitable treatment of interests: notably, if participants in constitutional bargaining are seriously unequal in terms of their power or resources—also a standard feature of postconflict procedures—we might also worry about the particular susceptibility of vulnerable parties to threats. Constitutional negotiations often feature dominant external forces, raising wider worries about the autonomy of the resulting process. Broadly speaking, we can characterize many of these circumstances as posing challenges akin to that of duress.

Duress and the Challenge of Imposed Constitutions

Identifying the point at which the imposition of a constitution threatens legitimacy is challenging, in part because of the difficulty of characterizing full autonomy and the rarity of "an ideal type of autonomous constituent agent utterly free from external influence" (Hahm and Kim 2010, 848). Indeed, many scholars have argued that basically all constitutions are imposed, and that to try to distinguish between "imposed" and "unimposed" with regard to a constitution is "a false dichotomy" (Law 2013, 264). For instance, Andrew Arato (2009) argues that imposition is an inescapable feature of constitution-making, because of the unequal power relations among actors. According to Arato, there are essentially no fully autonomous constitutions, because a qualified-majority vote on the part of the population still entails the imposition of those preferences over the minority opposing it; the question is when imposition raises a challenge to legitimacy. To Jon Elster's dyadic account of the key mechanisms in constituent assemblies—"arguing and bargaining" (Elster 2000a)—Arato adds imposition to form a requisite triad for successful negotiations, because it is impossible to imagine that under conditions of inequality, different sides would be able to persuade each other on all issues.[24] Arato distinguishes imposition from bargaining in the following ways: (1) in imposition, an actor's "credible threats cannot be met by effective counterthreats"; (2) "threats play a much greater role than promises"; (3) the bargaining is "monological" rather than "genuinely interactive"; and (4) the result involves no "exchange" of concessions (Arato 2009). We share Arato's skepticism about the possibility of full autonomy evinced by other scholars, and we agree that most constitutions will include a degree of imposition. But from our standpoint, there is an important difference between those bargains that satisfy the prospective standard of equitable treatment of interests—even when some of those terms do not meet with the assent of all parties—and those that would lead us to believe that the resulting constitution will surely run afoul of this standard.

The paradigmatic case of duress entails the "gun to the head" defense; that is, one is not obliged by contractual commitments made under the threat of physical coercion. That the framers of constitutions would themselves resort to violence during negotiations would seem to be an outlandish scenario. But troops and security forces are a familiar concern at constituent assemblies, and the specter of violence is often invoked, directly or indirectly, during constitutional bargaining. Jon Elster distinguishes between "visceral fear" and "rational or prudential fear"

(Elster 2012). The latter, "rational fear," may obtain in any circumstance that might lead to political action: if we do not act, some undesirable consequence will follow. In contrast, visceral fear may generate conditions ripe for duress. If actors are unequally situated with respect to some physical threat—some lives are imperiled in a way that others are not—we may doubt that bargains reached by the parties can possibly reflect the requisite volition.[25] Of course, in principle, a constitutional process marked by violent threats—for example, "Reject bicameralism or else!"—should not be the basis of a political order. If we thought that framers' fear for their own safety, or the safety of their families, affected their judgments, it might seem clear that the bargain was coerced. Yet even here we should try to distinguish between the risk of short-term violence versus long-term violence. Historically, one key reason for a constitution-making process is to quell violent conflict. Indeed, few constitution-making processes are not shaped in some way by the aim of avoiding bloody civil war, whether in the short term or the long term. But this means that constitution-making regularly occurs under duress, in which the framers fear for themselves, their families, and their communities if they fail.

Under circumstances of persistent violence, there may be no alternative to accepting settlements under duress; this is the Hobbesian insight. But the more severe the coercive conditions that mark constitutional bargaining, the more skeptical we should be about whether the resulting constitution will treat interests equitably. Of course, it may be that key actors and ordinary citizens alike have good prudential reasons to abide by an imposed constitution. Indeed, if key actors recognize that resistance will plunge the community back into civil war, they may even have moral reason to continue to abide by the imposed constitution, at least provisionally, until the possibility of peaceful renegotiation emerges. That said, we need not capitulate to the Hobbesian view that physical safety produces political obligation, nor must we insist that we cannot meaningfully distinguish between imposition and bargaining under asymmetric power. The value of treating a constitution created under conditions of coercion—whether produced by external forces or produced by internal violence—as a bright-line case of duress is that it removes any normative question as to whether the constitution is justifiable, and whether the agents who might decline to enforce it act rightly, from the democratic perspective.

In sum, constitutions created under duress, or wholly imposed constitutions, are highly unlikely to yield bargains that satisfy the conditions of equitable treatment of interests. Even if they did, those disadvantaged by the bargains would have good reason to suspect that their interests had not been treated equitably, and that these asymmetries would bleed into future lawmaking in that community, posing a challenge to the perceived, or "sociological," legitimacy of the constitution. This may well mean that the constitution itself ought rightly to be revised or replaced entirely. But where that is infeasible, the best strategy may be to create institutions able to scrutinize the bargains that emerge from constitutional provisions that would not have arisen but for duress or for grave asymmetries in the bargaining process. In these cases, "structural due process" review for equitable treatment of interests— ensuring that the bargaining enabled by the constitution does not run afoul of what we take to be the democratic baseline—is essential, as we discuss in Chapters 3–5.

Conclusion

We have sought to draw from the constitutional experience in Canada, and from constitutional thought more generally, grounds for a bargaining theory of constitutionalism, which takes seriously the notion of contract while adapting it to a large-scale setting marked by conflict among asymmetrical parties. We have argued that a constitution itself must satisfy the prospective standard of equitable treatment of interests. But we have also used concepts such as consideration, duress, unconscionability, and good faith from the private law of contracting to highlight reasons why a constitution may not reliably satisfy this standard, or why it will permit future decisions that are likely to fall short. The conditions of constitutional bargaining and the institutional bargaining that it enables must mitigate against grave inequalities of bargaining power. In the constitutional setting, these concerns are most likely to arise with respect to permanent minorities, and especially Indigenous populations.

Our bargaining theory of constitutionalism holds that the primary aim of a democratic constitution should be to secure the fundamental interests of citizens, and to provide a framework for the distribution of power across relevant parties and groups, subject to ongoing contestation and redistribution. Our contention is that a constitution that satisfies these conditions is democratically legitimate even if it reflects and enshrines unequal power relations, including, but not restricted to, the inequality of power between citizens and representatives. But to be democratic, the constitution itself, along with its subsidiary institutions, does require the creation of norms that manifest the standard of equitable treatment of interests. What this looks like within and among the institutions created by a constitution is the subject of the rest of the book.

3

The Scope and Limits of Legislative Bargaining

ON FEBRUARY 15, 2019, President Donald J. Trump declared that unlawful migration through the southern border of the United States constituted a national emergency. Responding in an op-ed in the *Washington Post*, Senator Thom Tillis (R-NC) wrote that he opposed on principled grounds the use of emergency declarations to promote policy aims. He argued that the use of emergency declarations was a form of executive overreach that weakened Congress's power, and that just as he had opposed such overreach under the Democratic administration of President Barack Obama, he had "grave concerns" about its use by Trump, and could not "justify providing the executive with more ways to bypass Congress." He wrote that those who sought to make Trump's emergency declaration a "simple political litmus test" of support for the president and his policies were missing the mark, and that as such he would vote in favor of the resolution disapproving of the president's national emergency declaration (Tillis 2019). Although Trump had warned that Republicans who opposed him on the national emergency would "'put themselves at great jeopardy'" (Werner and Wagner 2019) and had repeatedly tweeted that Republicans who defied him were standing with Democratic House Speaker Nancy Pelosi, Tillis remained firm, telling a reporter, "It's never a tough vote for me when I'm standing on principle" (Kim and Werner 2019).

Conservative Republican Party leaders and outside groups such as the Club for Growth began to raise the prospect of primary challengers.

The chairwoman of the Rockingham County Republican Party, Diane Parnell, argued, "When you have a Republican president, you expect your Republican senators to follow suit. The state of North Carolina elected him to go to Washington, DC, and support our conservative values. We want this immigration problem fixed. We want him to support our president. And we want America to remain a great country" (Wong and Bolton 2019). She said that she had encouraged Rep. Mark Walker (R-NC) to challenge Tillis. By March 14, Tillis had changed course and voted to approve the emergency declaration, saying that "a lot has changed over the last three weeks," although he failed to reach any agreement to curtail these powers (Blake 2019).

On July 25, 2017, Sen. Lisa Murkowski (R-AK) voted against her party on a crucial procedural vote allowing the Senate to open debate on repealing and replacing the Affordable Care Act. After President Trump himself called Murkowski to pressure her to support the effort, Interior Secretary Ryan Zinke called both Murkowski and Alaska's other senator, Dan Sullivan, to threaten to withhold support for expanded oil drilling—a top priority for Alaska Republicans and their constituents—and the nominations of Alaskans to administrative posts. More generally, Sullivan reported, Zinke warned them that Murkowski's vote had "put Alaska's future with the administration in jeopardy" (Martinson 2017). In response, House Democrats requested an investigation by the Interior Department's Office of Inspector General into what they identified as an ethical violation on the part of the agency to withhold economic development as a punishment for votes by that state's lawmakers, but the investigation was dropped after the senators refused to cooperate.

These cases exemplify ordinary politics: the vile sausage-making that citizens and scholars alike associate with the legislative process. Specifically, legislation derives from bargaining between parties, and among legislators with unequal power. As we have argued in the Introduction and Chapters 1 and 2, we challenge both the assumption of political scientists that all outcomes of legislative bargains should be treated as justified (subject to constitutional constraints) and the claim of political theorists, primarily in the deliberative tradition, that the exercise of asymmetric power undisciplined by reason-giving yields illegitimate outcomes. In this chapter, we take up the invitation, extended by both Rawls and Habermas but basically neglected,[1] to think seriously about the scope and limits of bargaining in the legislative context.

Of course, a significant literature in political science, especially in positive political theory, is devoted to the study of legislative bargaining.[2] But the normative analysis of legislative bargaining is crucial, because legislatures are the paramount institution in democracies. Legislatures are the means by which citizens' interests have the most direct influence on the laws that will bind them. Their influence derives from the electoral relationship, that is, the fact that their representatives will ultimately (if imperfectly) be accountable to them. In principle, at least, representation is the primary means of treating interests equitably. This is so for three reasons. The first two are familiar. First, if the right to participate politically is distributed equally (which in the United States it is not), then in principle, a majority vote will reflect the distribution of preferences in the community. Second, under egalitarian conditions, a pluralistic, large body of representatives means that—as Dahl suggested—most interests will emerge and find advocates. Third, less familiarly, the bargaining that well-designed legislatures enable allows the wider satisfaction of ordinary interests, and a broader distribution of gains, than is found in other institutions. Although, as Chapter 4 argues, the judiciary and the bureaucracy often engage in bargaining with an aim toward enacting their preferred interpretation or implementation strategy, these bodies are secondary in most respects, derived from the need to ensure that legislation on the ground conforms to legislative intent.

Because we accept that asymmetrical power in legislatures is ineliminable, and under certain conditions salutary, our argument does not proceed along standard lines. We do not seek to eliminate the effects of power on law, or to focus solely on the unequal distribution of such power. Rather, we aim to distinguish among sources and types of asymmetric power to analyze whether there are in fact power inequalities that should be excluded in the legislative domain. When these sources or types are themselves worrying, we consider whether we can or should mitigate those asymmetries directly; in some cases, reducing inequalities in power may jeopardize other significant values. Yet we are not solely concerned with limning the difference between troubling and untroubling power asymmetries, because, as we have seen, certain bargaining strategies—most obviously, the use of significant threats—may produce unjustifiable outcomes even if the source of the power asymmetry is prima facie untroubling.

Our argument depends on the claim that democratic representatives possess the authority to bargain among themselves to produce binding legislation, so long as the representatives are responsible for their votes to their constituents via the electoral mechanism, and so long as the laws pass constitutional muster. We accept these conditions as necessary for the products of legislative bargains to be justifiably enforceable. But we do doubt that they are sufficient, because we believe that the *process* of bargaining also matters: that not every bargained-for outcome in the legislative arena should bind us. Particularly once embedded in institutional rules, certain forms of power asymmetries, and the exercise of some forms of coercion over legislators, produce unjustifiable outcomes. These two forms of procedural deficiencies track, respectively, the unconscionability and duress constraints discussed in the Introduction and Chapters 1 and 2.

As we will see, these deficiencies often derive from partisanship; although parties are valuable, even necessary, they depend for their efficacy on strategies of cohesion. Representative democracies require parties to identify shared priorities and to solve collective action problems, but to operate effectively, parties must be able to provide their members with incentives for remaining unified rather than fragmenting. In particular, powerful party leaders seek to whip rank-and-file members through threats and offers so as to secure legislative victories. Leaders' power may derive from their seniority or expertise, from the "war chests" they possess, or from the size of their constituencies; the sources of these power disparities partially affect our judgment as to whether we think the exercise of this power over members might be justifiable. Just as important, if less noticed, are the specific tools that leaders wield: threats and offers vary, and they do so in a way that may be more or less troubling from a democratic (and sometimes a moral) perspective.

In both cases, Republican Party leaders pressured rank-and-file members to change their vote: successfully in the case of Tillis, unsuccessfully in the case of Murkowski. Whereas Tillis was threatened with a primary challenge for breaking with his party, Murkowski was threatened with the removal of support for the oil pipeline—a priority for Alaskan constituents, but also a policy closely aligned with the main goals of the Republican administration. One key aim of this chapter is to isolate the scope of permissible offers and threats—the exercise of party discipline—with an eye toward the limits of intraparty bargains. We seek to enforce these limits not through an approach to political ethics reliant on the hope that leaders will internalize this conception of their duties, but through institutional reform.

Of course, intraparty bargaining is merely one step in the legislative process, which centrally involves bargaining across the aisle or through the construction of coalitions. Parties possess unequal power, depending on whether they hold a majority or a minority of legislative seats, and whether they share a party with the executive in a presidential system. Insofar as the distribution of partisan power within the legislature reflects the distribution of preferences within the population, unequal power may be not only justifiable but normatively attractive. However, as in the intraparty case (and in contracting more generally, as discussed in Chapter 1), powerful agents may offer only certain types of offers and threats, and only under certain conditions, for interparty bargains to be justifiable. Here we return to the logic of "take or leave it" contracts to highlight limits to legislative bargaining, with particular attention in the US context to congressional rules governing debate, amendment, and information availability. We also consider the expanded power of party leaders under closed-list proportional representation systems, in comparison to open-list systems, as a source of potential concern, arguing that allowing scope for a "personal vote" is more likely to yield the equitable treatment of interests.

In analyzing these forms of unequal power, and these specific legislative institutions, we do not imagine that we provide an exhaustive account of legislative bargaining. Rather, our aim is to illustrate the theoretical argument for democratic bargaining, identifying some predictable ways in which it can secure citizens' interests, and the conditions under which it is more likely to fall short. Others may believe that different features of the bargaining process, or alternative institutions, are more salient in explaining legislative outcomes; we take our main contribution to be a conceptual framework that could guide their normative assessment of those elements.

Chapter 3 proceeds as follows. First, we restate the conception of partisan, representative democracy on which the rest of the argument depends. This account seeks to justify the role of parties and representatives in terms of their ability to identify and to advocate for citizens' significant (though ordinary rather than fundamental) interests in a large, heterogeneous community. Second, we use this basic framework to help us examine when threats and offers constitute a form of wrongful coercion in the intraparty context. We then turn to the interparty context to examine legislative institutions that exacerbate disparities among parties, including, in the US Congress, closed amendment rules, self-executing rules, and restricted layover. We look carefully at the example of the Affordable Care Act to highlight how these rules interact in ways that we find troubling. Finally, we consider what routes reformers might take to eliminate wrongful threats and offers and information-restricting institutions.

Representation and Bargaining

If one accepts both the ineliminable quality of legislative bargaining, and its potential justifiability, a particular conception of representation becomes salient. As in Chapter 2, this concept of representation rests on the notion that citizens better protect their interests—both fundamental and ordinary—through deputizing agents to bargain on their behalf than they would by acting directly. Although the bargaining focus is unusual, the twin claims that representation is justified both by the promotion of constituents' interests and by some form of distinctive (if institutionally induced) capacity on the part of representatives are familiar. First, whether representatives are characterized as "delegates," "trustees," or "gyroscopic"—whether their approach is "anticipatory," "promissory," or "surrogate"—their role is to advance their constituents' interests (Mansbridge 2003; 2011). To be sure, these approaches differ in terms of (1) how they conceptualize constituents' interests—notably, the extent to which constituents possess preexisting interests over policy questions or whether such specific policy aims are inchoate—and (2) the extent to which constituents may direct their representatives to vote in specific ways that they believe will promote these interests (and sanction them for deviating from these directives) or allow their representatives to render their own judgments. That the goal of representatives should be to *promote* interests—again, whether by their own lights or as directed—is essentially uncontroversial, even if the claim that they should do so by means of bargaining is less so.

That representation should be justified by reference to *distinction* in some respect is also widely if not universally accepted. Drawing on Aristotle, Bernard Manin identified electoral representation as an aristocratic mechanism, one designed to select the best (the "principle of distinction"). Manin argued that the salient criterion—the dimension on which one candidate outstripped others—depended upon the subjective judgment of voters (Manin 1997, 149), though he also thought that the differences among candidates on the basis of this attribute were objective ("election selects perceived superiorities and actual differences"). The criterion of distinction is sensitive both to the positively valued attributes among citizens and to the specific representative body in which these agents will operate. So, where bargaining is the central mechanism yielding legislative outcomes, citizens rationally ought to use the ability to advocate effectively for their interests in such a domain as the salient criterion; certain features of political campaigns, such as performance in public debates, may enable voters to (imperfectly) assess candidates on these dimensions.

Contemporary work in political theory, influenced by Manin, frequently contrasts electoral institutions with sortition ("lottocratic" bodies).[3] Were representatives chosen by lottery, they might better reflect the distribution of interests in a political community; optimally, they would serve as a microcosm of such interests. Yet mere descriptive representation in this microcosmic fashion is insufficient to promote the equitable treatment of such interests, because a randomly selected representative will have no constituency to which she is accountable; she has no institutional reason to promote their interests, nor any systematic means of identifying what such interests might be, apart from looking within.[4] Even if a representative is a member of a marginalized group, a core insight of intersectionality scholars (for example, Crenshaw 1989) is that such groups do not have monolithic interests. By contrast, electoral representatives will have an incentive to acquire a bird's-eye view of the important interests of their own constituents, as shaped by their constituents and their parties, and can effectively realize these interests through the creation of legislation; if they fail to do so, they can be sanctioned by voters. Further, this means that even if they lack prior expertise in advocating for interests, the prospect of electoral accountability should strongly motivate them to develop such skills (Landa and Pevnick 2020).

In contemporary representative democracies, parties help coordinate members on legislation in the service of these interests.[5] Parties serve a valuable sorting role in identifying and vetting prospective candidates, as well as informing candidates about the key issues, while using their organizational apparatus to make new candidates salient to the wider population. Further, insofar as deliberation retains a role in contemporary legislatures marked by bargaining, it is through the operation of parties. As Nancy Rosenblum has argued, "Parties do the work philosophy cannot: determine the range of matters for discussion and decision" (Rosenblum 2008, 307). Conflict among parties sharpens disagreement, reducing the scope of alternatives and identifying the key points of contestation. In joint work with James Johnson, one of us has argued that democratic deliberation may reduce dimensionality, increasing the likelihood of single-peaked preferences and decreasing the frequency of cyclical social orderings (Knight and Johnson 1994). But in a large, heterogeneous electorate, a party structure may itself be a necessary precondition of deliberation's efficacy in this regard, especially with respect to agenda-setting. Parties, and partisan conflict, help to promote accountability, by highlighting the costs and benefits of prospective legislation, particularly during political campaigns. Within legislatures, parties identify priorities and solve collective action problems; in so doing, they also enhance clarity of responsibility for outcomes. necessary to enable ordinary citizens to assess whether a legislative bargain supported by their representatives promotes their interests.

Yet as Emilee Booth Chapman has recently argued, much of the new literature on parties and partisanship neglects the role of party leaders and strenuous internal discipline (Chapman 2020). Parties require leaders and disciplining tools to solve collective action problems, including agenda-setting and coherence among members and their strategies. But this requires asymmetric power among leaders and rank-and-file members. Under many circumstances, both sets of asymmetries—between majority and minority parties, and between party leaders and rank-and-file members—may conduce to the equitable treatment of interests. When they do, they are justifiable in terms of those gains; when they fall short, such asymmetries may reasonably be challenged. In the book's Introduction, we discussed the potential benefits of cycling for the protection of minorities. Drawing on this logic, Yuhui Li characterizes the bargaining power of minorities in terms of defection costs—specifically, the costs associated with switching coalition partners (Li 2019). When a minority is able to split an incumbent majority coalition and join a new coalition, cycling can generate protection. A proportional representative system under parliamentarism will be more likely to produce the low defection costs that enable minorities to secure their advantage. Yet particularly under a two-party system, the cost of members defecting to another party may be quite high, and so in order to disincentivize dissent they may seek to impose such costs on individual legislators who buck leadership. This is where some of the most worrying elements of party discipline tend to arise. Even if the threats do not approach what we typically take to be contract-defeating forms of duress, they may still be experienced as coercive. More troublingly, these threats may impact not just legislators' own interests, but their constituents' interests as well. So insofar as party discipline may jeopardize the equitable treatment of interests, and thus the justifiability of resulting legislation, it is important to examine the tools available to legislators.

Threats and Offers in Legislatures

A representative system that secures equal voting weight under a fair system of districting is necessary for the equitable treatment of interests in legislative bargaining. But it is insufficient, in part because of the role that political parties play in the bargaining process. As we have argued, parties are valuable insofar as they help citizens to discern their interests, they enable legislators to effectively advocate on their behalf, and they identify when representatives have fallen short. However, because a party's interests may not always align with what a specific partisan legislator takes to be in her interests or, more crucially, the interests of her constituents, it is important to try to define the scope of threats and offers that parties may make to their own members as they bargain over legislation.

The fields of comparative politics and American politics share the assumption that party leaders rationally seek to increase their control over rank-and-file members; party cohesion improves their ability to dictate policy and reap organizational benefits. As Keith Krehbiel argues, there is an important difference between parties that are cohesive because of underlying agreement among the members on policy questions, and those that are cohesive because leaders impose discipline on their members (Krehbiel 1993). This distinction also emerges between closed-list and open-list proportional representation systems, although somewhat counterintuitively: as Carroll and Nalepa (2020) have argued, because leaders are less able to enforce party discipline under open-list proportional representation systems, they may have a stronger incentive to recruit ideologically unified members than under closed-list systems.

In closed-list (CLPR) systems, voters cast ballots for parties, who have ranked their candidates in advance of the election. Parties who receive *n* seats assign those seats according to their rank. In open-list (OLPR) systems, voters cast ballots for individual candidates running under a party label. Parties receive seats in proportion to the aggregate number of votes their candidates receive, and those seats are assigned according to the individual votes each candidate received. By virtue of their control of the ballot, party leaders under CLPR have substantially greater ability to discipline their members than those in OLPR, in which the party's success derives from their members' personal votes. A CLPR system secures the order in which candidates are elected from multicandidate ballots, whereas party leaders have weaker control in systems with open or flexible lists (in which candidates who receive more votes than a predefined quota receive priority over others). Members of Parliament (MPs) under a party system that rewards the cultivation of a "personal vote" have an incentive to respond to constituent demands more consistently than do MPs under a party system that values loyal soldiers; a substantial literature demonstrates that the personal vote tends to promote particularistic spending (Carey and Shugart 1995). Even where party leaders seek to constrain "disloyal" MPs by threatening to remove them from a list, the party depends upon popular members to secure seats under an open-list system: the MP's own success contributes to the party's electoral fortunes as a whole. This means that certain threats, such as removal from the list, may not be credible (Carroll and Nalepa 2021). Instead, party leaders may decide to extend offers, including pork barrel spending, to induce loyalty. Insofar as open or flexible lists constrain threat power on the part of leaders, while providing an incentive to satisfy the interests of wider constituencies through both policy and pork concessions, they may be more attractive than closed-list systems.

In parliamentary systems, party leaders—most notably, prime ministers—also have an especially important disciplining tool in the form of the vote of confidence. Diermeier and Feddersen identify this as the key explanation for party cohesion in such systems, because it "creates an incentive for all those who profit from the current government to vote for the government's proposals" (Diermeier and Feddersen 1998). This grants tremendous power to the prime minister, who is empowered to make the final policy proposal without amendments, and to link the adoption of the bill to the survival of the coalition (Huber 1996). Christopher Kam characterizes this tool as a two-pronged instrument, which presents members of the governing majority a "threat of early elections and the inducement of continued access to the perks of office" (Kam 2014). Agenda-setting powers may also induce party cohesion, because party leaders may identify policy domains on which there is broad consensus to mask or stifle dissent (Tsebelis 2002; Cox and McCubbins 2005).

Arguing that there are a variety of formal and informal mechanisms leaders can use to induce cohesive behavior among individual MPs, Kam provides a model of parliamentary behavior termed "LEADS": the MPs' Loyalty Elicited through Advancement, Discipline, and Socialization

(Kam 2011). Because MPs may derive electoral benefits from defection, party leaders choose different strategies by which to induce behavior. For MPs early in their career, advancement opportunities, such as cabinet positions, may be proffered or withdrawn; Kam provides a detailed account of how Liberal Canadian prime minister Jean Chrétien withheld government positions from a large number of incumbent MPs at the start of the 1993–1997 Parliament, in part to reward loyalists and to punish dissenters. Again, in CLPR systems—whether parliamentary or presidential (as in Argentina)—party leaders have especially strong means of sanctioning dissenters through rank.

In the United States (and other presidential systems with open party lists), party discipline necessarily takes different forms than in parliamentary systems. Again, scholars such as Krehbiel once questioned whether parties in the United States actually induced behavior on the part of their members, rather than simply reflecting ideological cohesion; in 1974, David Mayhew wrote that "no theoretical treatment of the United States Congress that posits parties as analytic units could go very far" (Mayhew 1974, 27), although he wrote during a nadir of party cohesion. Today, however, there is little question that parties in the United States—and party leaders in particular—do exert power over legislators, even if that power has been attenuated in recent years. In 2015, Kathryn Pearson observed that, as a result of reforms that began in the 1970s, party leaders in the House of Representatives wielded more power over the careers of rank-and-file members than they had in 100 years (Pearson 2015, 19). Since the election of President Donald Trump and the rise of the Freedom Caucus, however, the power of GOP party leaders has diminished. In early 2023, the House of Representatives passed a set of rules that significantly weakened the speaker's power, notably including a provision allowing a single lawmaker to bring a "motion to vacate the chair." Such a motion leads to a vote of the House on whether to remove the speaker, producing complex and iterated bargaining that will surely occupy scholars of Congress for years to come.[6]

Nonetheless, the literature on Congress emphasizes three main forms of partisan power: (1) control over the legislative process, in terms of deciding which members' proposed legislation to consider on the House floor (corresponding to the agenda-setting power of leaders); (2) the allocation of campaign resources (corresponding to the electoral power of leaders); and (3) the assignment of committee chairmanships (corresponding to the career or organizational power of leaders). Note that leaders' exercise of power over members in these domains typically takes the form of offers and threats: for instance, a party leader can offer a committee chairmanship to a member in exchange for her vote, or a leader can threaten to block the appointment of, or strip a chairmanship from, a member. For instance, in 1996, Speaker Newt Gingrich canceled fundraising visits to the districts of four GOP freshmen to punish them for voting against legislation to end a partial shutdown of the federal government (Pearson 2015, 158). In 2012, Speaker John Boehner removed four Republican members from important committees after they persistently challenged GOP leaders on key issues.

Under certain circumstances, the exercise of power by leaders over backbenchers can be characterized as coercive (Bowler, Farrell, and Katz 1999, 5, 13). Of course, coercion is a thorny question in political philosophy, and throughout this work, we have often chosen to adopt the strategy that Alan Wertheimer (1987) recommended, beginning with judicial reasoning rather than with our linguistic or moral intuitions. To analyze whether political threats entail coercion, however, we have limited case law and we lack obvious moral intuitions. Even legislative ethics guidelines tend to be spare in their guidance concerning the use of threats, as we discuss in the conclusion to this chapter.[7] So rather than focusing on the moral wrong of coercion, our analysis will emphasize the challenges that certain forms of party discipline may pose to the equitable treatment of interests.[8]

To clarify this, let us return to the example of Lisa Murkowski. To begin, did Murkowski find herself coerced with respect to the ACA vote? Some (like Robert Nozick) would argue that insofar as she was able to resist her party's pressure, and voted against the ACA, she was not—if the coercion is unsuccessful, that is, the coercee does not act as the coercer insists, there has in fact been no coercion. We are skeptical. A ubiquitous example of coercion involves a person confronted by a robber: "Your money or your life." Virtually everyone accepts that a person who hands over her wallet has been coerced into doing so. But one might also believe that a person who successfully escapes the robber has been subject to coercion, even if the attempt failed to yield the desired result.[9] Some coercees may be braver, foolhardier, or stronger; that a coercive action did not succeed against a given subject should be irrelevant to determining both the character of the action and its wrongful nature (though under some conditions it may speak to its credibility). In our view, that Murkowski did not capitulate to Zinke does not mean that she was not coerced; indeed, that she later voted to repeal the ACA's individual mandate may indicate that her resistance to ongoing coercion had flagged.

Yet whether or not Murkowski has been coerced by party leaders bears only partially on the issue of whether resulting legislation may run afoul of the equitable treatment of interests. Our argument in Chapter 1 would seem to give us reason to resist in general the use of coercive threats, partially on the grounds that they are unlikely to yield outcomes that reflect the recipients' considered views of their interests. But the nature of agency relationships in legislatures complicates this assessment. As we have argued, party leaders have a claim to exert discipline over their members; such discipline is essential for parties to achieve their aims. If for institutional reasons (such as proportional representation) or due to polarization, citizens generally vote for parties rather than for distinctive candidates, their interest may lie in enabling such parties to act consistent with their policy agendas more generally, even when they depart from constituents' preferences with respect to a specific policy. Yet sometimes legislators may have good reasons to defect. They may wish to follow the dictates of their conscience, to pursue their own judgments of the common good, or to advance their own judgments of their constituents' interest. (They may also have bad reasons, such as the interests of donors or a handful of powerful constituents.) Ultimately, in these cases, representatives will need to choose, and bear the electoral or professional costs where they fall.

Nonetheless, the character of threats and offers remains important, largely because the exercise of certain forms of discipline may make it less likely that citizens' interests will be treated equitably. Consistent with much of the literature, we characterize a "threat" to be a proposal to take an action that makes the recipient worse off than she was before the intervention (her "baseline," as per Nozick and Wertheimer), whereas an "offer" is a proposal to take an action that makes the recipient better off than she was before intervention. From our standpoint, party discipline in the form of offers—that is, inducements to make a member better off if she votes with the party—is typically acceptable. This is the sort of context in which a party leader often offers to appoint a member to a sought-after committee. The member may have to choose between her constituents' preferences and her personal ambitions, which may induce some psychological pressure, but it does not reduce her effective set of choices in any way that we would regard as tantamount to duress. Specifically, it is unlikely to result in procedurally compromised legislation resulting from coercion, which would be subject to scrutiny by courts under a form of structural due process, as we discuss shortly. If political rivals later accuse her of choosing her personal ambitions over the interests of her members, and if members find these arguments persuasive—and find that the prospective benefits to the community as a result of her membership on that committee do not outweigh the costs of the outcome of her vote, by their lights—they can remove her from office via the electoral sanction.

Threats are more complicated. For instance, we believe a threat to replace a member on a desirable committee if she does not vote with the party is likely to be a permissible exercise of power. It is true that the consequences of the loss of a powerful committee position may affect constituents at least as much as it impedes the representative's own interests. But here the notion of a "moral" baseline, one that acknowledges the normative quality of the expectation on the part of the agent, is also helpful. Relative to the member's "nonmoral" baseline,[10] the leader is making a threat. But because no representative has a right to join a given committee, nor does a community have a right to have their representative do so, it is also possible to regard it as an offer: the leader tells the member that she may remain on the committee only if she votes with the party. The representative is likely to feel, as a subjective matter, that she has been coerced, and she may reasonably believe that she has been wrongly forced to choose between two different ways of advancing her constituents' interests. But whether she made the right decision in the face of this pressure is a case that the representative herself will now need to make during her campaign, and is a matter for her constituents to decide.

What of Thom Tillis, who supported the emergency declaration in the face of a "threat" of a primary challenge? If we take the standpoint of Tillis's own interests, we might think he was made worse off by these threats relative to his expectation of an uncontested primary. But—adopting again a moralized baseline perspective—we believe he had no such claim to the Republican nomination. As such, we can also characterize the chairwoman's statements as making Tillis an offer: if you vote with the party, we will not support primary challengers. Moreover, if we turn our attention to the constituents' interests, it is difficult to argue that a contested primary makes them worse off. To be sure, we might worry that party leadership may be manipulating the alternatives available to the constituency in a way that might seem troubling, and that it would be better to exclude this category of threat. Yet parties typically exert control over the eligibility of prospective candidates to run under their party list or receive their endorsement, and indeed such control is likely necessary to ensure ideological coherence.

The Murkowski example is in certain respects different. One might think that the pipeline itself is merely an offer: the Alaskans lack it, and the Republicans have offered to provide it in exchange for Murkowski's support. But let us stipulate that, across party lines, Alaskan legislators and residents have overwhelmingly favored drilling, and Republicans in particular, within and outside of Alaska, have argued that it is an urgent priority. Republicans regularly and repeatedly characterized this as an important, if not fundamental, interest for the country as a whole—not merely for Alaskans—on the grounds that energy independence fostered by the pipeline is essential for national security. Because Murkowski and her constituents relied on Republican promises of support for such interests, from their standpoint it is a threat, making both Murkowski and her constituents worse off relative to their baseline.

To whom is the threat directed? This is the main question that governs our analysis of when threats may be inconsistent with the equitable treatment of interests. Although Murkowski likely experiences the threat to the pipeline as a personal threat to her political career, she has no claim to her office independent of the support of a majority of her constituents. She may believe that Zinke makes her worse off with respect to her baseline, in which she expects to be reelected—perhaps largely due to the advantages of incumbency—but she has no right to her seat except through a fair election. Her constituents can decide whether her choice to support the ACA at the cost of the pipeline was the right one. Yet Zinke's threats against *citizens'* interests—indeed, what he and his copartisans have publicly identified as their important, if not fundamental, interests—is where troubling features arise.[11] Directly targeting threats of harm at the interests of a particular community so as to affect the actions of their legislator undermines equitable treatment, in part because it forecloses bargaining. Rather, as a gratuitous threat, it constitutes a type of extortion—"Your vote, or your constituents will get it"—one akin to duress.

Not all threats are gratuitous in this respect. To illuminate the difference, consider a case in which the Department of Defense recommends to Congress the closure of three military bases.[12] If the DoD identifies specific bases for closure on the grounds that they are no longer necessary for national security, there are few grounds for complaint. No particular constituency has any claim to retain its military base, even though the constituency would be made worse off relative to its expectations by a base's closure, on the moralized baseline account. By contrast, consider a case in which the Department of Defense calls for three closures, but then leaves to Congress the decision of which bases should be targeted for closure. This decision provides party leaders with a valuable weapon.[13] It allows them to target threatened closures to the constituencies of recalcitrant members, and to secure some interests at the expenses of others. So here the question of threats becomes more complicated. The justification for any closure should be in terms of national interests, notably in security and economic efficiency. Targeting a base that is almost universally recognized as strategically paramount—say, the Wheeler Army Airfield, in Hawaii—so as to discipline a senator would raise significant concerns about the treatment of interests, among Hawaiians and the nation as a whole. This is analogous to the Alaska Pipeline example: it is a threat to gratuitously harm both the specific interests of the constituency and (by the GOP's lights) the interests of the nation, as construed by the party.

In other cases, though, the case will be indeterminate: there will be a number of bases that it might be reasonable to close, and so party leaders can make this choice with an eye toward rewarding or sanctioning representatives without necessarily engaging in extortion. Would a threat of base closure in order to discipline representatives in a case where the closure might be warranted necessarily run afoul of the equitable treatment of interests? This is a harder case, but we believe that it does not: rather, it may merely open a new domain of negotiations in which trade-offs and concessions might be generated. To be sure, a representative will likely experience the threat of closure subjectively as coercive. She will no doubt face consequences at the polls for whatever she chooses, whether she changes her vote on a matter important to her constituents so as to protect the base, or stands her ground and loses the base. But she has no grounds for complaint; this is the electoral sanction operating as it should.

Now, let us characterize the example as an offer, rather than a threat. In this case, a representative is offered the opportunity to keep a base scheduled for closure open if she votes in favor of a piece of legislation that she and her constituents oppose. The representative again faces a difficult question, again one that she will likely experience as a "coercive offer"[14]: Do the benefits to her constituents' interests from the base outweigh the cost to their interests from the proposed legislation? But such an offer does not run afoul of the equitable treatment of interests—it is merely a means by which competing interests can be weighed. Of course, whether the representative chooses to decline the offer and vote against the measure as she intended or to accept the offer and vote in favor, she will have to answer to her constituents. But this too is merely the electoral sanction operating as it should.

So, from the standpoint of both legislators and constituents, the use of threats and offers does not undermine the justification of legislative bargains, except at the limit, in which such threats take the form of gratuitous injury to a constituency's interests and thus becomes tantamount to extortion. Again, the wrong of coercion in the legislative context primarily lies in the distorting effects it may have on the equitable treatment of interests, rather than (for instance) in the direct autonomy interests of representatives. Insofar as these autonomy interests on the part of representatives are implicated by party discipline, it is because it may undermine the interests of constituents promoted by legislators' freedom to strike bargains that they take to be in their constituents' interests.

Are there any cases in which a leader's use of otherwise impermissible threats against members' constituents might be permissible, given the consequences? Even were we to accept the possibility of dirty hands,[15] in which the only way to achieve some morally crucial end is through what would otherwise be a wrongful action, these cases would be exceptionally rare; most such matters that generate the dirty-hands problem (for example, ticking bomb scenarios) would not obtain in the legislative domain or, if they did, would not find their resolution through the use of individual threats. Even a case in which one individual legislator held up a crucial bill targeting climate change—about as important an interest as could be identified in the legislative domain—would ordinarily not rise to this level, and other inducements and threats specifically to that individual legislator's political future could be deployed: see, most recently, tax and fossil fuel concessions, respectively, to Sen. Kyrsten Sinema (D-AZ) and Sen. Joe Manchin III (D-WV) to secure their agreements to a climate bill. It is also worth noting that high-stakes issues such as raising the debt ceiling produce predictable incentives for legislators to hold out, given the extraordinary costs to citizens' interests for failure to agree.[16] Such circumstances warrant institutional remedies other than anticipated, iterated hardball, and this is in part where the structural due process analysis we develop in Chapter 4 has its bite. So, a court judging whether the debt ceiling violates the Fourteenth Amendment provision that the "validity of the public debt . . . shall not be questioned" should assess the effect the debt limit has on legislative bargaining, and its consequences for the treatment of interests.

So far, we have examined the use of threats and offers as a means of ensuring internal party cohesion. But legislative bargaining is typically an interparty affair. Although the prohibition on extortion remains, parties obviously disagree about what they take to be the interests of constituents. In bargaining with other parties, of course, the nature of the carrots and sticks at leaders' disposal differs, and the scope of impermissible threats and offers will differ. Democrats may resist oil drilling in Alaska and believe that it is not in the long-term interests of the local or national community; offers they might make to protect the Arctic National Wildlife Refuge would not constitute extortion, even though Republicans in Alaska might well regard such an attempt as a form of harm to their interests (and punish Democratic candidates as a result). The equitable treatment of interests never constitutes a guarantee that a constituency will receive its preferred policy outcome.[17] Outcomes derive in part from the distribution of preferences both within the party and across the aisle. Yet they also emerge from institutional features of the bargaining process, which we now explore.

Interparty Bargaining

Interparty bargaining poses distinctive challenges, because power is distributed asymmetrically not merely between leaders and rank-and-file members but between a majority and a minority party or coalition. These asymmetries can be exacerbated by the specific institutional and procedural features of a particular legislative body. In partisan legislatures, a majority party, or majority coalition, possesses greater control over the legislative agenda than a minority party or minority coalition. There are a variety of ways to measure this control, both "positive"—that is, that a matter gets onto the legislative agenda and is considered via a final-passage vote—and "negative," meaning that a bill does not receive floor consideration. Legislative bodies differ in terms of the relative control, both positive and negative, that a majority possesses. In the United States, the standard view has been that the institutional rules of the Senate, such as unanimous consent agreements and the filibuster, provide the majority with less control than it possesses in the House, although more recent scholarship suggests that majority party negative agenda control in the Senate may be stronger than is often appreciated (Gailmard and Jenkins 2007). Insofar as disparities in party control reflect the underlying political preferences of the electorate, we have argued that such control is not only untroubling but salutary. However, as we discussed in the intraparty context, disparities may reflect partisan efforts to entrench their political advantages or immunize their members from electoral control. They may result from institutional rules that produce malapportionment, or that secure disproportionate distributions of power. We believe that these types of disparities in a representative system, if significant, may affect the justifiability of resulting political bargains.

But we are not merely interested in power disparities among individual legislators or parties; as we have argued throughout, we are also interested in the bargaining process, and for this we need to turn to the nitty-gritty rules governing the creation of legislation. These internal norms of legislatures condition the bargains that emerge, whether in proportional representative or first-past-the post systems, and so it is important to examine whether they exacerbate asymmetries or mitigate them.

In this section, we turn to the rules that shape legislative decision-making in the US House of Representatives; these rules, little studied by political theorists and of limited interest even to most political scientists, shape the legislative bargains that emerge from the House. These rules give rise, however, to worries analogous to those posed by adhesion contracts, because they produce "take it or leave it" forms of legislation: they restrict information, debate, and amendments. These often raise immediate concerns in terms of the equitable treatment of interests, because they restrict bargaining outside of the committee, but the opacity of the legislative process makes it especially difficult for constituents—and, often, even their representatives—to ascertain whether a given legislative bargain might be in their interest. Opacity generates further problems in terms of the structural due process review of legislation, as we discuss in Chapters 4 and 5.

Beginning with the now-canonical Baron-Ferejohn model (1989), a substantial literature in political science has compared open and closed amendment rules. Briefly and synoptically, Baron and Ferejohn develop a model of distributive politics featuring a sequential structure and a rule by which legislators are recognized. The model generates different predictions under a closed amendment rule and an open amendment rule. Under a closed rule, a randomly chosen member makes a proposal and no amendments are allowed; the legislature instead votes on the resolution of the motion on the floor immediately. If it fails, the status quo remains intact; if it passes, the legislature adjourns. The process repeats when the legislature's next session begins. Under an open rule, members can amend a motion on the floor or move the previous question (that is, bringing the motion to an immediate vote). Open rules produce delay, and depending upon the cost of such delays, members may prefer a closed rule.

However, there is theoretical and empirical evidence to support the view that open rules result in a more equitable distribution of benefits. Baron and Ferejohn themselves suggest the normative implications of their findings: "An open rule results in more equal ex post distributions than does a closed rule, so it might be chosen to further equity considerations. . . . Furthermore, an open rule seems to comport better with democratic theory in the sense that it allows greater opportunity to members than does a closed rule, which immediately closes the amendment process when a proposal is made" (Baron and Ferejohn 1989, 1199). These findings have been supported by experimental work, demonstrating that open amendment rules produce a more egalitarian distribution of benefits, if at the cost of greater delays in the bargaining process (Fréchette, Kagel, and Lehrer 2003).

When Baron and Ferejohn published their paper, the use of closed rules was relatively rare. However, in the contemporary House, most rules are at least somewhat restrictive. From 1993 to 2008, on average 78 percent of major bills were considered under a highly restrictive rule (structured or closed); in the 109th Congress and 110th Congress, 96 percent of rules were substantially restrictive, and in the 111th, 99 percent. In 2015, the late Rep. Louise Slaughter (D-NY), the ranking Democrat on the House Rules Committee, lambasted Republicans for passing the most closed rules in the history of Congress (though, to be sure, Congress under Democratic control did not refrain from using such rules).[18]

The majority party tends to control the Rules Committee—indeed, Cox and McCubbins (2005) describe it as a "weapon" of the majority party—which means that closed rules ensure virtually no opportunities for deliberation or negotiation on the part of the minority party. Cox and McCubbins (2005) provide particularly egregious examples; one is the House's passage of the Partial Birth Abortion Ban of 2002. Republicans on the Rules Committee ensured that the bill was considered under a closed rule, preventing six Democratic amendments from being added, despite the fact that (as the Democrats argued) the absence of an amendment providing a health exception would make the bill unconstitutional. The rule also waived all points of order and the requirement of a three-day layover of a committee report; as a result, the bill was considered one day after the Judiciary Committee produced its report, and it passed on a near-party-line vote of 274–251.

Scholars provide various explanations for the use of closed amendment rules, including the goals of securing logrolls made at the committee level and of ensuring that committees retain an incentive to develop policy expertise (Krehbiel 1992). Regardless of the explanation, the use of closed rules ensures that legislation is effectively "take it or leave it," disabling either any form of public argumentation or further bargaining. We explored why such norms have worrying implications in the private bargaining context in our discussion of adhesion contracts, and in Chapter 2, in the duty to negotiate under Canadian constitutional jurisprudence: a "take it or leave it" contractual environment broadly entails the absence of meaningful choice.

An additional procedural rule—"restricted layover," in which leaders release long, complicated bills immediately prior to the vote, keeping rank-and-file members from seeing the legislation until that point (what James Curry [2015] refers to as "legislating in the dark")—exacerbates these issues, as the rank-and-file effectively lacks knowledge about the legislation before them. Senator Jeff Merkley (D-OR) shares an anecdote in which Sen. Barbara Mikulski (D-MD), then chair of the Senate Appropriations Committee, "extolled in a caucus meeting the good things she had gotten in the omnibus we were about to vote on." Merkley asked Mikulski "what was hidden in the bill that we would learn about and hate a week later." Mikulski responded to him, "'I'm not telling you. That's not how the process works.'"[19]

The problem is especially severe when restricted layover is combined with norms of self-execution (a rule we discuss shortly that "deems" some measure passed without demanding separate debate, amendment, or voting), and when it pertains to highly complex bills. Indeed, this was (putatively) part of the House Freedom Caucus's objection to Speaker John Boehner; the caucus demanded that the House should return to "regular order," providing time for public arguments. In this context, Rep. Justin Amash complained, "[Boehner] operated a top-down system. Which means that he figures out what outcome he wants, and he goes to members and attempts to compel and coerce us to vote for that outcome" (Drutman 2016). In 2009, however, Boehner had himself denounced the 340,000-word conference report on the American Recovery and Reinvestment Act of 2009. As Curry writes, "Slamming his copy onto the chamber floor, Boehner raged, 'Here we are with 1,100 pages—1,100 pages not one member of this body has read. Not one. There may be some staffer over in the Appropriations Committee that read all of this last night—I don't know how you could read 1,100 pages between midnight and now. Not one member has read this'" (Curry 2015, 1).

Members of the minority party might object to these procedural norms, not only because they cannot enact amendments but also because the absence of public debate means that they lack an opportunity to place on the record their disagreement and provide reasons why the proposed legislation is flawed. As Chapter 4 discusses, the creation of a robust legislative record is essential in shaping the interpretation and enforcement of the law. The interests of legislators in public debate do not require any commitment to the value of deliberation or reason-giving as such. Rather, such speech enables legislators to send a variety of signals to their copartisans, to other state and national leaders, and to constituents. The opportunity to speak on the floor concerning a given policy is an especially important resource for individual legislators seeking to build alliances, particularly for the least powerful backbenchers. These norms also constrain the rank-and-file members of the majority party from engaging in bargaining that might advantage their constituents. Both the use of restricted layover and the use of the closed rule for the majority of controversial measures—including, in the 109th and 110th Congresses, measures pertaining to the war in Iraq, flag desecration, oil exploitation in the Arctic National Wildlife Refuge, and the permanent repeal of the estate tax—shift power away from the rank-and-file to party leaders (Doran 2010). However, it is also true that under certain circumstances, information-restricting norms may well increase the prospect that bills will arise that distribute gains widely, if through lobbyist efforts to introduce provisions that benefit special interests. Indeed, this is the implication of Senator Merkley's anecdote. Systematically promoting the equitable treatment of interests, through norms allowing scrutiny and revision, may sometimes involve sacrificing certain beneficial bargains that can emerge only by disabling these norms.

Finally, lest this seem merely a parochial argument, one purely specific to the US Congress, recent scholarship proves that legislative institutions also condition the formation of policy under parliamentary democracies more generally (Martin and Vanberg 2020). Multiparty governments typically must delegate policymaking power to cabinet ministers, but controlling ministerial discretion is difficult. Per Martin and Vanberg (2020), where parliamentary institutions enable coalition partners to challenge and amend ministerial bills, policies that distribute gains more widely are more likely to emerge. There is good reason to believe that these arguments about the value of constrained informational asymmetries and revisability for the equitable treatment of interests transcend the American context.

Summing up, the main worries posed by "information-restricting" rules are as follows. These rules exacerbate power disparities between leaders and party members, and enable majorities to pass legislation in a fashion that disables debate and amendment. The equitable treatment of interests would seem to require a public opportunity to contest and negotiate the scope of proposed legislation, even if the outcome is largely determined by the distribution of political power across parties. Such public contestation is essential for citizens to assess whether their representatives have in fact advocated for their interests and whether a given bargain advantages or disadvantages them. Information restrictions inhibit monitoring and accountability. Moreover, insofar as we have confidence in the Baron-Ferejohn findings, we may think that a rule that distributes the benefits of a given policy more widely is likely to better satisfy the equitable treatment of interests, and that the costs of delay would typically be outweighed by such gains.

Bargaining over the Passage of the Affordable Care Act

Our focus in this chapter has been to identify the scope conditions on legislative bargaining. We began by examining intraparty bargaining, specifically the types of threats and offers that party leaders could offer rank-and-file members without running afoul of the democratic baseline of equitable treatment of interests. We then turned to interparty bargaining in the House, and specifically the institutions that shape the resulting agreements, some of which exacerbate existing power inequalities. Now we can turn to bargaining in a bicameral legislature with a partisan executive capable of placing a thumb on the scales. To do so, we turn to President Barack Obama's own account, in his memoir *A Promised Land* (2020), of his role in the passage of the ACA, the types of threats and offers he used, and how the rules of the Senate in particular shaped the bargain that emerged.

In a chapter of his book devoted to the passage of the ACA, President Obama writes at length about the challenge of getting a bill through the Senate Finance Committee. He describes his attempts to help Max Baucus, chair of the Finance Committee, persuade the two GOP senators involved in bipartisan talks: Olympia Snowe and Chuck Grassley. His appeal to Snowe took the form of offers: specifically, he joked to Nancy Pelosi, he would offer the chance to "write the whole damn bill! We'll call it the Snowe plan! Tell her if she votes for the bill, she can have the White House. . . . Michelle and I will move to an apartment." He found his efforts at soliciting Grassley's vote to be more frustrating, in part because he suspected Grassley was negotiating in bad faith: "He'd hem and haw about this or that problem he had with the bill without ever telling us what exactly it would take to get him to yes" (Obama 2020, 400). (Eventually, Obama would ask Grassley whether if he had accepted all of Grassley's suggestions, Grassley could support the bill. "Are there any changes—any at all that would get us your vote?" . . . "I guess not, Mr. President.") Baucus disagreed with Obama, and remained firm in his belief that Chuck Grassley would eventually come around. Obama writes of his frustration and his temptation to threaten Baucus:

> A part of me wanted to get up, grab Baucus by the shoulder, and shake him till he came to his senses. I decided that this wouldn't work. Another part of me considered threatening to withhold my political support the next time he ran for election, but since he polled higher than I did in his home state of Montana, I figured that wouldn't work either. Instead, I argued and cajoled for another half hour, finally agreeing to his plan to delay an immediate party-line vote and instead call the bill to the vote within the first two weeks of Congress's reconvening in September. (Obama 2020, 401)

Eventually, the bill passed out of the Senate Finance Committee by a 14–9 vote, supported by Snowe but not Grassley.

The House passed a bill over GOP opposition, and Obama hoped that the full Senate could pass a similar version of the bill before the

Christmas recess in 2009; they could then spend January negotiating the differences between the Senate and House versions of the bill, send the merged bill to both chambers, and have the legislation ready for his signature by February. But Obama needed to rely on Senate majority leader Harry Reid to hang onto a 60-vote majority sufficient to overcome the possibility of a filibuster: Obama noted that "this fact gave each one of those members enormous leverage to demand changes to the bill, regardless of how parochial or ill-considered their requests might be." This was a situation that was "fine with Harry, who could maneuver, cut deals, and apply pressure like nobody else." Although the Senate debates were occupied by procedural matters, "the only action that really mattered took place behind closed doors in Harry's office, where he met with the holdouts one by one to find out what it would take to get them to yes" (Obama 2020).

Obama describes the deals cut through the use of offers: most famously, the Medicaid dollars secured by Sen. Mary Landrieu ("the Louisiana Purchase," D-LA) and Sen. Ben Nelson ("the Cornhusker kickback," D-NE). He defends Reid's methods as "relatively benign" compared to the "egregious pork-barreling, logrolling, and patronage dispensing tactics Senate leaders had traditionally used to get big, controversial bills like the Civil Rights Act or Ronald Reagan's 1986 Tax Reform Act, or a package like the New Deal, passed." He also defends the decision to remove the "public option" from the bill, necessary to keep Senator Joe Lieberman's vote, which raised objections from the left. Obama implies that some of these objections were personal to Lieberman, who had supported McCain in the last presidential election and had been defeated in the 2006 primary in the wake of his support for the Iraq War.

Specifically, Obama argues that he and Reid resisted the use of threats against Lieberman: "Harry and I had quashed calls to strip him of various committee assignments, figuring we couldn't afford to have him bolt the caucus and cost us a reliable vote." Obama says he was right and that Lieberman had voted reliably with his domestic agenda: "But his apparent power to dictate the terms of health-care reform reinforced the view among some Democrats that I treated enemies better than allies and was turning my back on the progressives who'd put me in office."

He continues: "I found the whole brouhaha exasperating. 'What is it about sixty votes these folks don't understand?' I groused to my staff. Should I tell the thirty million people who can't get covered that they're going to have to wait another ten years because we can't get them a public option?" (Obama 2020).

Obama writes at length about the final stage in the House: the challenge of keeping on board the House Democrats who represented swing districts, identifying in particular the courage of specific members of Congress who resisted opposition from home; ultimately the vote passed by a margin of seven votes in the House.

President Obama's memoir tends to characterize the project of lawmaking as one of individual negotiations to hold together a caucus, shaped by the threats and offers leaders have at their disposal. Of course, Obama is far from alone in this characterization of lawmaking—to read Robert Caro's massive volume (Caro 2013) on Lyndon Johnson's Senate career is to be confronted repeatedly with the exercise of personal power, marked by individual persuasion and the obsessive counting and recounting of votes. To be sure, the specific tools that leaders have at their disposal do yield results, and ones that do not necessarily secure the equitable treatment of interests; otherwise, we would not have scrutinized the use of what we characterize as extortion, gratuitous threats against the interests of constituents.

But, as we have also seen, the distribution of power across parties is a function of the institutional rules of the legislature or chamber as well. Major substantive changes to bills are worked out via informal processes engineered by the majority party and are then considered under highly restrictive rules (Sinclair 1997); such was clearly the case in debate over the ACA. We have already discussed several of these rules, but now we turn to one of the most important: "self-executing" or "deem-and-pass" rules. Self-executing rules enable the House to pass a bill by approving a special rule governing debating, amending, and voting on a bill, and "deeming" it thereby passed, rather than directly voting on the bill itself. They are typically used to avoid direct votes on controversial measures, enabling last-minute amendments to be incorporated. During the late-stage negotiations described by Obama, Democrats weighed passing health-care reform merely through self-executing rules. This would have allowed the House to pass a version of the legislation that would fix items in the Senate health-care bill without confronting the specter of a subsequent Senate filibuster, or obliging Democrats to vote for particularly unpopular provisions of the bill, including those concessions won by Nelson and Landrieu. That it would shield members from having to publicly support the bill with these features, in fact, was how House Speaker Nancy Pelosi explained the appeal.

But in the end, the ACA passed through the budget reconciliation process. The Democratic House would not accept the Senate version of the bill without modifications, and the Senate—especially having lost Sen. Ted Kennedy's seat to Republican Scott Brown—would not pass any changes the House made. So, an entirely separate bill, amending House Bill 3590, would be negotiated in the House, constrained by what could command a Senate majority. Ultimately this language did not emerge from a committee, but from negotiation between White House officials and Democratic congressional leaders; it took shape through amendments published by the House Rules Committee. On March 20, 2018, the Rules Committee published "Amendment to the Amendment in the Nature of a Substitute to House Bill 4872."

Under the Rules Committee, the House would vote to concur with the Senate version of the bill, and if that passed, would move to the House's reconciliation package under a closed rule. Debate was limited to two hours between the parties, without opportunity to offer amendments. But the Senate parliamentarian ruled that the House had to pass the bill, and the President sign it into law, before the Senate could take up the reconciliation rule. This too posed obstacles: debate was limited to 20 hours and senators could offer unlimited amendments, termed "vote-a-rama." Each proponent had a minute to explain a proposed amendment, and an opponent had a minute to disagree, followed by a vote. Finally, House Bill 4872 passed the Senate on March 25, though even then it needed to return to the House so that the identical piece of legislation could be passed, following 10 minutes of debate. It was ultimately passed at 9:02 on March 25.

But for vote-buying within these opaque procedures, it is likely that the Affordable Care Act—and other pieces of important legislation— would never have been enacted. In the case of the ACA, we observed intraparty and interparty bargaining, but with minimal transparency, and often with limited formal opportunities for amendment. Does this undermine the justifiability of resulting legislation from the standpoint of the equitable treatment of interests?

The collective power of Blue Dog Democrats protected them from intraparty threats, suggesting that the power disparities between leaders and rank-and-file members were not a central cause of concern—moderate Senators, such as Joe Lieberman and Ben Nelson, wielded outsized power relative to leadership and to other politically "reliable" Democratic members. Insofar as there are worries presented by the account of the ACA, we believe they rest on the microlevel institutions, rules that shield debates from public scrutiny and that prevent amendments from receiving fair hearings. As we have argued, transparency is essential for the accountability of legislators to constituents: it is especially important when legislation is as significant, and as controversial, as the ACA. To be sure, more open rules may occasionally enable minority parties to derail legislation. But an open amendment rule may nonetheless be crucial, not only for distributive and accountability reasons but also to make an account of the legislative process available for courts and other actors to examine.

During the debate over the ACA, Michael W. McConnell wrote in the *Wall Street Journal* that the self-executing rule violated Article I, Section 7 of the US Constitution; he argued that this section "clearly states" that bills cannot be presented to the president for signature without having been approved by both houses of Congress "in the same form" (McConnell 2010). We are skeptical of some features of McConnell's argument—including the assertion that the presentment clause is unambiguous on the point—but we do share the basic view that these norms pose a challenge to the democratic justifiability of legislative outcomes. As we just saw, a key benefit of the self-executing rule is that it undermines accountability. In a high-profile case such as the ACA, we tend to share Sarah Binder's assessment that it would "make little difference to voters whether Democrats explicitly voted for the Senate-passed bill or voted for a procedure that allowed it to be passed" (Binder 2010). But Binder also recognizes that legislators themselves believe very strongly that it matters, and so they deliberately seek to shield themselves from responsibility through their use. Insofar as this tool undermines voters' ability to determine whether their representatives are acting in the voters' interest, as they understand it, we take it to be at odds with the democratic baseline. More generally, as we discussed above, the use of information-restricting rules generates an opaque legislative history. Opacity undermines one strategy the courts might adopt in their review of administrative actions, raising further concerns about the compatibility of legislative bargains with the equitable treatment of interests, as we discuss in Chapter 4.

Conclusion

Although we have argued that legislation almost invariably emerges from bargains, not all bargains will treat interests equitably. We have argued that intraparty bargaining through the use of party discipline, including the use of threats and offers, is generally permissible, so long as it does not extend to coercion in the form of threatened harm to constituents' interests. That said, just as we rejected a focus on individual-level motivations and mindsets as a means of reaching compromise, we also doubt that constraints on bargaining can emerge from leaders' dispositions to refrain from the use of impermissible threats. Of course, party leaders will not unilaterally disarm; they will not surrender the expansive power to threaten their own members if they do not believe that the other party will also commit to such constraints.

In conclusion, we focus on the resources for constraining intra- and interparty bargaining in the US Congress. To begin, more aggressive enforcement of legislative ethics might partially remedy these concerns about the use of gratuitous threats. Congressional ethics rules do already preclude threats against members for failing to vote in a particular fashion. Rule 23, Clause 1, of the Code of Official Conduct of the House of Representatives requires that "a Member, Delegate, Resident Commissioner, officer, or employee of the House shall behave at all times in a manner that shall reflect creditably on the House" (Committee on Standards of Official Conduct 2008). This clause has been read expansively to preclude certain types of threats and offers, and it is not without bite, although the scope has been too narrow from our vantage point. For instance, the clause was used to challenge an offer extended by Majority Leader Tom DeLay to endorse Representative Nick Smith's son in exchange for Smith's vote in favor of a Medicare bill. This offer was deemed impermissible; the Investigative Subcommittee concluded that "it is improper for a Member to offer or link support for the personal interests of another member as part of a quid pro quo to achieve a legislative goal" (Committee on Standards of Official Conduct 2004). In turn, the Subcommittee also determined that certain forms of threats run afoul of ethics guidelines. "Representative Candice Miller made a statement to Representative Smith on the House floor during the vote on the Medicare legislation that referenced the congressional candidacy of Representative Smith's son. Representative Smith fairly interpreted Representative Miller's statements to him during the vote as a threat of retaliation against him for voting in opposition to the bill" (Committee on Standards of Official Conduct 2004). Both DeLay and Miller were rebuked by the House Ethics Committee, and DeLay eventually resigned in response to this and other ethics violations.

We have defended the use of threats and offers that pertain to a member's own political ambitions as a justifiable means of securing party loyalty. But threatening the ambitions of a member's son constitutes a form of gratuitous harm to the interests of a third party, and it was rightly rebuked by the Ethics Committee. Our argument would defend a more expansive understanding of Clause 1 to include what we take to be more significant threats to the interests of ordinary citizens. But an effective and independent office would be required in order to enforce such rules, given the disincentives on the part of partisan legislators to hold their comembers accountable (as Dennis Thompson [1995] has long argued), and so far such offices have been repeatedly undermined.[20]

Second, the value of particularistic benefits, such as earmarks, as a means of mitigating policy loss for constituents ought not to be underestimated: pork "greases the wheels" of the legislative process (Evans 2004; Lazarus 2010; 2018). There are both observational and experimental studies demonstrating that legislators trade off pork for policy gains. Members of majority parties who "lose" when their party pursues policies with which they disagree—in principle, because their constituents oppose such a policy, or whose constituents support bills that the leadership will not propose—receive compensation in the form of nonpolicy benefits, that is, pork-barrel spending (for example, Lee 2003; Carroll and Kim 2010). Indeed, recent experimental evidence predicts that in fact members of an ideological minority benefit most from the inclusion of pork in bargaining: banning targeted spending disproportionately hurts their bargaining prospects (Baranski, Haas, and Morton 2023). Insofar as earmarks help to distribute gains more widely and compensate those who do not benefit from legislation, they may well advance the equitable treatment of interests. We return to this argument in the conclusion of the book.

Finally, constraints on interparty bargaining may require change in institutional rules, though these rules are quite sticky. We have argued that majority rule is a necessary condition for the equitable treatment of interests, particularly in the legislative domain, and so the Senate filibuster obviously runs afoul of it. To be sure, the filibuster also affects legislative strategy in the House: as we saw in the discussion of the ACA, to evade a Senate filibuster, the House had to avoid sending a further amended bill to the Senate. The incentive to use information-restricting tactics that exacerbate the inequality of bargaining power both within and across parties is enhanced by the filibuster, but these tactics themselves warrant scrutiny and reform, because of the essential quality of transparency for the electoral sanction to operate effectively. There is bipartisan support in principle for such changes, but securing the commitment is difficult: as in the filibuster, the party disadvantaged by the use of deem-and-pass in a given context invariably decries its use—and challenges its constitutionality—but both parties have relied on it over time. Because it also constitutes a weapon in the arsenal of party leaders, it is difficult for members to commit to its reform, and so the other branches have a role to play in ensuring that legislation satisfies the condition of equitable treatment of interests. In Chapter 4 we discuss judicial scrutiny of legislative bargaining within a structural due process account of the interpretation and implementation of law.

4

Interpretation, Implementation, and Enforcement

Since the Affordable Care Act was enacted on March 23, 2010, it has been the subject of more litigation than any other statute in American history (Gluck, Regan, and Turret 2020, 1472). Overall, more than 2,000 legal challenges to the statute have been filed in federal and state courts in the United States. Seven of these challenges have already found their way to the US Supreme Court. The legal questions that underlie these challenges encompass a wide range of issues related to the ways in which the complex statute should be interpreted as well as to the appropriateness of how it has been administratively implemented. As Gluck and his coauthors colorfully describe this period, "Along the way, the statute has been rebelled against by the states charged with implementing it, sabotaged by the second President to administer it, and financially starved by Congress" (Gluck, Regan, and Turret 2020, 1473). And yet, despite the unprecedented efforts to undermine or change it, it remains the law, albeit in altered form.

Democracy is defined by a specific standard of collective decision-making, which in our view requires formal equality of voting rights along with a set of institutions designed to promote the equitable treatment of interests. That standard serves as the normative criterion for assessing the justifiability of law in democratic societies. Of equal importance, democracy also involves an ongoing struggle to sustain that criterion. For the normative dictates of democratic legitimacy do not end at the election of political representatives. Nor do they end at the creation of the laws that those representatives enact. Rather, the normative dictates extend to govern the ways in which democratically enacted laws are interpreted and enforced in everyday life.

Democratic governance involves law creation, implementation, interpretation, and enforcement. Normative democratic theory tends to treat these different tasks as part of a coherent whole. The focus tends to be on the process of law creation. The assumption then seems to be, more often than not, that the law is subsequently implemented and interpreted in a manner consistent with its intended purpose. But in most democratic societies, governance is characterized by a division of labor among these various tasks. And this division of labor creates new difficulties for democratic theory.

In Chapters 2 and 3, we analyzed the role of the constitution in establishing the terms of public bargaining throughout the system of democratic governance. There we articulated a defense of legislative supremacy, grounded in the basic fact that the agents who engage in legislative bargaining are authorized by and accountable to ordinary citizens as principals. And we defended the normative criterion of equitable treatment of citizens' interests that democracy requires of these representatives. However, unlike legislators, state actors who undertake the tasks of interpretation, implementation, and enforcement need not be directly authorized or accountable in such a fashion; this is the primary reason why we argue that they should be subordinate to the legislative branch in a democratic system.

And yet, this division of labor extends the opportunity to influence the form and substance of democratic laws to these directly unaccountable state actors. In doing so, it raises additional normative questions for any justification of democracy. The possibility that political actors who have been unsuccessful in achieving their goals in the legislative process will resort to these other aspects of governance as alternative strategies for influence has been proven throughout history to be a substantial one. In the face of this possibility, theories of democracy must confront questions like these. If the judge who interprets the law makes a decision inconsistent with the purpose of the statute, what does it say about the democratic legitimacy of the law? If the bureaucrat who implements the law does so in a manner that changes the purpose of the statute, what does it say about democratic legitimacy?

In this chapter, we will argue that state actors who are not directly accountable to voters are still subject to the normative constraints of the democratic criterion of equitable treatment of interests as well as the "defensive" doctrines governing public bargaining. Our task is to unpack the implications of the democratic criterion for these other aspects of governance. To do so, we will analyze the primary places in the democratic system where issues of interpretation, implementation, and enforcement are resolved. We will demonstrate that these secondary tasks are best understood as bargains between legislators and other state actors who are not directly accountable to voters, actors who constitute the judiciary and the administrative bureaucracy. We will identify those places in the system in which bargaining is most consequential, places where the defensive doctrine of unconscionability is most important. And we will show how, in those places, the concern with the unconscionability of relative bargaining power is in large part the product of a mix of two factors, institutional authority and public opinion, where the effect of public opinion may be distorted by how the availability of resources for political lobbying is distributed in the society. This obviously has important implications for issues of institutional design. Specifically, we will demonstrate the ways in which the democratic criterion of equitable treatment of interests dictates both which tasks should and should not be delegated to nonlegislative actors and how these tasks ought to be institutionalized to diminish unjustifiable political bargaining.

To start, how do we conceptualize interpretation and implementation as instances of bargaining? As we set out in Chapters 2 and 3, political bargaining involves a strategic interaction among actors who differ in the power that they bring to the process. Like the others, our analysis in this chapter is grounded in an assessment of the implications of the asymmetries of power in these relationships. However, unlike the bargains analyzed in those chapters, bargaining over issues of interpretation and implementation involves more complex relationships.

Up to this point in our discussion, we have focused on instances of bargaining that have a well-defined structure. In both the constitutional and legislative cases, the bargaining took place among actors engaged in the explicit task of creating or modifying a constitution or enacting a law. In these cases, negotiations took place among the members of a single decision-making body. It was fairly easy to see when bargaining took place and when it reached a conclusion.

When we extend the analysis beyond the enactment of laws to the ways in which the other tasks of governance influence the day-to-day effects of democratically enacted laws in citizens' lives, we can see that they basically involve ongoing bargaining over the future meaning and purpose of those laws. But the structure of such bargaining often becomes much less clear. In most systems of democratic governance, the tasks of interpretation and implementation are assigned to different government officials and different institutional bodies. The specifics of this distribution of responsibilities are commonly, but not exclusively, detailed in the country's constitution. The separation of powers framework in the United States is a well-known example, in which interpretation is primarily the responsibility of the judicial branch and implementation primarily the responsibility of the administrative arm of the executive branch. This creates some new issues for the identification of relevant instances of bargaining.

For example, when the members of the US Congress were formulating and enacting the Affordable Care Act, they knew that their work would be interpreted and implemented by a different set of actors in the future, but they didn't necessarily know by whom or when. These representatives presumably had an interest in how their statute would be treated in the future. That is, they preferred, to the extent possible, to have the laws interpreted and implemented in the ways in which they were intended at the time of their enactment. This is the perspective that courts take in instances of private bargaining and contracting, seeking to answer the question, How do we facilitate the intentions and goals of the actors to the bargain?

More importantly, this would also seem to be what a commitment to democracy, understood in terms of legislative supremacy, would require of the future interpretation and implementation of democratically enacted laws like the ACA. For what is the point of being concerned about how laws are enacted if we are not also concerned about how they actually play out in the lives of citizens? Therefore, we think that it is important to take account of these longer-term interactions in an assessment of the role of public bargaining in a democratic society.

For the purposes of this analysis, we identify an interagency interaction, either explicit or implicit, as a bargain when it (1) produces an interpretation or an implementation of the democratically enacted statute and (2) is characterized by asymmetries of power among the relevant actors, asymmetries that appear to influence the final form and substance of that interpretation or implementation. These more extended interactions may seem less like the types of bargains that courts often assess in the private contracting case, but we feel confident they are nonetheless best treated as a bargain. Treating these long-term interactions as bargains is the most fruitful way, we believe, to assess the role that power plays in the long-range interactions that are a central part of democratic governance. And, thus, their consideration is necessary for a comprehensive assessment of the normative legitimacy of the democratic state.

In our earlier discussion we emphasized that bargaining power can influence many aspects of the democratic process within a legislature. Often the influence of power is transparent and explicit; other times it is not as readily observable and involves an anticipated reaction on the part of the weaker parties. While less transparent, these influences of bargaining must be included in any assessment of the normative significance of political bargaining in democratic politics. With this in mind, let's briefly identify the types of interactions which we consider in this chapter. For ease of discussion, we treat the tasks of enactment, interpretation, and implementation as the responsibilities of different branches of government, as set out in the separation of powers system in the United States.[1]

Our analysis covers both short-term bargaining within a branch and long-term ongoing bargaining between branches. We primarily focus on the following types of interactions. First, we are interested in the implications, if any, of intrabranch bargaining within the nonlegislative branches. For example, even in the short history of the ACA, there is evidence that such bargaining took place among the members of the Supreme Court in regard to the proper interpretation of the enabling statute. The speculation among reporters who cover the court centered on the likelihood that Chief Justice Roberts had switched his vote late in the decision-making process in *National Federation of Independent Business v. Sebelius* (567 U.S. 519 [2012]), and, in doing so, changed the outcome of the case.[2] In addition to such negotiations among the judges on a collegial court like the Supreme Court, we are also interested in negotiations among bureaucrats within the hierarchy of an administrative agency.

Second, we consider two features of interbranch bargaining that might influence the initial enactment of legislation. Both of these possibilities challenge the independence of the legislature and, thus, raise questions about legislative supremacy. One feature involves explicit bargaining at the enactment stage with an executive who threatens a veto. For a president to threaten to veto proposed legislation has been a recurring feature of the history of executive-legislative relations in the United States (Cameron 2000). The second feature highlights the anticipated reaction effects on the legislature in which they anticipate the relative responses of the other branches to their new laws. In the case of the ACA, for example, this would involve amendments on the part of the Democratic coalition in Congress to their most preferred version of the healthcare reform act in order to offset any anticipated negative reactions by the courts.

Third, we consider the reactions of the other branches when they anticipate the future responses of the legislature to their own acts of interpretation and implementation. Here we are primarily interested to see the ways in which the future anticipation of interbranch bargaining can influence the capacity and willingness of the nonlegislative branches to hold the legislature accountable according to the democratic criterion. A classic example of this type of anticipated reaction can be found in Chief Justice Marshall's decision in *Marbury v. Madison* (5 U.S. 137 [1803]). Justice Marshall struck a delicate balance in the case, asserting, on the one hand, that the court had the constitutional authority to review the constitutionality of legislative enactments and yet concluding, on the other hand, that the executive branch did have the authority to make the disputed personnel decisions that were at the center of the case. The historical circumstances surrounding the case suggest that

Marshall adopted the mixed strategy in order to avoid retaliation against the court by President Jefferson (Knight and Epstein 1996).

Finally, and most importantly, we consider instances of implicit bargaining over time, a characteristic feature of democratic governance. Here a common example would be the ongoing interactions between Congress and executive administrative agencies over implementation questions in various policy areas. To give some structure to these ongoing interactions, we focus on instances in which one branch acts in what we take to be an undemocratic manner and ask the question, What can the other branches do in response to enhance the democratic legitimacy of the law?

Throughout this book, our underlying normative concern is that asymmetries of power too often determine both the nature and substance of democratic politics without any justification. The normative task becomes one of determining when the outcomes of asymmetric bargaining should be deemed unjustifiable and thus unacceptable for democratic politics. In this chapter the relevant question is, What makes an interbranch bargain undemocratic? Although this is similar to our concern in Chapters 2 and 3, the assessment of the illegitimacy of a bargain is more complicated. In the constitutional and legislative settings, we have focused primarily on the process of bargaining, emphasizing the roles that duress and unconscionability play in influencing the decisions of the relevant parties. After assessing the process, we turned to a consideration of the substance of the bargain, to see if there might be some competing value that offers a countervailing reason for accepting it as normatively legitimate.

Given the priority that our account of a democratic commitment places on legislative supremacy, we reverse the order of the analysis in instances of interbranch bargaining. In our assessment of the interbranch cases, we place primary emphasis on the substance of the bargain. We ask, How does the resulting interpretation or implementation reflect the democratic criterion established by the elected representatives? If the outcome of the bargaining constitutes a deviation from the criterion, then we assess whether or not it was a product of unconscionable asymmetric bargaining.

In assessing legislative bargains, we focused on the process by which legislation was produced and we assessed the extent to which that process treated the significant interests of the community in an equitable manner. We acknowledged that the criterion of equitable treatment of interests would often be difficult to employ without appealing to such standards as equal respect or concern for citizens, stricter standards that we sought to avoid endorsing. We argued that the best way of applying the criterion would be to make sure that representatives set aside important interests only when they were seeking to realize other, even more important values.

So, what is the role of the criterion of equitable treatment of interests in the interbranch bargaining case? Basically, it serves as the baseline of comparison for the assessment of subsequent acts of interpretation and implementation. If we determine that the representative legislature satisfied this democratic criterion, then the enacted statute serves as the normative baseline for subsequent actions by the other branches. Both the courts and the administrative agencies must strive to instantiate the meanings and purposes of the legislature in their own decisions. To the extent that they deviate from that standard, either by mistake or by an intentional effort to replace legislative purposes with ones reflecting their own preferences, they must be judged as committing a democratically unjustifiable action. If, on the other hand, we determine that the representative legislature failed to satisfy the democratic criterion, then the enacted statute does not provide an adequate normative baseline for subsequent action. And this introduces the opportunity for the nonlegislative branches to enhance the democratic nature of the legislation through their own actions. However, this also leaves open the important question of how the nonlegislative actors would go about determining what changes in the enacted statute would better satisfy the democratic criterion, a question that we address in more detail later in this chapter.

The outcomes of interbranch bargaining may be influenced directly by asymmetries of power among the relevant actors and indirectly by institutional rules that are themselves the product of prior bargaining among asymmetric actors. In order to identify instances of asymmetric bargaining in interbranch cases, we need to focus on the actions that deviate from the democratic baseline. Why are officials deviating? Do they see it in their personal interests to deviate from the interests of the electorate? And do they have the power to establish the deviation as the new policy? Or is it a function of an exercise of asymmetric power against them? And are they forced to accept it? We can get a good sense of the effects of asymmetric power by looking at the series of interactions that take place between the initial instance of deviation from the democratic baseline and the end of the possible responses. If a deviation from the democratic baseline becomes the settled law in the society and it is a product of an asymmetric power relationship, then it is an unjustifiable bargain and must be deemed unenforceable unless it reinforces an even more important value for the community as a whole.

But here it is important to keep in mind that there are a number of different bargains that may result from this process, some of which will not be considered unjustifiable on our theory of the dictates of democracy. As we will show, there are both good and bad bargains in the interbranch case. On the one hand, bargains that produce future meanings and purposes that deviate from the democratic baseline are normatively problematic. A recent example would be the efforts of the administrative agencies during the Trump administration to undermine the effectiveness of the ACA. On the other hand, similar bargains that ultimately correct actions (by any of the government branches) that initially produce deviations are not problematic. Here the recent actions by the Biden administration to reinforce the effective implementation of the ACA are relevant examples. Only the former types of bargains are potentially unjustifiable according to a commitment to democracy.

The democratic condition of good faith has important implications here. Under this condition the members of the legislature are committed to the terms of the political bargain once it is enacted. This means that they should not seek to change the terms of the bargain through future interpretation or implementation. Their only legitimate recourse is to return to the legislature and seek to change the terms of the policy. That is what the Republican majority in Congress attempted unsuccessfully to do in regard to the ACA after Trump was elected. Such is the reflexive nature of democracy.

And this condition of good faith places a secondary constraint on the officials in the other branches. Given the priority established by legislative supremacy, the officials tasked with the responsibilities for interpretation and implementation are, in an important sense, agents of the legislative branch. And thus they should seek to instantiate the democratic criterion in their own decisions. The only exception to this would be in those cases in which the legislature itself enacts unjustifiable bargains. Therefore, these officials should not seek to facilitate changes to the terms of legislative bargains unless the legislative bargain itself fails to satisfy the democratic criterion.

If, however, the condition of good faith is violated by an actor in any of the branches, it is possible that interbranch bargaining will produce a bad bargain. Such bargains can be produced by those officials who have the power to establish a statute's meaning and purpose in terms of their own interests and not the interests instantiated in the democratic criterion. The greater the asymmetries in bargaining, the greater the opportunity for there to be a deviation from the criterion. Here duress and unconscionability serve as evidence of the conditions that create the opportunities to pursue bad bargains. But, to repeat, that requires the more powerful actors to want to establish a disproportionate treatment of interests. That may not be the fact of the matter. Here, it is important to reemphasize, our analysis in this chapter sets out the ways in which unjustifiable bargains can occur. Not that they necessarily will occur.

What are the factors that influence bargaining power in these interbranch cases? The single most important factor is institutional authority, which, in a democratic society, is primarily established by the constitution. The institutional rules distribute the authority to interpret, implement, and enforce democratically enacted laws. They determine who makes the decisions and they define the qualifications of the people who fill those roles. And more often than not, they establish the procedures by which such decisions are made. Most importantly, these rules establish the degree of independence enjoyed by these primary decision-makers. Similarly, these same institutional rules create procedures that allow government officials in the other branches to respond to those decisions. In doing so, they allow potential constraints on the primary decision-makers, establishing direct mechanisms of accountability.

As we will see in the following analysis, one of the most important features of the system of institutional authority is the cost involved in exercising these constraining strategies. The greater the cost of constraint, the greater the independence of those who interpret and implement the laws. This calls our attention to the factors that influence the cost of such strategies. In a democracy one of the most important factors turns out to be public opinion. And public opinion can cut both ways in its influence.

On the one hand, if public opinion is weighted by the distribution of lobbying resources in a society, then the effect can be to distort it disproportionately in favor of the more powerful members of that society. This would reinforce the efforts of some citizens to undermine the democratic criterion. If, on the other hand, the effect of public opinion is institutionalized in such a way as to mirror the actual distribution of interests, then it can have a positive effect on the maintenance of the democratic criterion. In the latter case, interpreters and implementors who seek to alter the democratic criterion through their actions may face the costs of adverse public opinion. Or public opinion may bolster their efforts to sustain it. And this is as it should be. To the extent that public opinion affects interbranch bargaining in this way, it provides an additional important means for citizens to influence democratic governance.

The institutional balance between independence and accountability is one of the most important features of a constitutional democracy. Establishing the appropriate balance is the subject of ongoing negotiation and bargaining throughout the life of a democracy. By separating the tasks of enactment, interpretation, and implementation/enforcement, the constitutional framework serves to distribute and balance the relevant power of the democratic state. This requires that a certain degree of independence will be enjoyed by each of the different branches. But, in any institutional system, there has to be some common value or goal that structures and defines the interworkings of government. And this will, in an important sense, give some degree of priority to one of the branches. We have argued that the priority in a democracy rests with the legislative branch. That is the definition of legislative supremacy. Through the analysis in this chapter, we further demonstrate the implications of legislative supremacy for a commitment to democracy.

We proceed as follows. As we noted earlier, although it might be the case in some constitutional systems that the same actors could be responsible for more than one of the postenactment tasks, we separate them for purposes of analysis and consider the task of interpretation first and then implementation and enforcement. This allows us to draw on the extensive theoretical literature on the separation-of-powers system in the United States. Within each section we begin with a consideration of bargaining within the relevant branch of government and its implications for the normative legitimacy of democratic governance. Then we look at the possibilities of bargaining between the legislature and one of the other branches. Here we address the implications of both direct and indirect interbranch bargaining; in the latter cases we must take account of the anticipated reactions of the legislature to their beliefs about the future actions of the other branches.

Since we have already addressed in Chapter 3 what a democratically unjustifiable act would be for the legislature in the case of intrabranch bargaining, in the present chapter we start, for the sake of argument, with the assumption that the legislature has acted democratically in enacting a new law. This allows us to keep the primary focus on acts of the other branches that can adversely influence democratic legitimacy, as well as the possibilities for the legislature to constrain undemocratic actions by the other branches. After that, we turn to a brief consideration of ways in which, and by what criterion, the other branches can act to improve the legitimacy of undemocratic legislative action. Finally, we make the case for the best ways to minimize unjustifiable interbranch bargains in a democratic system.

Judicial Interpretation

When we think about the possibility of intrabranch bargaining, the first question that comes to mind is, Does it matter? Does it matter that a group of judges on a collegial court, judges who differ in their degree of bargaining power, bargain over the outcome and decision in a particular case? The answer, of course, is that it depends. It depends on the nature of the ultimate decision. For democracy does not require that the initial decisions on interpretation (and implementation and enforcement, for that matter) be made according to democratic procedures. It does require that the resulting decisions appropriately serve democratic aims. So, while it may turn out to be the case that intrabranch decision-making would benefit from democratic procedures, it will be a normative requirement of democracy only if we found it necessary to achieve the primary goal of final interpretations that satisfied democratic interests.

Let's focus first on bargaining within the judicial system. Explicit bargaining generally takes place on collegial courts, where judges use various procedural rules to try to influence the substantive outcome of cases. There is substantial evidence from both legal and social science research of explicit bargaining in the judicial system. Before turning to a more detailed analysis of this kind of intrabranch bargaining, we should clarify the distinction among three different types of decisions that judges might face.

The first two of these relate to general questions about the substantive implications of a specific statute. The first type arises when courts are asked to resolve questions of whether the legislative enactment violates certain substantive rights guaranteed to individuals under the constitution. Here we have in mind what are considered private rights, like a right to property or freedom of religion, which we treat as fundamental interests. In those cases, the constitution may give the judicial system authority to overturn the decision of the legislature, even when the legislature has satisfied the baseline democratic criterion.

This is what is commonly referred to as constitutional, or judicial, review. And it is the subject of some controversy in discussions about the implications of a commitment to democracy. Given the fact that this form of review can result in the complete nullification of the decision of the legislature, one could reasonably ask, What does a commitment to democracy have to say about the distribution of authority for constitutional review? Questions about the scope of the judiciary's power of constitutional review are usually governed by an explicit provision in a country's constitution. In these countries, the power is granted either to courts in the regular judicial system or to special courts and/or other governmental tribunals created explicitly for that purpose. If the constitution grants the judiciary this power, it will be allowed to render judgments as to when a statute violates a right that is protected by the constitution. In other countries, the question of who holds the power of constitutional review is less clear. For example, the US Constitution is silent on the specific issue of constitutional review. The basis for constitutional review in the United States was initially an assertion by the

Supreme Court in *Marbury v. Madison* (1803) that it had this authority. Since then, the emerging norm of judicial review has generally been respected by the other branches of government.

As we have already stated, our view is that everyone who acts on behalf of the democratic state, whether elected or not, must respect the dictates of the democratic criterion. And we think that it is also obviously so in regard to the dictates of the constitution. So, regardless of whether you are a legislator or a judge, you have a good faith responsibility to maintain and enforce the rules and procedures of the constitutional democracy. This is the logic that has led some constitutional scholars to argue that the authority over constitutional review should rest with the legislature and not the judiciary (Waldron 1999; 2006). We see considerable merit in this argument, but we also understand the concern with holding the legislature accountable within a constitutional democracy. We realize that this trade-off must ultimately be resolved by a bargain in the constitution-making process.

The second type of substantive question involves explicit statutory interpretation, when judges are asked to interpret the meaning of a statute and thus the implications of that statute for the factual controversy that led to the case. This is the most common type of question that judges face and it is an important focus of our analysis. It is central, we would argue, to any assessment of democratic legitimacy. Here the baseline democratic criterion is the appropriate measure for assessing the substantive implications of the statute and, thus, the legitimacy of the judicial decision.

The third type of decision that judges are asked to undertake focuses explicitly on the procedural aspects of the democratic decision-making process. Here they address basic questions as to whether the legislature followed constitutionally prescribed procedures of statutory enactment. These procedures commonly detail the formal methods by which the legislators can legitimately enact laws. But we would argue that this procedural inquiry should extend far beyond the minimal institutional requirements of legislative enactment. In a democratic system of governance, these should also include the procedural guarantees that affect the ability of individual citizens to participate effectively in the democratic process—their most fundamental interest—as well as the legislative bargain itself.

As now exists in some jurisdictions, judges may have broader authority to inquire into the statutory enactment process. Many democratic governance systems have enacted explicit procedures that institutionalize protections against unjustifiable political bargains. They may take the form of statutory procedures that specifically regulate the legislative process (for example, restrictions on lobbying activities). Or they may take the form of a more general right, either constitutional or statutory, to equitable democratic procedures. Some scholars have argued that such a right can be read into the due process and equal protection requirements of the US Constitution, but this is a subject of considerable debate. Others have argued that a right to democracy has been instantiated in many state constitutions in the United States (Bulman-Pozen and Seifter 2021). In our subsequent discussion, we will set out how we think judges can resolve these procedural questions consistent with the dictates of the democratic criterion. Central to this discussion will be our support for a structural due process approach to statutory analysis.

Bargaining on Collegial Courts

Bargaining is an important feature of decision-making on collegial courts. Such courts are the primary form of appellate review of judicial decisions throughout the world. In the United States the rules and procedures of collegial courts structure the process of interpretation in both state and federal systems. There has been a great deal of social scientific research on the general question of the dynamic of collegial decision-making. The predominance of the research has focused on the United States and the federal appellate courts but there is a growing body of research on state court systems in the United States as well as the appellate courts of other countries. This research identifies several ways in which bargaining among the members of the collegial court can significantly influence the final decision on the merits.

At the outset of this discussion, we anticipate a question that drove some of the early debate in research about collegial courts: When are the justices bargaining and when are they merely deliberating? This follows from the underlying idea that deliberation, as a debate over ideas, is what judges should be doing under any common conception of the rule of law, whereas bargaining, as the strategic use of whatever power they may have over other judges, is a normatively inappropriate form of judicial behavior. This text is not the place to rehash that debate. Epstein and Knight (1998) offer a detailed analysis of what distinguishes judicial bargaining from judicial deliberation, highlighting the differences between merely offering a substantive suggestion about the merits of a proposed argument and invoking a procedural rule of decision-making to pressure a change in the opinion. Employing the private papers of a number of US Supreme Court justices (Brennan, Douglas, Marshall, and Powell), they were able to demonstrate numerous instances over several terms of the court in which the justices used the internal rules of the court to their strategic advantage in influencing the interpretations of statutes. This finding, as we show below, has been substantially reinforced by subsequent research.

For our purposes here, we think that it is enough to say that there is sufficient evidence of bargaining among judges on collegial courts to justify a normative assessment of its implications for democratic legitimacy. And we would add that the same conceptual questions that arise about our ability to discern the underlying mindset of representatives in the legislative process are relevant to the analysis of judges. In fact, it is difficult to distinguish deliberation from bargaining when we try to assess the behavior of a judge in a particular case. Given the strategic incentives, it is better for the normative analysis to characterize judicial interactions as bargaining, even if the contours of those bargains are given by ideas. It enables us to identify a prospective role for courts in securing the equitable treatment of interests even if they individually and collectively fall short of Herculean judgments, or their purported role as the "exemplar of public reason" more broadly.[3]

Bargaining among judges can influence the substance of an interpretive decision about a statute in a number of ways. Such bargaining closely tracks the rules and practices of the collegial courts. Here we want to briefly highlight two such practices: rules governing the initial decision on whether to decide the case on the merits, and rules governing how the court produces its final written opinions. Judicial systems vary in the ways that the rules regulate these tasks. As opposed to making a comprehensive assessment of the different implications across institutional practices, we will focus here on a few examples from existing research that further our general argument that these institutional procedures lend themselves to strategic bargaining.

Consider, for example, the initial decision as to whether or not to hear a case. Many collegial courts have little control over their dockets. They are obligated to consider all of the petitions raising statutory questions that come before them. They may decide, and often do, that it is not necessary to consider a case on its merits, resolving the conflict on procedural grounds instead. If not, they must consider the substantive questions in dispute and render a decision on the merits. This is not the case, however, for the US Supreme Court, which has a very precise procedure for selecting the cases that it hears. It provides a great deal of autonomy for the members of the court and thus the opportunity for some bargaining over the ultimate outcomes of the case.

The procedure is commonly described as the Rule of Four. The rule establishes the following criterion for hearing a case: the only petitions that will be accepted for consideration by the court are those that receive the support of at least four of the justices. Any petitions that fail to meet this standard are deemed to be resolved according to the decisions of the lower court from which the appeal originated. So, the initial choice facing the justices is binary, between the substantive decision of the lower court and the yet to be determined decision of their own court.

The US Supreme Court receives thousands of petitions every year appealing the decisions of lower courts. In recent years it has ended up hearing fewer than a hundred cases per year on the merits ("CQ Press Supreme Court Collection" 2022). We can reasonably assume that individual justices are influenced by the importance of the subject matter of such petitions as well as what they expect the final decision on the merits to be. To the extent that justices are concerned about the future effects of their decisions, we would expect them to vote to deny or grant review based on what they think will happen at the merits stage.

If they believe that their preferred interpretation of the relevant statute will be the majority view on the final decision on the merits of the case, they are likely to vote in favor of cert in hopes of establishing a precedential interpretation for the future that matches their understanding of the statute. On the other hand, if they believe that their preferred interpretation will not be the basis of the court's decision on the merits, they may prefer to pass on the petition even if they may not agree with the decision of the lower court. In such situations, given the possibility of establishing an unfavorable interpretation of the statute, they are likely to vote against hearing the case.

Social science research on the cert process of the US Supreme Court has demonstrated that this initial decision has generated bargaining in pursuit of the fourth vote needed to satisfy the Rule of Four (Epstein and Knight 1998). A strategy that has proved successful at this initial stage is the threat to issue a published opinion dissenting from a denial of certiorari. The threat is intended to influence those justices who might be concerned about being called out for their failure to be willing to decide a case. Justice John Paul Stevens once explained that the threat to issue a dissent in this situation challenges the basic institutional integrity of the court, in the sense that the justices prefer that they not make public their private disagreements.

Here it is important to note that the initial decision on how a court will treat a conflict over the meaning of a statute can have a significant effect on the day-to-day treatment of a democratically enacted law. At the level of an ultimate appeals court like the US Supreme Court, it is a decision to either leave the lower court's decision in place, with the possibility of there being continuing conflict over the proper meaning of the statute, or resolve it, setting a precedential meaning for the future. A decision not to hear a case would be especially problematic when the lower court has issued a decision that violates the democratic criterion. Nonetheless, bargaining over this initial question does not necessarily tell us what the exact implications would be for the baseline democratic criterion. That depends on the specific preferences of the justices in the particular case. But it does show us one important way in which the institutional rules of the court foster bargaining, which might have significant implications for democratic legitimacy.

A second important area of the rules of a collegial court that is especially relevant to our discussion is the procedures governing how the court produces its final opinion on the merits. More specifically, we have in mind the decision on who will write the opinion articulating the decision on the merits of the case, as well as the rules governing the availability of options of writing alternative opinions for those judges who might disagree with the majority decision. On the question of initial opinion assignment, the rules on most courts are fairly straightforward. On the US Supreme Court, for example, the justices meet in conference right after hearing the oral arguments on a case and take an initial straw vote on the merits. Then the task of drafting an initial opinion is assigned to one of the justices in the majority. If the chief justice is in the majority, they have the authority to make the specific assignment. If the chief justice is in the minority, then the authority to assign the opinion rests with the justice in the majority who has the most seniority on the court.

The initial opinion assignment can have significant influence over the final interpretation offered by the court. Clearly, the preferred interpretation of the opinion author will set the framework for the collective opinion of the court. However, the author is always constrained by the requirement of maintaining the support of a majority of the justices, the threshold necessary to establish the opinion's interpretation as a precedent for future cases. The task of maintaining a majority creates significant space for bargaining over the final interpretation of the court. Typically bargaining on the merits begins after the opinion writer sends the first draft of an opinion to the full court. From there, the justices may attempt to bargain over the language of the opinion, including the rationale it invokes and the substantive interpretation that it adopts.

The research about bargaining over the merits on collegial courts is quite extensive.[4] It illustrates how justices use two strategic tools, explicit bargaining statements and threats to publish separate accompanying opinions, to try to influence the opinion author. Explicit bargaining statements by the justices offer a switch in a vote on the merits in exchange for amendments to the draft opinion. Such statements are transmitted in the form of private memos between the justices. Epstein and Knight (1998) found the use of bargaining statements in more than two-thirds of the most important cases before the US Supreme Court in the 1970s and 1980s.

Threats to publish separate opinions are an alternative, and a somewhat less explicit, strategy. Once the opinion author has submitted a first draft, the other justices are free to issue their own potential opinions.[5] Such draft opinions may be offered merely to inform the primary opinion author of another justice's plan to publish an accompanying opinion, or such opinions may be intended as part of a bargaining strategy to elicit changes in the majority opinion. Obviously, it is often hard to discern what the motivation is for a justice to write a secondary opinion. But one way to possibly identify a bargaining motivation is to see how often the secondary opinions are introduced in the prepublished opinion review period and then withdrawn before the court announces its decision on the merits. Epstein and Knight (1998) looked for the number of instances in which an opinion written by a justice other than the assigned opinion author changed in form or was retracted during the decision-making process. They found that in 17.7 percent of the cases in their sample justices suppressed their writings or changed them during the circulation. This behavior was significantly higher for the landmark cases (26.4 percent) than for those decided during the 1983 term (10.8 percent). All of these might not be conclusive evidence of an effort to bargain over the main opinion but, given the complaints raised by many of the justices over their workloads, the fact that such secondary opinions are produced and then retracted or altered in nearly 20 percent of the cases lends significant support to the idea that the justices are using them as tools to bargain over the interpretation of statutes.[6]

Having presented the case for the existence of intrabranch bargaining on collegial courts, we should acknowledge that there remains a debate in the social science literature as to whether this bargaining really affects the final outcome of the case. One line of argument among scholars of judicial decision-making holds that, at the end of the deliberative process, regardless of who gets assigned to write the opinion or how much internal bargaining takes place, as long as the judges vote according to their true individual preferences, the final decision of the court will reflect the ideal preferences of the median judge. This is the classic logic of spatial voting in a democratic decision-making environment. If this argument is correct, then the only thing that democratic theorists would have to do to assess the normative implications of interpretative decisions of courts on the legitimacy of the democratic process would be to compare the baseline democratic criterion with the ideal preferences of the median judge in every case.

But from our perspective the better argument rests with those researchers who have identified various ways in which such bargaining forces the collective decision of the court away from the position of the median judge and toward a decision that reflects the preferences of the more powerful judges. Their power in these cases is primarily a function of the special authority that the institutional rules and practices of the court system, like the deference to seniority, provides them.[7] While there is no reason to assume that these rules skew the interpretive decision of the court in any particular substantive ideological direction, it is clear that they introduce the space for asymmetric relations of power to influence judicial decision-making on collegial courts.

And, yet, this alone does not tell us what effects intrabranch bargaining has on the legitimacy of the democratic process. The evidence of the potential for a wide range of different views influencing the court's collective interpretive decision raises significant questions but does not provide sufficient support for a direct challenge to democratic legitimacy. The existing research on collegial courts demonstrates that there is a high probability that substantial bargaining occurs in the interpretive stage of democratic governance. But much of this bargaining may be easily tolerated by the normative dictates of democracy.

For, as we have already argued, the equitable treatment of interests baseline does not offer anything in principle to directly constrain *the process by which* collegial courts make their decisions. Judges may have different degrees of power depending on seniority, institutional authority, rules and practices of collegial decision-making, and public opinion. These factors may determine who among the judges has the greater capacity to fashion a decision in a way consistent with their own preferences. In principle, it is not the process of intrabranch bargaining that matters but rather the outcome of that process.

But this does not mean that "anything goes" when it comes to intrabranch bargaining on the court. Just because we argue that a democratic commitment does not explicitly dictate the terms for judicial bargaining, it does not mean that we should not be attentive to the bargaining strategies employed by the judges. For there may be particular strategies that undermine the capacity of the court to render an opinion that satisfies the democratic criterion. If we find that a particular bargaining strategy (like coercive threats, for example) would have the effect of producing a substantive opinion that is democratically unjustifiable, then we have a normative reason for prohibiting the use of that strategy. In these cases, however, the primary issue remains: Is the collegial decision consistent with the democratic baseline, the equitable treatment of citizens' interests?

Getting at the question of how courts render decisions consistent with the democratic baseline begins to focus our attention on the broader implications of our account of legislative supremacy. Legislative supremacy has been the basis for a wide range of proposed theories of statutory interpretation. The primary alternatives on offer tend to focus on the plain meaning of the text, on the intentions of the enacting legislators, or on some objective purpose that can be inferred from the statute (Eskridge and Frickey 2012). On the plain meaning account, judges look to the meaning of the words in the text itself, and only that, to decide how the statute is to be interpreted. On the legislative intent account, judges can look to the legislative history of the statute in order to discern how the legislators intended for the law to be interpreted. On the purposivism account, when it is distinguishable from intentionalism approaches, judges attempt to determine a general purpose that a reasonable legislature would have sought to achieve through the statute and then interpret it accordingly.

Each of these approaches has its advocates among students of the judiciary. And each has its critics. It is not clear to us that a commitment to democracy alone can adequately resolve the conflicting precepts of the alternative theories.[8] However, we will say more in the next section about how we think our bargaining justification of democracy might influence the ways in which courts choose to interpret statutes. The main idea to keep in mind at the outset of our analysis is that a commitment to democracy does place constraints on how courts can legitimately interpret statutes. If their decisions are consistent with the democratic baseline, then the judicial interpretation is democratically acceptable. If the interpretation is different from that standard, it is a problem for democracy. The potential for undemocratic bargains leads us on to interbranch questions.

Interbranch Bargaining: Courts and Legislatures

We start this discussion with the assumption that the legislature seeks to satisfy the democratic baseline and treat the interests of citizens equitably. This allows us to focus on the ways in which the judicial branch might undermine democracy through its interpretations. Here we distinguish two types of bargaining that might lead to undemocratic judicial influence on democratic governance: anticipated reaction effects on the initial enactment of the legislature, and long-term bargaining through statutory interpretation by the courts.

As we have argued, legislators presumably make certain assumptions about how the statutes they enact will be interpreted in the future. Their preference would be that future judges interpret the statutes in a way consistent with the initial legislative enactment. If they assume that their intended enactment will shape future judicial interpretations, then the legislature can confidently enact legislation that satisfies the democratic baseline. If, on the other hand, they assume that future judges will render interpretations that reflect their own policy preferences, this creates a legislative dilemma. Should the representatives continue to pursue the statute that satisfies the democratic obligation of equitable treatment of citizens' interests? Or should they modify the statute, thus favoring the interests of some citizens over others, in a direction that would diminish the probability of an even worse interpretation by the court? By adopting a strategy of modification, the representatives would anticipate the damaging effects of an undemocratic judiciary and yet somewhat diminish the normative legitimacy of their own actions.

The separation of powers system in the United States has been the subject of significant research on this question. And there is evidence that these anticipated reaction effects do occur. In 1988, Brian Marks proposed a spatial model of judicial-legislative bargaining and used it to analyze how the judiciary might influence the collective decisions of Congress (Marks 1988). The underlying logic of his analysis was that the expectation of future judicial interpretation could constrain the internal dynamics of legislative bargaining. Marks assumed that the legislators were aware of the preferences of the judges who would be interpreting the statute in the future. The task for the legislators was to find a collective decision that was as close as possible to their own preferred law but could also survive efforts by the court to interpret it differently. The implication of the legislators' strategic choice was to effectively change the substance of the law and thus undermine the optimal collective preference of the legislature. In Marks's analysis, the likelihood of success or failure for the legislature was a function of the distribution of preferences among the members of the collegial court and the pivotal members of the legislature. This research led to a number of important studies that pursued various aspects of the legislative-judicial relationship, focusing primarily on the influence of the expectations of future statutory interpretation on legislative decision-making.[9] These studies reinforced the basic notion that if elected representatives take the future influence of interpretive decisions into account when they are engaged in their initial decision-making, the resulting statutes may undermine the normative requirements of democracy.

Given the normative implications of this anticipated reaction strategy, why would a legislature intent on satisfying their democratic obligation ever choose it? Why wouldn't they, as an alternative, merely enact the statute that satisfies the requirements of democratic legitimacy, establishing the democratic baseline, and wait and see how it plays out in the future? We don't actually know which of the alternatives the legislature will take when confronted by such a choice. But we do know that the choice either way has implications for our normative analysis. If legislators adopt the reactive strategy, they acquiesce to the unequal treatment of the interests of citizens and undermine the normative requirements of democracy. If they choose instead to maintain the dictates of democratic legitimacy, they must anticipate their future responses to any judicial interpretations that seek to alter the effects of their statutes. This constitutes the long-term bargaining game over the process of interpretation.

The rules of this long-term bargaining process are commonly set by a nation's constitution through an institutional structure that distributes authority among governmental entities. The separation of powers system in the United States is but one example. If the courts are granted independent authority to interpret the laws, they will be free to establish whatever meaning and purpose they prefer to the enactments of the legislature. The greater the independence, the more power enjoyed by the courts to establish their own preferences if they so choose. The relevant question here is, What institutional options are available to the legislature to respond to a court that seeks to undermine the democratic baseline?

The most obvious response is that they can enact new legislation that explicitly rejects the existing interpretation of the court. By doing so they can reinforce the purpose of their previous legislation and clarify the relationship between their enactments and the dictates of the democratic criterion of legitimacy. In doing so, they introduce the important role that public opinion plays in defining the power relationship between the legislative and judicial branches. The existing research on judicial-legislative relations in the United States suggests that the willingness of either branch of government to engage in this type of challenge and response is a function of their relative standing in the eyes of the public (Bartels and Johnston 2020). From the perspective of the legislature, the expected value of new legislation to overturn unfavorable judicial decisions depends significantly on the level of support it enjoys relative to the courts.

Under the right circumstances, the new legislation response might be the most effective way of directly addressing the problem of an undemocratic court. However, it might turn out to be a very costly way of legislating if there are many areas in which the preferences of the courts are different from those of the elected representatives. This seems like a very time-consuming approach to dealing with this problem of democratic legitimacy. An alternative strategy available to legislatures in a number of countries is the institutional control that elected representatives have over judicial appointments and funding. To the extent that the elected representatives have the institutional authority to appoint judges as well as the authority to control the funding and budgets of courts, they can use more general threats to the independence of the courts as a way of discouraging statutory interpretations that fail to satisfy the democratic baseline.

And there is research that supports the idea that courts might respond to these kinds of threats to their institutional authority. These studies analyze the ways in which judicial interpretation might be constrained by expectations of legislative or executive responses to their own judicial decisions. Epstein and Knight (1998) assessed the claims of these studies as they apply to both constitutional and statutory review by the US Supreme Court and found evidence in the private papers of some of the justices that in making their own decisions they did take into account the potential reactions of the other branches of government. On the other hand, Segal and his collaborators (Segal 1997; Segal, Westerland, and Lindquist 2011) raised questions about the degree to which the justices actually acted strategically in the face of the anticipated reactions of political actors. In his first study, Segal (1997) argued that in the case of statutory interpretation, where it is easiest for Congress to respond to a decision of the court by merely enacting a new statute, the empirical evidence did not support the view that the Justices altered their decision from what they would choose without the threat of Congressional reaction. But in the later study, Segal, Westerland, and Lindquist (2011) analyzed the possibility of strategic decision-making in the case of constitutional review and found that there is evidence of a strategic calculation on the part of the Justices in response to potential Congressional reaction. Segal and his collaborators continued to argue against the explanation that the strategic behavior was a result of the court's concern that Congress would try to change the substantive nature of their particular decision. They argued instead that it was a more general response to a fear that Congress would try to attack the court more directly, seeking to undermine its basic legitimacy.

In the end we can see that there are strategies by which the legislature can respond to an undemocratic interpretation of the legitimately enacted statute. Some strategies focus directly on the substantive content of the statute in question. Others focus more on the rules and procedures that structure the independence of the interpretive process. Whether or not the strategies will prove successful in maintaining the democratic baseline depends on the relative bargaining power of the different actors. In these situations, relative bargaining power is primarily a function of the institutional authority granted to the actors as well as the degree of support that the different actors enjoy in the public at large (Bartels and Johnston 2020).

These are roughly the same conditions that govern the ability of a court to respond to an instance of the legislature enacting a statute that fails to satisfy the basic democratic criterion of equitable treatment of citizens' interests. Thinking about cases in which the legislature fails to meet the criterion offers some additional insights into the complicated role of courts in the democratic process. The basic question is, How do courts assess whether the legislature has satisfied the democratic criterion? This has implications for the debate over the best approach to statutory interpretation. It is not our goal here to resolve the general disagreement over whether a judge should focus primarily on text, intention, or purpose when interpreting the implications of a statute. And, as we said above, we doubt that a commitment to democracy alone provides a basis for doing so. But we argue that such a commitment does place an obligation on courts to assess the democratic legitimacy of the statute as part of the interpretive task, regardless of their substantive theory. It is an essential feature of any process of holding the legislature accountable in a democratic society. Given the role that unequal bargaining generally plays in the democratic legislative process, we think that judges must look to see if the democratic criterion has been satisfied. For our purposes, we can distinguish two different approaches the court may take in analyzing the legitimacy of the statute.

One approach is for the court to focus on the substantive content of the law. This is the approach that courts commonly use in the United States and many other countries when they are asked to assess the constitutional legitimacy of a statute. If judges were to employ this approach to resolve questions of legitimacy in terms of our argument here, the task would be to determine if the law instantiates an equitable treatment of citizens' interests. To do this the court would have to answer several empirical questions: Which citizens' interests are relevant to the statute in question? How are those interests distributed within the society? How successful was the legislature in considering these interests and then crafting a law that closely approximates them? And, if the substance of the law fails to adequately take account of these interests, is there another value, held by the community, that is furthered by the law and is worthy of priority treatment in this case? Answers to each of these questions would be needed for a court to adequately assess the democratic legitimacy of the statute by means of analyzing the substantive content of the law. Frankly, it is hard to see how most judges would be able to adequately answer such questions. And, therefore, we believe that there are better institutional alternatives than authorizing the courts to rewrite the substantive content of the law.

The Structural Due Process Approach

An alternative that we find more promising is for the court to focus on the process by which the legislation was produced. Rather than determining whether the substantive content of the law accurately reflects the interests of citizens, the court can focus on whether all relevant interests had an opportunity for real consideration in the legislative process.[10] This would involve an analysis of the rules and procedures that governed the process as well as an assessment of the extent to which asymmetries in power had a disproportionate influence on the legislative bargaining outcome. This would explicitly entail an analysis of public bargaining that would mirror the approach undertaken by judges in private contracting cases.

What we have in mind is a variation on the "structural due process" approach originally advocated by Tribe (1975).[11] The analysis of the legislative process is something that courts seem better equipped to undertake.[12] And there is substantial evidence of past judicial behavior that lends support to this view. Consider the following examples. European courts, in particular, often examine the legislative process as a part of their determination of substantive constitutionality (Bar-Siman-Tov 2011). To be sure, courts in the United States regularly review and set aside executive agency actions on procedural grounds. In the 1970s many courts followed the lead of the DC Circuit in taking a "hard look" at agency decision-making (*Greater Boston Television Corp. v. FCC*, 444 F.2d 841 [1970], 85). In 1983, the US Supreme Court clarified the dictates of the Administrative Procedure Act, concluding that it established a scheme of "reasoned decision-making" that prohibited agency decisions that are "arbitrary and capricious" (*Motor Vehicles Manufacturers Association v. State Farm Mutual Automobile Insurance Co.*, 463 U.S. 29 [1983]). Crucially, in *Allentown Mack Sales & Service, Inc. v. NLRB* (522 U.S. 359 [1998]), the court held, "Not only must an agency's decreed result be within the scope of its lawful authority, but the process by which it reaches that result must be logical and rational" (374).

In recent decades, the US Supreme Court has turned to the legislative record, and therefore the process of lawmaking, not just for the review of agency actions but in its determinations of the constitutionality of legislation. Sometimes it has been employed to explicitly resolve procedural legitimacy in federalism cases. In *United States v. Lopez* (1.514 U.S. 549 [1985]), the court invalidated the federal Gun Free School

Zones Act of 1990 on the grounds that it exceeded congressional authority under the commerce power; the opinion held that even though the rule on its face did not have any substantive effect on interstate commerce, congressional findings would have provided the court some basis for accepting a link to interstate commerce. In other cases, the court used procedural analysis to give further content to claims about legislative purpose and intent. In *Seminole Tribe v. Florida* (517 U.S. 44 [1996]) and *City of Boerne v. Flores* (521 U.S. 507 [1997]), for example, the court suggested that legislative history, including careful evidence of findings, might be of importance in persuading the court to uphold a statute (Frickey and Smith 2001). In *Kimel v. Florida Board of Regents* (528 U.S. 62 [2000]), the court made it explicit that it uses the "legislative record to infer the 'reasons for Congress' action.'"

And, in other cases, the court has employed procedural analysis to resolve other kinds of constitutional questions. For example, in *Board of Trustees of the University of Alabama v. Garrett* (531 U.S. 356 [2001]), the court held that Congress had "assembled only such minimal evidence of unconstitutional state discrimination in employment against the disabled," and that as such, Congress's authority to enact legislation under Section 5 of the Fourteenth Amendment to remedy failures of accommodations for the disabled under the Americans with Disabilities Act failed to exhibit "congruence and proportionality between the injury to be prevented or remedied and the means exhibited to that end" (365), as prescribed under *City of Boerne*. Justice Breyer's dissent complained that "the Court's failure to find sufficient evidentiary support may well rest upon its decision to hold Congress to a strict, judicially created evidentiary standard, particularly in respect to lack of justification" (382).

For our purposes, judicial interest in the legislative record, and the prescription of an "evidentiary standard" for Congressional action, supports the view that an analysis of legislative process can be effectively employed in the judicial assessment of the justifiability of statutes. But we must admit that previous recommendations for this kind of judicial analysis have received little support from judicial scholars. For example, Frickey and Smith (2002) argued that judicial investigations of legislative decision-making tend to violate some of the basic premises of contemporary political science's understanding of the legislative process. Their most compelling example notes that in cases of statutory interpretation, judges mistakenly treat statutes as if they are the product of a single author with a unique intent. We agree that the fact of bicameralism alone gives us reason to think that the legislative record will be multivocal. But these challenges to incorporating procedural concerns into statutory interpretation are more relevant to interpretative approaches that seek primarily to identify "the" intention or "the" purpose of the legislature, an issue that is most relevant to resolving questions about the substantive content of the statute. We would argue that they are less relevant to the more explicitly procedural analysis that we envision for public bargaining.

We believe that this structural due process approach can provide a clear method for courts to assess whether the legislature satisfied the democratic criterion. And, here it is important to emphasize, it would provide additional justification for greater transparency requirements in the political process. For the primary focus would be on the question of unconscionability, investigating whether the appropriate legislative process was undermined by the influence of asymmetric bargaining power. The court's analysis would rest on the notion that the greater the bargaining asymmetries, the greater the likelihood of an inequitable treatment of interests. If the court identified the influence of substantial power asymmetries, it would be required to investigate the source of those asymmetries to further determine if they are deemed legitimate or illegitimate by the criterion of democracy. If the court, after reviewing the procedural history of a statute, determined that the procedural prerequisites of a democratically justifiable statute were satisfied, that would be enough for it to conclude that the legislation satisfied the democratic criterion. This alternative approach requires the court to answer certain empirical questions about the process (questions that could be answered only if the legislative process was openly transparent), but it relieves it of the burden of determining the relevant content and distribution of interests in every case.

If a court were to determine that the legislature has failed to meet the democratic criterion, then it must decide what, if anything, it wants to do to rectify the problem in the case at hand. The strategies available to a court in this circumstance will also be a function of the institutional authority granted to judges by the constitution and relevant procedural statutes. Two strategies are especially relevant to our discussion and they are related to the interpretive approaches that we discussed above. On the one hand, judges could offer a substantive interpretation of the statute that better reflects the equitable interests of the public. While this might be the most immediately effective way of moving closer to the democratic baseline, it requires judges to rely on their own judgments of the relevant interests of the public. We have noted, as a practical matter, how difficult it may be to arrive at such a judgment. Substantive interpretations are relevant and appropriate when the task is merely one of assessing the implications of a justified statute for a specific set of facts in the case. But it is not the best approach when the normative status of the statute is in question.

On the other hand, if the courts have the explicit authority, granted either by the constitution or by statute, to assess whether rights of democratic participation and legitimate political bargaining have been satisfied, they will have other remedial alternatives. In a jurisdiction in which such a right is available, it can be used as an alternative response to unjustifiable behavior on the part of the legislature (Bulman-Pozen and Seifter 2021). If a court finds, employing the structural due process approach, that the legislature failed to satisfy the institutional procedures established to guarantee the democratic criterion, it could strike the statute as illegal or unconstitutional depending on the basis of the procedures, and then send the unjustifiable statute back to the legislature. This then puts the responsibility back on the elected representatives to craft legislation that more closely approximates the equitable treatment of citizens' interests.

To the extent that we have demonstrated that the assessment of questions of duress and unconscionability is a necessary feature of determining the legitimacy of democratic governance, we have also demonstrated the fundamental importance of an institutional approach to assessing the justifiability of public bargains. If we choose to acknowledge the role of bargaining in the democratic process and thus allow its political legitimacy, we will need to incorporate a structural due process approach to judicial review of legislation. It would become a centerpiece of statutory interpretation in a truly democratic society.

Summary

Our discussion of bargaining in the process of interpretation introduces ways in which the judicial branch can both undermine and enhance the normative legitimacy of the democratic process. An independent judiciary, considered a cornerstone of most conceptions of the rule of law, may counterintuitively serve as a hindrance to the achievement of a democratically legitimate political process. And not just in its traditionally conceived role as the guarantor of constitutionally protected rights. Independent judges can, if they so choose, replace the elected representatives' best judgment of an equitable balance of citizens' interests with their own preferences for favoring some citizens' interests over others. When they do so, it places a burden on the legislature to respond to these judicial interventions and maintain a commitment to the democratic criterion. Or the judiciary may serve an important remedial role, enhancing the democratic legitimacy of the law when the legislature has failed to satisfy the normative requirements of democracy.

Efforts by either branch to remedy undemocratic actions may focus on either the substance of a particular statute or the general process by which the statute was enacted. The probability of success in any situation will be in large part a function of the relative power differentials between the actors. That is the nature of bargaining. But the wisdom of the choices between the two approaches—that is, what would be more effective in the best of circumstances, the substantive or the institutional—will depend on factors related to the differences in the roles that the actors play in the overall governance scheme. We return to this last question at the end of the chapter, after we assess bargaining between the legislative and executive branches of government.

Implementation and Enforcement

While the elected representatives in the legislature are responsible for enacting laws, the tasks of implementation and enforcement are generally considered executive functions of government. To the extent that the legislative and executive functions are separated in the governance scheme, the opportunities for asymmetric bargaining to influence the actual application of democratically enacted laws in everyday life are numerous. So, a comprehensive account of democratic legitimacy must take account of these opportunities.

In this section we focus on two areas of executive activity that are especially relevant to this concern. Our primary interest is in the role of bureaucratic agencies in the implementation of the laws and policies enacted by the legislature. Much of the actual work in a democratic society involves this form of implementation and thus raises important normative questions. As with our analysis of judicial decision-making, we conceive the process from enactment to implementation and enforcement as one of long-term and ongoing bargaining. A second area of executive activity that we briefly consider is the explicit bargaining that often goes on in systems in which the executive has some power of veto over legislative enactments. This issue directly addresses a challenge to the idea of legislative supremacy in a democratic society.

Executive branch bureaucracies are large and often decentralized organizations. The coordination necessary to implement the law commonly involves many actors. And the task of agreeing on a shared approach for implementation introduces significant collective action problems, problems that are often resolved through bargaining among actors with different political interests. The dictates of democracy suggest that this shared approach should incorporate the legislative purpose instantiated in the statute. That is, the bureaucracy should satisfy the democratic baseline.

As in the case of interpretation, the important normative question is not, in principle, how the bureaucrats arrive at their common purpose but rather whether their common purpose is consistent with the democratic criterion we proposed in earlier chapters. If bureaucracies implement and enforce the law as the legislature intended, assuming that the legislature satisfied the democratic criterion, then the dictates of democracy are satisfied. As a general rule, it doesn't matter how they get there as long as they get there. The one exception to this rule would be, as we explained in the case of intrabranch bargaining among judges, if we discovered that particular intrabranch strategies had a negative effect on administrative decisions. In such cases, a constraint on that bargaining strategy itself would be warranted. Here it is important to reiterate that while implementors need not be procedurally democratic in their own decision-making, they must satisfy the condition of good faith in the exercise of their implementation and enforcement authority. If they choose to favor some interests other than those instantiated by the legislature, significant normative questions must be faced. Only implementation and enforcement actions that displace these legislative aims are worthy of concern.

The fundamental empirical question for our normative analysis is, Whose interests control the bureaucracy? To see the different potential answers to this question, it is helpful to briefly consider how administrative law in the United States since the early twentieth century has addressed this issue (Tushnet 2011; DeCell 2011). Initially, it was assumed that administrative agencies did follow the dictates of the legislature, that the interests chosen by the elected representatives would be those motivating bureaucratic implementation. But in the early decades of the twentieth century, the Progressive movement argued for the importance of greater independence for these agencies. The argument behind this movement was that the ever more quickly changing conditions of a rapidly growing society necessitated that more authority for implementation of democratically enacted laws should rest with experts in the relevant fields. Giving experts greater independent authority would diminish the significance of political preferences in the implementation process and thus enhance the beneficial value of legislation for the society as a whole. This was a highly contentious view and the subject of many court battles during the New Deal period. As Tushnet (2011) notes, while many advocates of the Progressive view felt that they were losing the battle in the courtroom, the actual degree of bureaucratic independence continued to grow.

After World War II, however, the greater discretion enjoyed by bureaucrats did not lead to implementation merely by the experts. Bureaucratic decision-making became the target of considerable political activity.

Interest groups began to turn their attention more directly to the implementation process as a means of achieving disproportionately favorable treatment under the law. What they could not get from their elected representatives, they sought from the bureaucracy. In administrative law circles, this led to new questions about the democratic accountability of the bureaucracy.

Recommendations for how to institutionalize greater accountability highlight three different areas of interests. Some argued that legitimacy concerns about an independent bureaucracy could be satisfied by instantiating the interests of the president in implementation decisions. This followed from the idea that the president was also elected through a democratic process, in fact being the only government official relevant to the process who was elected by all of the citizens. Others argued that the administrative agencies should be conceived of as quasi-legislative bodies who are required to answer to the interest groups relevant to their regulatory issues. This approach sought in a sense to justify the increasing influence of interest groups by arguing that they had a legitimate interest in the special treatment that they sought, given their intense interest in the questions under consideration. And, finally, a third group argued that the requirements of democracy hinged on the interests of all citizens and that the best approach was for bureaucracies to implement procedures that allowed them to get input on the interests of the full spectrum of citizens.

Here we see four plausible answers to the question of bureaucratic interests. In addition to the elected representative's judgment of public interests instantiated in the enacted legislation, there are three other possibilities: the scientific recommendations of experts, the policy preferences of the executive, and the policy preferences established by the bureaucrats themselves. If any of these three diverge from a normatively legitimate baseline, it raises questions for democracy. For the first two of these alternatives, there are plausible normative justifications for divergence. The third alternative, the personal preferences of the bureaucrats, is more problematic. This is the main normative concern of those who highlight the role that private interest group politics plays in the implementation of the law. Efforts to shift public policy away from the democratic baseline and in a direction more favorable to the interests of highly affected interest groups run counter to the dictates of democracy (Lowi 1979).

Scientific expertise raises a difficult question for democracy. On the one hand, we are committed to the equitable treatment of citizens' interests. That means in part that everyone's vote—as the primary means of conveying such interests—counts equally. On the other hand, we want to base our decisions on the best information and knowledge that we can acquire on a question. Surely that means that we need to be open to the testimony of experts and to use their evidence in deciding important policy questions. And in doing so we may give disproportionate influence to some citizens over others. We have argued that democratic governance often requires us to face value trade-offs, including trade-offs between giving the interests of individual citizens equal weight, and realizing interests and values that are deemed more important in particular circumstances. And that is basically what we face in thinking about the role of expertise in a democratic society. We may be justified in giving special authorization to experts in the process of implementation.[13] But even if we accept the reasonableness of this trade-off, we are left with the question, Who should make the decision of when and how experts are to be allowed to influence that process? The appointed heads of agencies or our elected representatives?

If one accepts the traditional view that the election of representatives and the enactment of legislation is the primary focus of democratic theory, then it is reasonable to ask, What are the normative implications of a bureaucracy that implements the law according to the interests of the executive rather the legislative purpose instantiated in the law? This will primarily be a question in those democratic systems that separate the executive and legislative functions. In unified systems the main concern will be those rogue bureaucracies that pursue implementation based on their own preferences. In separation of power systems, the problem for democracy is that both the legislature and the executive are elected by the people. If they differ in their judgments about what equitable treatment of citizens' interests would entail for the law, which branch should prevail?

As we see in the following discussion of interbranch bargaining, the actual resolution of this dilemma is a function of the relative bargaining power of the two branches. It is the result of an ongoing struggle to control administrative agencies. From the normative perspective, we would argue that the question is best answered by focusing on two important issues: which branch is better equipped to assess and weigh the interests of all citizens in an equitable manner, and which branch is easier to constrain when it fails to meet the democratic baseline. The effectiveness of efforts to constrain the implementation decisions of bureaucrats in order to maintain the democratic baseline is in large part a function of the rules of institutional authority in the system. Largely dependent on the ways in which the authority over implementation is distributed within the governance structure, the relative bargaining power of the legislative and executive branches will determine the extent to which the democratic baseline is maintained. This raises important normative questions about the relationship between the legislative branch and executive administrative agencies and about the processes of administrative decision-making and the ways that bureaucrats are held accountable.

As in our earlier discussion of legislative-judicial bargaining, it is important to consider transparent instances of bargaining as well as the influence of anticipated reactions to real and implicit threats of future actions. The most transparent instance of bargaining between the legislative and executive branches occurs in those systems that allow the executive to veto an enactment of the legislature. A second type of bargaining, which can be either explicit or implicit, involves the efforts of the legislature to oversee and control the implementation process of the bureaucracy. Both types are characterized by the opportunity for asymmetric bargaining to influence implementation, through explicit threats or anticipated reaction, in democratically illegitimate ways.

Consider first the exercise of an executive veto. In principle, one might consider the veto to be the limiting case of undemocratic implementation. It serves to thwart the legitimate effort to instantiate the interests of the citizens in a new law or governmental policy. At times we can see the veto bargaining in action. The legislature enacts a new statute, the executive vetoes it, and the legislature seeks to override that veto and save the statute. Other times the bargaining works less transparently. As the legislature is involved in the process of making new legislation, the executive observes its negotiations and threatens a veto. In response, the legislature either ignores the threat and proceeds as it wishes or it anticipates the effects of the threatened veto and changes the terms of the legislation to diminish the possibility that the veto will be employed.

In the first case, if the veto is not overridden, then it might seem that the normative implication of interbranch bargaining is to undermine the equitable treatment of interests. We note, however, that the executive might veto legislation because, in the executive's view, the legislature has not satisfied the democratic criterion. But we also note that this would be a judgment made by the executive as opposed to the elected representatives in the legislature. In the second case, if a modified statute is enacted, then the further the modified version of the legislation deviates from the version that the elected representatives would have originally judged to best satisfy the democratic criterion, the greater the question about the normative legitimacy of the political bargain. In both cases there is a risk that the bargain will produce an outcome that gives disproportionate treatment to a minority of the electorate.

Both of these scenarios have been the subject of significant research in the social sciences. Some of the most interesting work on the logic of legislative-executive bargaining has been done by positive political theory scholars. They seek to understand how various political conditions, conditions that will influence the relative bargaining power of the actors, influence how successful a threatened veto will be. These analyses have primarily used simple spatial models and noncooperative game theory to assess the possible equilibria outcomes from various configurations of interbranch bargaining. The research on veto bargaining analyzes the ways in which various distributions of preferences among the president and the main pivotal veto players in the House and the Senate influence the final content of legislation.[14] One version of these games focuses on the bargaining between the two houses of Congress, with the president's preferences serving merely as the limit for how far Congress can deviate from the status quo. A second version focuses more on the strategic behavior of the president, analyzing the ways in which the president's behavior can both influence the internal bargaining within Congress and set the possible limits on the terms of the final Congressional bargain (Cameron and McCarty 2004).

This research highlights the important role of uncertainty in determining bargaining strategies and outcomes. And it clarifies the strengths and weaknesses of the different branches given various configurations of political preferences. The success of the executive veto normally depends, understandably, on the relative bargaining power of the two branches. And, again, the balance of power is basically a function of the distribution of institutional authority (with special emphasis on the override threshold) and the relative standing enjoyed by the two branches in the opinion of the public.

Now let's turn to a more complex problem: the bargaining over bureaucratic implementation. The primary focus of this bargaining rests on the ways in which the legislature seeks to limit the ability of the executive agencies to choose their own goals for implementation. As we have already highlighted, there may be different normative implications if the bureaucrats are motivated by the preferences of the executive or by their own preferences. But, in either case, the strategies of the bureaucracy for deviating from legislative purposes remain basically the same. While the legislature always retains the option of responding to unjustifiable implementation by enacting a new corrective statute, this will often turn out to be a costly and inefficient approach. And it could lead to a series of back-and-forth actions between the two branches that undermines successful public policy.

This potential for perpetual conflict explains why the focus of legislative strategies for constraining the implementation efforts of the bureaucracy has primarily focused on ways of controlling the internal administrative decision-making process itself. There has been a large body of research on the struggle between the legislative and executive branches over control of the bureaucracy. Much of this work highlights the ways in which the legislature seeks to address what "McNollgast" famously called the "delegation dilemma" (McCubbins, Noll, and Weingast 1987; 1989). Although the legislature explicitly delegates the implementation task to the agency (commonly on the stated grounds of the importance of flexibility and the value of agency expertise), it retains the desire that implementation track legislative purposes. These studies analyze how and under what circumstances the legislature tries to address this dilemma. They have identified some important ways in which legislators and bureaucrats are engaged in both explicit and implicit bargaining.

The primary thrust of the findings is that legislators try to address the dilemma through both ex ante and ex post institutional mechanisms. The ex ante mechanisms try to take advantage of the legislature's influence over the general structure of governmental agencies, including such issues as agenda control and budgetary decisions. If legislators are concerned about the effects of bureaucratic action on a particular policy area, they can respond either explicitly (by limiting the bureaucracy's jurisdiction over that policy area) or implicitly (by shrinking the general budget of the agency.) The ex post mechanisms primarily involve oversight of agency actions. This is a more costly mechanism because it involves committing legislative resources to an ongoing review of bureaucratic action. The existing research has demonstrated that both approaches can have the desired effect to diminish bureaucratic influence but at the cost, in some instances, of administrative effectiveness.

And this is further complicated by explicit attempts by the executive branch to control the implementation process. Moe (1985), one of the leading exponents of the alternative view, emphasized strategies by which the US president sought to control the bureaucracy. He highlighted two general strategies. One involved centralizing the administrative process by shifting implementation authority from the agencies to a central office within the Executive Office of the President. A second involved explicitly politicizing the process by staffing the relevant positions of the agencies with political appointees who share the preferences of the executive. The implication of both efforts to enhance executive control of the bureaucracy is to increase the possibilities for interbranch bargaining between the executive and legislative branches.

However, even more troubling from the perspective of a commitment to democracy are the efforts of private interest groups to influence the statutory implementation process. The impact of these groups can be profound as they try to skew the balance of citizen interests that was established in the enactment of the law. There has also been a large body of research that documents the various ways in which these private groups seek to gain disproportionate influence over implementation (Sunstein

1985). This research, unsurprisingly, suggests that the success of these efforts at controlling the agencies and solving the delegation dilemma is a function of several factors, like initial institutional authority, the transparency of bureaucratic behavior, public opinion, and the willingness of the judiciary to intervene in the process of administrative oversight on behalf of the legislature. In the end, bargaining over implementation is a complicated, often three-way, competition for control over the implementation process. It is clear that this dilemma is never definitively resolved but rather is an issue that deserves constant attention.

Bargaining over the ways in which democratically enacted statutes are implemented and enforced is an ongoing and never-ending process. The opportunities to alter a law away from the meaning and purpose of the original statute are numerous. And the introduction of additional actors in the bargaining process adds increased complexity to the task of maintaining the democratic baseline. But there are a couple of basic issues related to the strategies of the legislature and the bureaucracies that are clear from the perspective of democratic theory. And they suggest that while the legislature might have the clear power advantage in this interbranch situation, the costs of exercising that advantage might be quite large.

The dictates of democracy recommend that the laws legitimately enacted by elected representatives should be implemented and enforced as they were intended. And this puts a considerable burden on those representatives to do everything they can to assure that this will happen. This obligates them to be attentive to both the nature and the substance of the laws that they enact and to the institutional rules and procedures that they create to govern implementation and enforcement. This means that, to the extent they want to assure that future implementation will accurately reflect their intended purposes, they need to explicitly address the trade-off between flexibility and democratic accountability. If they are most concerned about accountability, they should draft legislation that is as clear, precise, and detailed as possible. They should also minimize the tendency to be intentionally vague and to delegate excessive implementation authority directly to administrators. If, on the other hand, they are more concerned with allowing experts the flexibility to respond to changing circumstances, they should institutionalize adequate procedures to oversee and monitor administrative decision-making. And they should then seriously enforce them. This explicit attention to the rules and practices of bureaucratic decision-making can better structure the relationships of the executive and judicial branches with the bureaucracy. If they so choose, the elected representatives could clarify and answer many unclear questions about institutional authority and the role that separation of powers practices play in this case.

On the other hand, there is much less that the bureaucracy can do in response to a new statute that fails to satisfy the democratic baseline. The only mechanism that is really available to government bureaucracies when confronted with an unjustifiable statute is to try to diminish the degree to which the statute fails to meet the criterion. In most democratic systems there are not many other institutional mechanisms available to bureaucrats that will allow them to enhance the democratic nature of the law. In the end, we are left with the question of whether or not we should be asking unelected officials to make these basic decisions about citizens' interests and the best way to weigh them. Will they be effective in establishing the appropriate democratic baseline? And should they be asked to do so?

Conclusion

As our analysis demonstrates, interbranch bargaining over the future meaning and purpose of democratically enacted laws plays a major role in democratic governance. It raises challenging normative questions about democratic legitimacy, and the struggle to maintain it in a society. Throughout this chapter we highlighted places in the system where there were opportunities for directly unaccountable officials to establish their own interests over those of the population as a whole. And when we identified them, we sought to also identify strategic responses available to other officials that might constrain efforts to disproportionately skew the distribution of relevant interests in the democratic process.

The normative problem here is not bargaining per se, but rather what the bargains potentially do to the future effects of democratically enacted laws in the day-to-day lives of citizens. As we argued, we can distinguish good and bad bargains in the interbranch cases. Good bargains successfully stifle efforts to undermine the democratic baseline. Bad bargains instantiate those efforts in the future meaning and purpose of the statutes.

In principle, bad interbranch bargains undermine the legitimacy of the democratic process. These bargains are facilitated by asymmetries in bargaining power that are initially institutionalized in the rules and procedures of democratic governance and then exacerbated by other factors, like public opinion (and the effects of inequitable distributions of resources employed in lobbying), that influence the benefits and costs of exercising various institutional strategies. Our analysis, building on an impressive body of legal and social scientific research on democratic institutions, suggests that the greater the inequality in bargaining power among the different branches of government, the greater the opportunity of one branch to dominate the process in these cases. To the extent that the more powerful branch is committed to prioritizing the interests of a subset of citizens over equitable treatment of all citizens, we would expect an ongoing stream of bad bargains. Under these circumstances, we would be facing a major challenge to the legitimacy of democratic governance.

Given this possibility, what is the best way, from an institutional reform perspective, to address this challenge? We have already highlighted some of the specific recommendations, like the structural due process approach to judicial decision-making, that we propose for dealing with this challenge. Here we want to offer three general considerations that should guide our thinking on the problem of interbranch bargaining. Each of the three speaks to the fundamental problem of how to distribute political power in such a way as to most effectively foster the equitable treatment of all citizens' interests.

First, although it is important to focus on the substance of the bargain in assessing its normative implications in interbranch cases, it is more important to focus on the process of bargaining in thinking about how best to counteract the bargain's negative effects. When we are confronted with a bad bargain, our primary focus should always be on the institutional rules that create the opportunities for abuse, rather than on the specifics of any particular case. For example, if a judge is asked to resolve a dispute over a statute that, when enacted, failed to meet the democratic criterion, she should, whenever possible, try to identify the conditions in the legislature that created the opportunity for the problem rather than merely trying to reinterpret the statute to satisfy the baseline. Identifying these conditions is the crucial first step in enabling legislative reform: it is necessary, but far from sufficient, in part because legislators will often have personal reasons to resist such reforms. The real problem in assigning this power to judges, though, is the availability of an opportunity to impose a deviation from the democratic criterion. That opportunity is a product of asymmetric bargaining power. That is what needs to be rectified.

This recommends close attention to the distribution of institutional authority across the branches. The need to diminish the influence of asymmetric bargaining power on the exercise of postenactment tasks clearly justifies the institutionalization of an effective balance of powers approach in a democratic society. Institutional rules and practices that allow us to balance the competing demands of independence and accountability are a necessary feature of effective democratic governance. Achieving perfect equality among the three branches is an unrealistic and, given the democratic commitment to legislative supremacy, an undesirable goal. And yet the distribution of authority needs to be sufficiently balanced to maintain the effectiveness of the institutional mechanisms of democratic accountability. Institutional rules that fail to achieve some type of balance of decision-making authority are more likely to fail to allow the interests of all citizens the opportunity to influence these postenactment tasks. But we need not stop there.

In addition, democratic accountability can be enhanced through the creation of institutional mechanisms that allow citizens to actively participate in these tasks, and such mechanisms should be strongly encouraged. One such mechanism arises from the problem of political bargaining between bureaucrats and private interest groups. This is one area of the problem of political bargaining in a democratic society that Habermas (1989) has explicitly addressed. Early in his career, Habermas addressed the problem of the refeudalization of public affairs. One of the primary characteristics of the problem was the role that private interest groups played in influencing administrative decision-making. He argued at the time that these private influences undermined the legitimacy of the administrative state. He proposed that the only way to adequately address the problem was to institutionalize democratic decision-making procedures within various aspects of the administrative process. The idea would be to create public bodies within administrative agencies to advise bureaucrats about issues of implementation and enforcement. The goal would be to expand the range of citizens beyond special interest groups who might be able to influence these decisions.

An example of such a body would be the committees established by the Federal Advisory Committee Act in the United States. The act authorizes the creation of committees of various forms to gather opinions from a wide range of citizens and to advise agencies in the executive branch on policy questions. These committees are governed by standards set by Congress, standards intended to enhance the diversity of opinions considered by administrative agencies and to improve the transparency of the advisory process. A robust version of these committees could produce two important benefits for the implementation process: it would help governmental agencies to better articulate fundamental and ordinary interests, and it would help to redistribute bargaining power away from special interests and toward a broader range of citizens.[15]

A second possible mechanism would loosen the requirements of standing for lawsuits that challenge the democratic nature of legislative enactments. Traditionally in the United States, a citizen has been able to file a lawsuit challenging the overall legitimacy of a statute only when she has been able to demonstrate that the statute violated one of her constitutionally protected rights. As we noted earlier in this chapter, some states have envisioned a constitutional right to democracy in their state constitutions. And some scholars have argued for an interpretation of the US Constitution that would ground a right to democracy in its provisions. If an explicit right to democracy could be established, then it would open up the possibility that citizens could challenge the statutory enactment process and use the courts to call attention to problems of unjustifiable political bargains.

Our second consideration directly addresses the question of which branch of government is most appropriate for addressing the important questions about democratic legitimacy. Throughout this discussion, we have highlighted the fact that assessing the justifiability of a political bargain does not stop at the determination of its fairness, or even whether it satisfies the democratic criterion of equitable treatment of citizens' interests. We must always consider the possibility that there is another value facilitated by the bargain, a fundamental interest, that society would prioritize over the bargain in the particular case in question.[16] So, to fully address the issue of democratically legitimate laws, we need to ask not only what is recommended by an equitable treatment of citizens' interests but also whether there is another value that deserves priority if there are questions about the satisfaction of the equitable treatment standard. For both of these questions, it seems clear that the elected representatives in the legislature are the most appropriate group of governmental officials to answer them.

In a representative democratic system, the answer to these questions should always follow from a consideration of the interests and views of its citizens. One of the best ways to encourage this is through the accountability that follows from elections. That recommends the legislative and executive branches over the courts. Between the different elected representatives there are, in our opinion, good reasons to believe that the legislative branch will do a more effective job. One of the main reasons why the legislature is better than the executive for purposes of balancing values and assessing citizens' interests is a factual claim, that the array of relevant interests of citizens is more likely to be captured and assessed by a collection of elected representatives than by an individual executive. This is, of course, a probabilistic claim but we think that it is borne out by the evidence drawn from the majority of the research that compares individual versus group decision-making (Page 2010).

This recommends a lesser, but still essential, role for the judiciary. Judges are necessary to protect democratic processes. Somehow there need to be designated enforcers of the rules. Such is the importance of adding the structural due process analysis to a court's repertoire of interpretive approaches. Combining a right to democracy with the structural due process approach establishes an effective institutional mechanism for addressing failures by the legislature to satisfy the democratic criterion.

But this does not absolve the legislature from its ultimate responsibility to satisfy the requirements of justifiable legislative bargains. Courts are better at assessing individual violations of the rules rather than assessing the fundamental effectiveness of the system of rules as an institution (Knight and Johnson 2011). The general oversight of how the legislature handles the equitable treatment of citizens' interests is better done by the democratically elected representatives themselves acting in good faith. Courts can intervene in this significant way only when the legislature fails in its most basic responsibility, and, in doing so, the response will inevitably be less satisfactory when done at its best than it would have been if the legislature had done it when it acted at its best.

As we have already acknowledged, this emphasis creates some tension with our earlier consideration about the importance of a balance of power system among the branches. However, we would note that the two general questions that we highlighted are central to the basic legislative task as envisioned by the commitment to democracy. We acknowledge that this favoritism for the legislative branch can create problems. To the extent that the elected representatives are not fundamentally committed to the democratic criterion, it will create much bigger problems than those created by interbranch bargaining. And it suggests the extent to which the other branches are ultimately limited in their capacity to sustain democratic legitimacy in the long run without a committed legislature.

This last point leads us to our third, and perhaps most important, consideration. This is an issue that goes to the core of normative arguments that are grounded in recommendations of institutional reforms. In talking about the institutional mechanisms that are intended to enhance the legitimacy of bargains (for example, the mechanisms like checks and balances that are intended to provide a method for constraining undemocratic behavior), it is important to emphasize that their effectiveness hinges on the existence of an interest in respecting and enforcing the rules. This interest may follow from a natural difference of opinion among the officials of the different branches or from a commitment to the institutions of democracy themselves that is at least somewhat independent of the outcomes of the process. It is analogous to the condition of good faith in private contracting. Government officials must have a commitment to the future effectiveness of their institutional bargains. For whatever reason, they must have an interest in the role that they play in the institutional scheme of governance.

If such officials do not have an interest in the effective performance of their home institution, the likelihood of success of that institution as a constraint on the actions of another branch declines. A clear example of this in the United States would be where the same political party controls both the legislative and the executive branches. If the leaders of the two branches primarily identify with the political interests of their party instead of the interests of an effective system of democratic governance, the necessary balance between independence and accountability will be undermined (Levinson and Pildes 2006). This demonstrates a counterintuitive feature of separation of powers systems: if you create such a system and the actors within the system are not prepared to take the responsibilities that the roles anticipate, you can end up creating an even more unequal distribution of power and thus more powerful actors in a particular branch than they would otherwise have been. Without at least some degree of independent commitment to enforcing the rules, institutional reforms to sustain the democratic criterion of legitimacy will prove, in the long run, ineffective.

5

Bargaining "On the Ground"

FROM THE CREATION of a constitution through the various stages of governance—enactment of laws and policies, interpretation, implementation, and enforcement—we have set out an argument for when bargaining might yield democratically justifiable results. In doing so we have analyzed the role that unequal bargaining power plays in democratic decision-making and we have offered criteria for determining when the influence of such asymmetric power undermines the basic justification for democracy and when its influence should be tolerated. In this chapter we conclude our analysis of the stages of democratic governance by considering one final area of governmental action in which unequal bargaining power may play an important role. Here we focus on bargaining "on the ground," so to speak, where the state is an active participant in bargaining with its citizens.

Our discussion here relates to a growing body of work in normative political theory that seeks to address the question of the role of street-level bureaucrats in democratic society. One important instance of this work is that of Bernardo Zacka (2017). His work focuses on the roles played by social welfare workers, police officers, and educators, and in particular the operation of bureaucratic discretion. Zacka systematically assesses the types of dispositions and concurrent discretionary acts that influence the welfare of individual citizens. It is an illuminating argument that highlights the breadth of this discretion and thus the reasons why the role of street-level bureaucrats should be an important feature of normative analyses of democratic politics.

Our analysis shares the concern with bureaucratic discretion and how it influences the relationship between state actors and democratic citizens. And we should begin by acknowledging that such discretion is an inevitable feature of democratic governance. But we also want to note that, just like the elected representatives, the administrative hierarchy, and the judiciary, state actors who interact daily with citizens are similarly subject to the dictates of the democratic criterion of equitable treatment of interests and the defensive doctrines that we articulate in this book. And so, in this chapter, we seek to analyze how these doctrines affect the day-to-day discretion of street-level bureaucrats.

To do so, we analyze one important area of direct bargaining: plea bargaining in the criminal justice system. We offer this as a case study of how one should go about assessing the justifiability of direct bargains with the state in a democratic society. In this analysis we investigate the ways in which unequal bargaining power might influence the outcomes of the negotiating process. We pay particular attention to the ways in which state actors may use the power advantages enjoyed by the state, either to take undue advantage of citizens in the specific bargaining process or to negatively influence the future bargaining power of those citizens. Our basic question is, What normative constraints, if any, does a commitment to democracy place on state actors in these situations? In other words, how does a commitment to democracy constrain the actions of state officials in their day-to-day interactions with individual citizens? Note that this is a different question than those that ask what constraints a set of constitutional rights places on democracy. Rather, it invites a focus on the individual protections that a commitment to democracy may provide within its own system of governance.

The State as a Bargaining Actor: Plea Bargaining

The criminal justice system in a democratic society is a truly cooperative arrangement among the different branches of government. When the system is working effectively, the elected representatives in the legislature define the actions that warrant sanctions and punishment, the executive agencies enforce the rules and prosecute citizens that are accused of violating them, and the courts assess guilt and innocence and administer appropriate sentencing of the guilty. In principle, bargaining, either private or public, would seem to play no appropriate role in the process.

And yet, bargaining has come to define the criminal justice system in most democracies. In the United States, for example, the percentage of federal convictions that resulted from a plea of guilty as opposed to a trial was approximately 97 percent from 2012 to 2020 (United States Sentencing Commission 2020, 8). The plea rate at the state level was around 95 percent (Dervan 2019, 11). Similarly, the available statistics in England showed that in recent years about 85 percent of defendants charged with a crime pled guilty (Baldwin and McConville 1979, 287).

Plea bargaining, in some form or another, has been a feature of US legal systems since at least the late nineteenth century. Friedman (1979, 256–57) argues that the predominance of this practice has evolved in three stages. In the first stage, between roughly 1880 and the early years of the twentieth century, jury trials remained an important means of resolving criminal cases. At the same time there was an increase in the number of guilty pleas prior to trial, some by explicit agreement but more by implicit understanding that a guilty plea would produce a less severe penalty. In the second stage, covering most of the first half of the twentieth century, pleading guilty increasingly became the dominant response to criminal charges. Friedman describes the process as follows: "Trials became less common. Fewer cases were dismissed than before. The defendant had less (statistical) chance of acquittal if he went to trial. The guilty plea looked like the one chance for leniency; practically speaking, it was the only road to probation" (1979, 256).

While implicit bargaining remained a common source of these pleas, explicit bargaining with prosecutors became a more accepted practice. In the third stage, which extends from the 1950s to the present, explicit bargaining has become the norm. Understandings have been replaced by formal agreements. Charges lead to convictions in most cases. Jury trials are so rare as to be almost quaint. Their main purpose has become to shade the bargains that prosecutors strike with defendants and to cast a justificatory veneer over the outcomes. Here the bargaining is of a different kind than any we have considered up to this point. Plea bargaining involves direct negotiation between the state, specifically prosecutors in the executive branch, and individual citizens. Our understanding of these negotiations and the particular role of the prosecutor in them may differ depending on how we conceive of the purpose of bargaining in this situation.

In contemporary debates over the appropriateness of plea bargaining as an institution, it is characterized in two competing ways (Alschuler 1981). The first is the traditional understanding of plea bargaining as a sentencing device. As Kipnis describes it, the criminal sentencing system is characterized by two general principles: "only those individuals who are clearly guilty of certain serious specified wrongdoings deserve an officially administered punishment which is proportional to their wrongdoing" and "certain basic liberties shall not be violated in bringing the guilty to justice" (Kipnis, 1976, 101–2). For Kipnis, the effectiveness of plea bargaining as a sentencing device depends on the ability of the process to correctly distinguish between innocent and guilty defendants. And plea bargains are justified on the ground that defendants who acknowledge their guilt are entitled to a lesser penalty than those charged with similar crimes who insist on a costly trial to prove it.

Contrast this with an alternative conception that seems to have emerged in part to justify the growing dominance of the plea-bargaining system. In this conception, plea bargaining is justified as a dispute-resolution device. The dispute is between the prosecutor and the defendant, and the unresolved question is whether or not the court or jury would find the defendant guilty if the case went to trial. Given their inability to agree over the potential outcome, they bargain over a way of avoiding trial.

Alschuler persuasively argues that this conception fundamentally alters the role of the prosecutor in the process (1981, 684–85). In the sentencing conception, the prosecutor should be concerned about correctly answering the question of guilt or innocence. If she has significant doubt about the likelihood of a guilty verdict, Alschuler insists that she has a responsibility to dismiss the accusation. In the dispute resolution conception, on the other hand, the prosecutor does not appear to have such a responsibility. In the face of significant uncertainty, the prosecutor's task is to reach an agreement that will produce some form of punishment. The resulting plea bargain is justified as a voluntary agreement that made both parties better off than the expected utility of a trial.

For the purposes of our analysis here, we will focus primarily on the plea-bargaining process itself, asking the basic question, Does a commitment to democracy place normative constraints on the roles of state actors in this process? We will argue that issues related to the legitimacy of the bargaining process are the same regardless of what conception of plea bargaining is endorsed. Where the different conceptions may matter is if we determine that the plea bargain is the product of unjustifiable bargaining on the part of the state. In those circumstances we would need to assess if the illegitimacy of the plea bargain is outweighed by other values that should be given priority within the criminal justice system.

The Forms of Plea Bargains

Plea bargaining takes a number of different forms. Although it is commonly governed by a set of rules and procedures, it has seldom been the object of any formal institutional design. More often than not, it is, as best described by Crespo's account of the United States (2018, 1305), "a creature primarily of state law (not federal law), of court rules and statutes (not constitutional doctrine), and of procedures often seen as relevant only to a bygone era of trial-based litigation (not to the system of pleas that has replaced it)." The informality of the institutional framework places few constraints on the potential influence of power asymmetries and allows significant flexibility in the strategic choices of the bargainers.

Three actors are primarily relevant to plea-bargaining negotiations: the defendant, the prosecutor, and the judge. While the defendant's role is generally the same in all plea-bargaining situations, the role of the prosecutor and the judge may vary somewhat depending on the type of bargaining involved. A helpful way of characterizing these differences is to focus on the type of plea that the bargaining produces (Dervan 2019). There are four main forms of guilty pleas in the United States (Federal Rules of Criminal Procedure 11[c][1], 2017). The first type is the "open plea," in which the defendant pleads guilty even though there is no explicit promise of any kind from the prosecutor. Presumably, however, the defendant is motivated to offer the plea in anticipation of some leniency from the judge because of the voluntary confession.[1] With this type of plea, the prosecutor may or may not play a significant role in the process, depending on how much implicit information-sharing and bargaining goes on between the prosecutor and the defendant. Since there is no explicitly proffered agreement in these cases, the fact that the judge is not bound to offer any leniency for a voluntary guilty plea places the power to resolve the case entirely in the hands of the judge.

The second type is a "charge bargain," in which the defendant pleads guilty in exchange for the willingness of the prosecutor to drop some more serious charges or to agree to use the less serious of the charges available to her.[2] The third type is a "sentence bargain," in which the defendant pleads guilty in exchange for an agreement on the part of the prosecution to recommend a specific sentence. This remains the most common form of plea bargaining in many legal systems, especially those that do not rely on mandatory sentences and do allow judges a good deal of discretion in sentencing. With these two types of pleas, the prosecutor enjoys significant autonomy to bargain in any way that she desires. Flexibility over charges in the indictment phase and over sentence length in the negotiation phase opens up a wide range of strategic behavior for the prosecutor. In both of these types the judge ultimately retains the authority to reject or amend the sentencing terms of any plea agreement between the parties. However, given the fact that judges want plea agreements, in the overwhelming majority of cases they tend to encourage them informally and agree to their final terms.

Finally, the fourth type is a "binding plea," in which the prosecutor and the defendant bargain over the terms of the sentence and then present it to the judge as a "take it or leave it" deal. That is, in such cases, if the judge decides to accept the guilty plea, she is legally required to accept the terms of the plea agreement. This is the least frequent type of plea bargaining, primarily because many judges believe that this type of plea bargaining undermines their authority over sentencing.

For our purposes here, the most important types of bargaining are the "sentencing plea" and the "charge plea." They highlight the importance of the bargaining relationship between the prosecutor and the defendant, the relationship that is most relevant to the question of the implications of a commitment to democracy. Those are the bargains we will focus on. When the judge's participation in the negotiations serves to alter the relative bargaining power of the parties, we will identify and note it.

As we have emphasized throughout our analysis, normative assessments of bargaining have both a procedural component and a substantive component. In the case of plea bargaining, the process is really quite simple. It is characterized by a significant asymmetry in bargaining power and a small set of bargaining strategies. The enforcement power of the state is obviously a serious advantage enjoyed by the prosecutor. She has the authority to bring criminal charges against any citizen for whom there is probable cause to believe a crime has been committed. In the context of plea-bargaining negotiations, this basic power supports a few important strategies that can be used to induce a guilty plea. Both the courts and the legislatures have allowed prosecutors substantial autonomy to decide the extent to which these strategies can be used. We want to highlight two of the strategies in this analysis.

First, the prosecutor controls the information that the state collects about the evidence related to the alleged crime. The nature of this evidence, as well as the degree to which this evidence establishes a persuasive case of guilt, is fundamentally important for an assessment of the likelihood that the state would obtain a guilty verdict at trial. The probability of conviction is an important factor that a defendant must weigh in deciding whether or not to accept a plea bargain. In the discovery process before a trial, prosecutors have a duty to share some of the relevant information about the evidence at their disposal, especially the evidence that may serve to exonerate the defendant. But in most jurisdictions the discovery process does not begin until after any plea negotiations conclude, and so the prosecutor is commonly under no obligation to share that information with the defendant during the plea-bargaining process (Daughety and Reinganum 2020, 380). This discrepancy in relevant information works to the benefit of the prosecution (Waldstein 2020).

Second, the prosecutor controls the initial indictment, setting the terms for the number of charges to be brought and, except in jurisdictions that have minimum mandatory sentences enacted by the legislature, the severity of the penalties associated with the charges (Scott and Stuntz 1992). The strategic control of charges and sentences allows the prosecutor to set the initial parameters of any bargain. As we will discuss below, power over the baseline of negotiations is a significant determinant of the plea-bargaining process. When the authority over the initial indictment is combined with the autonomy to change its terms in the negotiating process, we get a real sense of how much bargaining leverage prosecutors have in these situations.

We can compare that with the bargaining position of the defendant. Certainly, defendants vary in their own bargaining power. Wealthy defendants may be able to draw on their resources to secure excellent representation, and anticipate that they may be advantaged at trial due to their ability to solicit expert witnesses, for instance. By contrast, until the early 2010s, defendants had no constitutional right to counsel for plea bargaining, meaning that impoverished defendants would be gravely disadvantaged. Further, members of racial minorities or other vulnerable groups may fear either that their chances of a fair trial may be impaired by societal racism or other forms of prejudice, or that they are being treated inequitably by prosecutors for those reasons. These factors will shape the bargains that emerge.

However, absent significant personal resources, all the defendant really has in the negotiations is the ability to diminish the costs of ongoing prosecution and trial. This may not seem like a lot when compared with the strategies available to the prosecutor, but it is exactly what most prosecutors are looking for. The research on plea bargaining suggests that administrative concern about crowded dockets and the cost of trials is one of the primary motivations, if not *the* primary motivation, for prosecutors to engage in plea bargaining. The significance of this motivation might well explain Alschuler's (1968, 60) observation that "the universal rule is that the sentence differential between guilty-plea and trial defendants increases in direct proportion to the likelihood of acquittal." That is, prosecutors bargain hardest when their cases are the weakest, as if they fear that the defendant with whom they are bargaining might decide to take their chances at trial rather than agreeing to a plea bargain.

Threats and Offers in Plea Bargaining

The most debated question in the literature on plea bargaining is, Are the plea agreements voluntary or coerced? Where you come down on this question seems to depend on (1) whether you think the prosecutor's plea proposal is an offer or a threat and (2) how you assess the gap between the proposed punishment in the plea proposal and the consequences for the defendant of rejecting it.

The standard view of the courts in the United States on this question is that the only proposals that may coerce a defendant are threats. And that plea proposals from prosecutors are merely offers, proposals that offer the benefit of a lesser sentence in exchange for an agreement to forgo the trial on the merits (Bowers 2016). Wertheimer (1979) argues, in his classic analysis of US Supreme Court decision-making on this question, that the threat-offer distinction rests on a closer assessment of the underlying morality of the prosecutor's proposal. He asserts that "the court has correctly concluded that the claim that a defendant voluntarily pleads guilty is not a purely empirical claim about the defendant's state of mind, or a purely empirical claim about the deprivations the defendant would suffer for refusing to plead guilty. Rather, the claim requires moral judgments about the context of the defendant's decision in the actions of the state" (206). This puts significant weight on the potential wrongfulness of the prosecutor's action. Young (2013) suggests that this leads to the following standard for coercion: it "demands a prior, independent view of what choices or options a person ought in general to have available to him, the denial or determination of which could then be understood as being wrongfully coercive. If this general view of coercion is correct, then unless the critic can show that plea bargaining leads to denying the defendant an option of that sort, he does not show 'coercion' in any morally meaningful or worrying sense" (263).

From our perspective the inclusion of a wrongfulness standard to the coercion analysis has two implications. First, it highlights the importance of assessing the underlying implications of the prosecutor's actions in the negotiation process. It requires us to look beyond the mere offer of a lesser sentence to a closer assessment of whether the prosecutor is bargaining in "good faith." Second, it complicates the assessment of the gap between the proposed punishment in the plea proposal and the consequences for the defendant of rejecting it. This follows from the fact that it increases the alternative baselines of consequences that may be used to assess the size of the gap.

Consider the task of selecting the proper baseline for comparison. As we saw in Chapter 3, Wertheimer offers two categories of baselines: predictive and normative. A predictive baseline "is what a person empirically would expect to happen in the ordinary course." A normative baseline, on the other hand, is "what a person legally, morally, or provincially is entitled to expect in the ordinary course" (1979, 204). At the time of publication in 1987, he found that the US Supreme Court had employed both of these baselines at different times. The predictive baseline was the anticipated punishment at trial. With that as the baseline of comparison, all plea proposals were considered to be beneficial offers. The normative baseline was anything that the prosecutor was legally entitled to do. This baseline treated any permissible criminal charge (supported by probable cause) as a nonthreat and thus the basis for a normatively acceptable offer. Wertheimer concluded that the Supreme Court was relying more on the normative baseline in its decision-making.

The effect of this normative baseline was to expand the power of the prosecutors. As Bowers notes, the normative baseline includes any charges that the state has a right to exercise (2016, 1095). It does not have to be the case that the charge is one that defendants typically face in similar situations. It is merely whatever the prosecutor could plausibly include in an indictment. Given the tendency of most courts to defer to the justifications offered by prosecutors in criminal cases, Bowers effectively argues that this baseline had the effect of turning the standard for plea bargaining into a formalistic one. The only judicial question would be, Is the technical criterion of probable cause for the alleged crime satisfied? If so, then the proposal is an acceptable offer and thus the end of the discussion about coercion.

In the years since Wertheimer's study, the Supreme Court has issued new decisions on the constitutionality of the plea-bargaining process that have complicated the determination of the proper baseline. In a set of cases in the early 2010s, the court addressed the question of whether the constitutional right to counsel should include the plea-bargaining stage of the process, which defendants in many jurisdictions lacked. In finding that the right does extend to plea bargaining, the court acknowledged something that most people in the criminal justice system already knew, that the practice of plea bargaining "is not some adjunct to a criminal justice system; it is the criminal justice system." This acceptance of the central role of plea bargaining led the court to a discussion of the ways in which plea bargaining affects the expectations of the actors in the bargain (Bowers 2016). No longer would the formal criminal code alone set the anticipated parameters for plea negotiations. Justice Scalia emphasized what he called "plea-bargaining law" as important new information that defendants and their counsel should take into consideration (*Lafler v. Cooper*, 566 U.S. 156 [2012]). This plea-bargaining law would include information about the actual practice of plea bargaining, including information about the prior accepted bargains in the jurisdiction. Most important was the realization that defendants were entitled to take account of the plea offers received by similarly situated defendants in previous cases in the jurisdiction.

The introduction of the reality of bargaining in the criminal justice system does make the assessment of the size of the bargaining gap more difficult. Prosecutors can continue to use the full range of crimes in the criminal code in preparing indictments. And yet the reasonableness of a plea proposal might be assessed according to a different baseline, one in which the expectations grounded in prior plea agreements set the comparative baseline. This suggests that there will continue to be a debate over the size of the bargaining gap and, thus, over the degree of coercion in the bargaining process.

However, what should not be lost in this debate over the proper baseline is that the state, through the actions of its prosecutors, retains the power to control the process. Prosecutors retain largely unconstrained authority to engage in charge bargaining, and they indirectly influence the "plea bargaining" law that sets defendant's expectations, given their control over past decisions in the jurisdiction. While the size of the gap may vary depending on the preferred baseline, the basic structure of the bargaining relationship has not changed. The assessment of coercion primarily rests, in our opinion, on the substantial power to set the terms of the bargain, which allows the prosecutor to create a significant gap in every case. The effect, from the perspective of the defendant, is to give the overwhelming majority of bargaining proposals a coercive character. From our standpoint, it also means that the distinction between "offers" and "threats" is moot, because from the defendant's standpoint, it is nearly impossible to ascertain the baseline, whether predictive or normative.

Let's unpack this claim by contrasting different approaches to the question of when the gap is evidence of a coercive offer. The first and simplest answer to the question is that any gap between the proposed bargain and the potential penalty from rejecting it constitutes a coercive bargain. It reduces the assessment to an empirical fact. It limits the analysis to the substantive outcome of the bargain. It renders the bargaining process irrelevant, placing no normative weight on the types of strategies employed by the prosecutor. In the end, it is grounded in the idea that the state confronts the defendant with a choice no one should have to face, and thus it is by definition coercive. This is a position adopted by certain advocates for the abolition of plea bargaining as a practice.

The second approach, more widely held in the literature, is the one best articulated by Wertheimer (1979). On this approach, a substantial gap is not enough. In fact, the substance of the bargain is not really the focus of the analysis. This approach puts the emphasis on the process. Coercion requires a wrongful act on the part of the state. To define such a wrongful act, Wertheimer applies the test for contractual duress: "Duress is defined as: (a) any wrongful act of one person that compels a manifestation of apparent assent by another to transaction without his volition, or (b) any wrongful threat of one person by words or conduct that induces another to enter into a transaction under the influence of such fear as precludes him from exercising free will and judgment, if the threat was intended or should reasonably have been expected to operate as an inducement" (215). Then, as we suggested above, he adopts the traditional standard of what constitutes a wrongful act. Only a clear threat on the part of the prosecutor will satisfy the standard.

This approach establishes a very narrow standard for coercion. Wertheimer explains later that "to show that X did Z under duress, it is not sufficient to show that Y's proposal left X with no other prudent choice, although that may be an adequate account of the first prong. It must be shown that Y's proposal was wrongful. . . . Acts or threats cannot constitute duress unless they are wrongful, even though they exert such pressure as to preclude the exercise of free judgment" (216). From this it seems clear that the mere size of the gap, presumably intended by the prosecutor to limit the possible choices available to the defendant, is insufficient evidence of duress. What would appear to satisfy the criteria would be a threat by the prosecutor that is not based on a charge or a punishment that is defined by the criminal code. For example, if the prosecutor threatened to have the defendant fired from his job if he failed to take the plea deal, an action that is beyond the scope of the prosecutor's official authority, that would seem to satisfy the criteria of wrongfulness. So, on Wertheimer's account, plea bargains, as a general rule, are voluntary and legitimate.

The third approach, developed from a law and economics perspective by Scott and Stuntz (1992), also applies traditional contract law to the analysis of plea bargaining. It applies the standards of duress and unconscionability to both the process and the substantive agreement. Unlike the Wertheimer approach, which places the focus almost exclusively on the actions of the prosecutor, Scott and Stuntz widen the scope of the analysis to take account of the conditions under which bargaining occurs. This allows for greater latitude in the assessment of the possibilities for voluntariness and coercion. It introduces the possibility that the plea bargain may be coercive even if the prosecutor's strategic choices remain within legally defined standards.

For example, in their analysis of the possibility that plea bargaining may violate the principle of unconscionability, they take care to assess whether the plea bargain may suffer from two problems that private contract law commonly associates with unconscionability: information deficits and market unresponsiveness. In the case of information deficits, the test usually is, Do the parties have the information necessary to understand the terms and conditions of the proposals and the future implications of their choices? Scott and Stuntz point out that the lack of adequate information can be grounds for identifying an unconscionable bargain. But they then assert that it applies in only those circumstances in which the deficit is created by one of the parties. They conclude that it does not apply in the case of plea bargaining because any deficits suffered by the defendant are not caused by any illegal behavior on the part of the prosecutor.

In the case of market unresponsiveness, the test usually is whether the feasible set of options available to either of the parties is practically limited to one option. "Take it or leave it" offers and adhesion contracts are examples of this type of market unresponsiveness. Scott and Stuntz ultimately reject this as a ground for unconscionability in the case of plea bargaining. They distinguish plea bargaining from the case of adhesion contracts by claiming that the plea-bargaining process lacks the conditions that make "take it or leave it" offers effective. They especially emphasize the individualized nature of the plea-bargaining process as opposed to the formalized set terms of an adhesion contract between, for example, a powerful corporation and disorganized consumers. They conclude that the market situation that determines the asymmetries of bargaining power in the adhesion case is different from that of plea bargaining. In the end, while Scott and Stuntz open up the analysis to allow for the possibility that plea bargains can be coercive, they find that instances of coercion are attributable to the specifics of particular cases rather than as a systemic problem of the plea-bargaining process.

A fourth approach is the one that we defend here. We agree that the gap alone is not enough to assess coercion; rather, some inappropriate strategy on the part of the prosecutor is necessary. We also agree that considering the conditions under which strategies are offered and choices are made is important to assessing this last point. But we disagree with the reasoning offered by Scott and Stuntz in making those assessments. The problem is in the way in which they employ private contract law. They bring the market along with them. But plea bargaining is not conducted in a competitive market environment. And thus the conditions under which issues of good faith, duress, and unconscionability are assessed are quite different. The asymmetries experienced by defendants are not market experiences.

As we have described, the prosecutor has extensive autonomy in the plea-bargaining process. Given the informal nature of the process, she establishes the initial terms around which the negotiations take place. In doing so, she also has significant influence over the conditions under which any choices are made. In the private contracting framework set out by Scott and Stuntz, the prosecutor is like a monopolist. The problem with these other approaches to the coercion question is that they fa l to appreciate the degree of control that the prosecutor has over the structure of the process itself.

The standard plea bargain violates two of the basic principles of fair contracting; taken together, they make a compelling case for the claim that the prosecutor's proposal constitutes a threat and that the choice to accept the bargain is, by any reasonable standard, coerced. The first is the principle of "good faith" bargaining. The prosecutor has a distinct advantage in terms of the relevant information that the parties have available to them. Of these advantages the most important is the nature of the evidence held by the state that could be used at trial. For the defendant, the decision to accept a plea proposal is a function of expectations about the probability of a guilty verdict, the maximum possible sentence, and the terms of the plea offer. The relative attractiveness of the choices is determined primarily by the probability of a conviction. But the parties have very different bases on which to assess this probability.

The prosecutor knows what evidence she has but is not required in most jurisdictions to share it with the defendant. In fact, there are no general requirements that the prosecutor even needs to be honest in her representations with the defendant in the negotiation process. This discrepancy creates a negotiating environment that encourages "bad faith" bargaining on the part of the prosecutor. She could share whatever evidence looks most damaging to the defendant's case, as a way of putting more pressure on the defendant to accept the deal. But she has no incentive to share exculpatory evidence if it exists. Therefore, any claims she makes to the defendant about the probability of a guilty verdict face serious credibility questions. Nonetheless, the defendant has little else other than these claims available to establish a probability about the outcome of a trial.

Given the control that the prosecutor has over the relevant information, she could find a way to resolve the credibility issue, reducing the informational asymmetries and enhancing the fairness of the bargaining, but she has no incentive within the bargaining framework to do so. While Scott and Stuntz examine the information discrepancy and conclude that it is not the product of actions by the parties, we attribute the discrepancy ultimately to the strategic choices of the prosecutor.

Under the traditional understanding of good faith bargaining, this would appear to constitute a ground for a finding of a coercive bargain.

The second relevant principle of fair bargaining that is in question here is unconscionability. This is straightforward. The prosecutor controls both sides of the gap. First, she creates the initial indictment of charges and potential sentences that establishes the upper bound of the gap. One might think that the appropriate strategy for the prosecutor would be a selection of charges that best match the available evidence of wrongdoing and that entail punishments that are proportional to those crimes. But prosecutors are not limited in their choice of charges in the initial indictment. A common strategy is to "inflate the quantity of charges the defendant faces, by piling on overlapping, largely duplicative offenses—increasing with each new charge the defendant's potential sentence, his risk of conviction, and the 'sticker shock' of intimidation that accompanies a hefty charging instrument" (Crespo 2018, 1313). Proportional indictments are seldom the best bargaining strategy given the power asymmetries. Draconian charges are more likely to make a trial unattractive and thus induce a plea.

Then, she also controls the terms of the plea proposal, establishing the lower bound of the gap and defining the size of the potential bargain. And, by doing so, "the prosecutor can capitalize on the ensuing leverage by sliding down from her initial threat to the lower set of charges that she actually prefers" (Crespo 2018, 1314). Here it is important to note that by controlling both boundaries of the gap, prosecutors have the potential to achieve a bargain without really giving up much from what you might expect they would gain by going to trial on more proportional charges.

Both the intentional lack of transparency and the charge manipulation are intended to affect the assessment of the available options. The manipulation increases the costs of going to trial while the lack of information increases the assessment of the probability of being found guilty. Both are intended to make the plea offer look better. This looks much like a "take it or leave it" contract to us. Unlike in a competitive market, there is nowhere else for the defendant to shop for an alternative. The prosecutor controls the process and the terms. The existing system fosters that and results in a bargain characterized by bad faith and unconscionability.

The Normative Implications of the Democratic Commitment

The commitment to democracy has important implications for how law is to be implemented and enforced on the ground. The example of plea bargaining raises interesting questions of whether direct bargaining with citizens is an appropriate way for the democratic state to implement criminal law. And, if it is an acceptable mechanism, what constraints, if any, does a commitment to democracy place on the bargaining strategies of state actors?

A number of opponents of plea bargaining argue that it is inherently unfair as a matter of sentencing policy. For example, Alschuler (1981) makes the case in its broadest form, arguing that criminal law should not be the object of contracting in principle. This is similar to Satz's (2010) argument about the market. The basic thrust is that there is a set of social interactions that should not, as a principle of justice, be governed by the mechanisms of contract law. Alschuler puts plea bargaining in that set of prohibited cases. We choose not to address this overarching implementation question here. We would point out that in a democratic society, absent a constitutional prohibition of plea bargaining, the initial decision about implementation would rest with the elected representatives in the legislature. However, it is our task to assess whether the bargaining strategies available to prosecutors are appropriate within the democratic system of governance.

Plea bargaining has been an evolving practice in democratic societies for over a century. What started out as an alternative criminal sentencing mechanism has emerged as the most common form of dispute resolution in the society today. But whether you conceive of it primarily as a sentence or as a contract, the normative problem remains the same. It is very hard to sustain the claim that plea bargaining produces a voluntary agreement and, thus, a legitimate bargain. In procedural terms, the case for coercion as the system is presently constituted seems clear. The excessive control of all aspects of the process enjoyed by the prosecutors allows bargaining strategies that violate the principles of good faith and unconscionability. These actions are not what a citizen in a democratic society should expect from a state that is obligated to seriously consider the citizen's fundamental interests. We believe that the commitment to democracy at the very least entails a commitment to good faith on the part of the state in its treatment of citizens on the ground.

And when we look at the substantive terms of the plea bargain, the argument for unconscionable treatment of citizens is made even stronger. Our first concern reflects a common complaint in the plea-bargaining literature (Alschuler 1981). The practice of plea bargaining with individual citizens creates a criminal justice system in which similarly situated citizens are treated differently by the state. Defendants who accept a guilty plea deal receive a different punishment from those who reject the deal and are found guilty at trial. The penalty differential violates the commitment to equitable treatment of citizens' interests. Defenders of the practice argue that the differential is merely a product of free and voluntary choices by the citizens themselves. But this fails to take account of the coercive nature of those choices.

Our second concern relates to the potential for collateral injury caused by the agreement. The potential consequences of the bargain can extend far beyond the details of the agreed-upon sentence. Edkins and Redlich offer a compelling description of this potential: "From disenfranchisement (that is, the loss of the right to vote) to denial of student loans to ineligibility to collect welfare or food stamps to a loss of professional licenses or certifications, individuals with a criminal record are prevented from fully participating in society as equal citizens" (2019, 5–6). This emphasizes how asymmetric bargains in one area of social life can serve to further instantiate inequality in other areas. This is especially relevant to any injuries a defendant may experience in their future capacity to participate effectively in the democratic process.

To put the point simply, bargaining begets bargaining which begets more bargaining. And unequal bargaining begets even more unequal bargaining in the future. Given the relevance of social and economic resources for the capacity of citizens to participate effectively in the political process, it is important in an analysis of democracy to consider the collateral consequences of state–citizen bargaining for the effectiveness of future participation in democratic politics. Our commitment to democracy should dictate that the state strives to maintain the necessary conditions for equal treatment in the society. To the extent that plea bargains undermine those conditions, it raises additional normative questions about the role of state actors in that process.

From this fact of the negative substantive consequences of plea bargaining in both the short term and the long term, we conclude there is a systemic problem in how plea bargaining is commonly structured in the United States and other countries that presumptively violates the equitable treatment of citizens' interests requirement of democracy. However, there may be other values that warrant priority in the case of plea bargaining that should be considered. Thus, the question is, Is there a competing value that overrides the claim about unfair bargaining that can legitimize the plea bargain as a legal institution? Our review of the literature suggests that there are at least three justifications of plea bargaining that need to be considered. They are social efficiency, preference maximization, and correcting an imbalanced system of substantive criminal law.

It does not take much thought to quickly reject two of these justifications. Preference maximization on the part of prosecutors and defendants is in principle a questionable justification for the plea-bargaining system. In the best of circumstances, why would that be the primary reason for maintaining plea bargaining, especially given the wider interests of the community in criminal justice? And when we take into account the good reasons for questioning the voluntariness of the agreement, it fails as a value to which democratic society should give priority in this case.

Those who justify retaining plea bargaining on the grounds that it serves to correct inappropriate imbalances in the criminal law code offer a more creative reason. Bowers (2016), for example, argues that the courts have come to see plea bargaining as a way of addressing a problem with democracy. The problem is that elected representatives have botched criminal law by creating an unjust system that overpunishes criminal defendants. So, as a way of addressing this injustice, prosecutors use the plea-bargaining system as a workaround for the democratic process that is failing. While we might agree with their indictment of the existing criminal justice system in the United States, we can question whether this is a good basis for defending the plea bargain. For the reasons that we set out in Chapter 4, we challenge the notion that prosecutors, unelected members of the executive branch, are the appropriate officials for making decisions about the substantive aspects of criminal law. Even if we were to accept the view that this is merely an implementation issue, in which the legislature defers to prosecutors who have greater expertise in the area of criminal justice, that deference cannot legitimately extend to substantive questions about the appropriateness of punishments for guilty defendants. That is a question that must be decided by the elected representatives of a democratic society.

Most advocates of plea bargaining base their support of the system on social efficiency. They argue that the system is administratively efficient because it costs less than a trial would and it is "inherently compatible with the public interest in securing adequate punishment for offenders" (Alschuler 1968, 105). The system may in one respect be cost-effective, in the sense that it produces more guilty verdicts for less money than the trial system, although the vast costs of mass incarceration may undermine even that claim.

Regardless of cost, though, there is little evidence in support of the claim that plea bargains do a better job of delivering appropriate sentences. The problem is that it is hard to adequately assess which system, plea bargain or trial, does a better job of distinguishing defendants who are innocent from those who are guilty. There is little concrete empirical evidence to support either side of the debate. Even those who advocate for the abolition of plea bargaining are not prepared to make the argument that trials do an adequate job of selecting out and protecting innocent defendants. Feeley (1979, 202) acknowledges that "unfortunately, we cannot answer these questions satisfactorily. The process of adjudication is an elaborate device for ascertaining truth and there is no instrument by which its accuracy can readily be measured." But Feely, like Baldwin and McConville (1979, 287), hastens to add that "it is also apparent from this body of research that there is no simple or neat correspondence between a guilty plea and legal culpability." We think it is fair to say that most scholars who have attempted to study the question empirically share the view of Kipnis that "while the conviction of the innocent would be a problem in any system we might devise, it appears to be a greater problem under plea-bargaining" (1976, 104).

Nonetheless, there appears to be at least some theoretical basis for expecting a trial to do this more effectively than a coerced bargain. The adversarial system of justice that is instantiated in the criminal trial gives the accused, at the very least, an opportunity to protect their own interests and to test the plausibility of the evidence offered against them. Without this due process protection, we are left with only one measure of the probability of guilt: the assessment and judgment of the prosecutor. Scott and Stuntz (1992, 1949) employ a formal bargaining model to analyze how the innocence question is handled by the plea-bargaining process. Their analysis highlights the inability of the prosecutor to know whether the defendant actually committed the crime or not. They conclude that "bargaining theory helps identify what we believe to be the most problematic feature of plea-bargaining: the dynamic of the parties' interaction makes it harder for innocent defendants to identify themselves." In the end, despite the uncertainty over whether the criminal trial does a good job of selecting the guilty and not the innocent, there seems to be good reason for rejecting the plea bargain as a better alternative for securing adequate and appropriate punishment for criminal offenders.

We argue, therefore, that none of the alleged benefits of the plea-bargaining system support a value worthy of priority over the requirements of fair bargaining in a democratic society. Given the substantial asymmetries in favor of the state that characterize these bargains, we strongly doubt that plea bargaining will conduce to the equitable treatment of fundamental interests. And thus we conclude that plea bargaining is a practice that undermines the dictates of democratic legitimacy. But as we have emphasized throughout this analysis, the ultimate responsibility for weighing this balance of values rests with the elected representatives in the legislature. In the event that these elected officials chose to retain plea bargaining as a legitimate practice in the criminal justice system, there are some institutional remedies that we believe should be imposed to diminish the unfairness of the system. Three that we will simply identify here are better discovery rules that would allow defendants greater transparency in the plea-bargaining process, institutional constraints on the prosecutor's ability to manipulate both charge and sentencing terms, and formal third-party monitoring of the negotiating process. Each of these would diminish the substantial asymmetries in power that undermine the interests of democratic citizens in these situations. We suspect, however, that these efforts to make plea bargaining more compatible with the commitment to democracy would make it ultimately a less attractive alternative for the state.

Conclusion

As we stated at the beginning of this chapter, street-level bureaucrats enjoy a good deal of discretion in their interactions with citizens. We believe that the analysis of plea bargaining demonstrates that democracy does place constraints on the behavior of state actors—all state actors—when they are engaged with individual citizens in these interactions. This demand follows directly from our understanding of the democratic commitment. We argue that the requirement of equitable treatment of interests crucially extends to state interaction with its individual citizens, given the inherent asymmetry of power between the state and those citizens. As we have applied it in our earlier analyses of decision-making by state officials, the commitment requires state decision-makers to take account of all citizen interests on equitable terms in deciding on a course of action.

In his penetrating analysis of other types of street-level interactions, Zacka (2017) emphasizes the importance of the standard of fairness in thinking about constraints on bureaucratic discretion. This is similar to what we have in mind in thinking about the exercise of state power. State actors "on the ground" are subject to the constraints of good faith, duress, and unconscionability. Establishing how they adequately satisfy these equity requirements in interactions with individual citizens is complicated. But it is often the case that although we don't know with certainty when we have adequately satisfied a behavioral standard, we do know when we have not. Our primary concern in these cases is that the existence of significant bargaining asymmetries in the decision-making process is important evidence of the possibility that the standard has not been met. Under those conditions, the behavior of state actors should be subject to the strictest scrutiny. These doctrines can serve as guidance of how bureaucratic discretion can go wrong.

To be more specific, we believe that the commitment to democracy establishes a presumptive constraint against government officials employing coercive bargaining strategies in those instances in which the democratic state acts as direct party to the bargain. When the government is bargaining with individual citizens, there are no natural asymmetries that should come into play other than its power to impartially enforce the law. This means that it should not employ bargaining strategies against private citizens that would result in bargains that violate the criteria of good faith, duress, or unconscionability.

In extending the reach of democratic constraints on bargaining, we emphasize in this chapter a necessary distinction. In analyzing bargaining in a democratic society, it is important to distinguish between the short-term effects *of* power asymmetries and the long-term effects *on* power asymmetries. Both types of effect create normative problems for democracy. But it is the latter, long-term effects, that is especially problematic when we turn to bargaining between private citizens and the state. For, as the case of plea bargaining makes clear, the consequences of unequal and thus unfair bargains in the present moment can have lasting effects on the distribution of various forms of power in the future, including political power over future democratic decisions. Felon disenfranchisement, which itself derives most often from plea bargaining, is the most obvious instantiation of this problem. This distinction is especially relevant when we note that democratic constraints on unequal bargaining always include the caveat that there may be, in specific circumstances, other values that are facilitated by the bargain that we prioritize in those circumstances. Highlighting the potential long-term effects of the bargain on a citizen's capacity to participate equally in democratic decision-making serves to emphasize how important these other values must be to override the criterion of equitable treatment.

In addition, the emphasis on long-term effects allows us to make one final point about the ways in which democratic states may influence bargaining, of either the public variety or the private. Put simply, a commitment to democracy precludes state action that exacerbates inequality but not state action that diminishes it. We believe that this long-term reasoning lends support for state action (in terms of either specific policies or more general institutional practices) that, under the appropriate conditions, diminishes the existing power asymmetries between the participants in various forms of public and private bargaining. The constraint on state actions, that they should not increase inequalities that result in future unjustifiable bargaining, should not preclude institutional rules that diminish relevant bargaining asymmetries, rules that would favor the weaker side of existing bargaining relationships.

We see no reason why a democratic state, absent some kind of constitutional prohibition, should be prevented from enhancing equality when it is institutionally possible. Here, consistent with our argument in Chapters 2, 3 and 4, the main normative task would be to distinguish democratically justifiable asymmetries from those that are problematic. Once that assessment has been completed, we argue that a commitment to democracy clearly allows institutional remedies that reduce problematic inequalities, especially those that implicate future political bargains.

Finally, having said this, we acknowledge that the balancing of these different asymmetries would ultimately be a decision best made by the democratically elected representatives in the legislature. And here it is important to note that in some similar situations, legislatures have authorized state intervention into private bargaining that diminishes the short-term bargaining advantages of the more powerful economic actors. The most prominent examples are the consumer protection laws that enacted detailed procedures to protect individual contractors from the unconscionable bargaining strategies employed by large corporations (Vogel 2012). A related example is the Credit Card Accountability Responsibility and Disclosure Act of 2009 (Credit CARD Act), the legislative politics of which we discussed at the beginning of this book's Introduction. The justifications for these reforms were grounded in large part in the unconscionable discrepancies between the bargaining capacities of unorganized consumers and those of unified, well-organized producers in the private contracting process. The bottom line for our analysis is that laws such as these would not appear to violate the normative constraint on the role of the state in either public or private bargaining.

Conclusion

In this book, we have sought to justify the use of bargaining within democracies under certain parameters. We have argued that bargaining is not merely an inescapable feature of politics, but that under certain conditions, members' interests may be better protected through bargaining than via other mechanisms of decision-making. Drawing on the law of contracts, we have treated both private and public bargaining as forms of exchange in which members are able to pursue their ends, both facilitating autonomy and potentially producing social welfare gains, and reflecting the wider value of good faith as a condition of democratic decision-making. But, as in contract law, we have also identified a set of conditions that such exchanges must satisfy to be justifiably enforced. Just as in private contracting, we permit certain asymmetries of power to affect the bargaining process and outcomes. However, again as in private contracting, we protect against grave asymmetries through the doctrines of substantive and especially procedural unconscionability, and through an expansive interpretation of the concept of duress.

Our argument here is intended as an opening gambit for a redirection of attention to bargaining power in democracy. We recognize that others may characterize the demands of equitable treatment and the institutional remedies for inequities differently. Nonetheless, we do think that the approach we have offered in this work helps to open lines of inquiry for political theory, political science, and law.

To begin, we have sought to recenter political theory on the questions that animated the pluralists: How should we explain, justify, and circumscribe political power and competing interests? To be sure, we are not alone in the spirit of this endeavor. In an influential review article, Marc Stears drew together a variety of theorists under the tradition of the "politics of compulsion," from antiliberal "agonists" such as William Connolly, Bonnie Honig, and Chantal Mouffe to sympathetic critics of liberalism such as John Gray and Jeremy Waldron (Stears 2007). These theorists are united by the view that politics is inescapably coercive; consensus is unachievable, even on fundamental questions of justice; and power, rather than reason, shapes political outcomes. As Stears rightly observes, such a position is liable to the charge that it is merely descriptive rather than normative, although he also notes that he takes this to be unfair: agonists embrace the unpredictability and creative possibilities of conflict, and democratic theorists such as Waldron defend the egalitarianism inherent in majority rule. Stears suggests that a realistic liberalism should accept that liberal ends may depend upon compulsive means.

In response, Andrew Sabl has argued that realist liberalism should acknowledge power and interests in a way that is closely akin to our project. Sabl suggests that "liberal institutions ought to favor everyone's interests equally, in spite of unequal social power and to a great extent in ways that render power less salient. . . . [For instance,] the benefits of the welfare state are available to all but in practice benefit the most vulnerable disproportionately by supplementing what would otherwise be their vastly inferior bargaining power. Powerful actors always try, with some success, to use their power to stack the system in favor of their own interests. . . . Correcting this requires, on a liberal realist view, countervailing power" (Sabl 2017, 377). In sum, Sabl argues that a primary normative ambition of realist liberalism is to recommend reforms that seek to remedy some of the biases that emerge from the asymmetric distribution of bargaining power (Sabl 2017, 399). Although the catholic nature of the "realist" umbrella leads us to resist the term, our project has sought to realize what Sabl characterizes as the ambitions of realist liberalism. Our bargaining approach to democracy emphasizes the redistribution of power rather than its elimination, and its institutional focus encourages attention to the varying ways in which powerful agents may seek to entrench their resources and how such attempts might be checked.

Political scientists have sometimes resisted political theorists' interventions in these debates over legislative practice on the grounds that they rely on motivations and dispositions that are unreliable or implausible, particularly in strategic environments. Focusing on institutions and their effects on politics enables us to avoid the difficult problems of insincerity and behavioral equivalence and makes available a more realistic and workable focus for the assessment of day-to-day politics in a democratic society. It acknowledges the inevitability of a certain amount of strategic behavior among democratic citizens, but by establishing normative standards to assess the bargaining process and its results, it allows us to characterize the features of the best contexts within which citizens can legitimately pursue their individual and collective interests.

We have relied heavily on insights from American and comparative politics for our accounts of legislative, judicial, and interbranch bargaining; happily, these are flourishing fields of inquiry in these disciplines. However, scholars in political science have tended to rely on a small cluster of normative concerns, such as responsiveness and stability of majority preferences, in their motivations for such work. We hope to have offered a new conceptual vocabulary and set of normative commitments to these scholars: specifically, we would encourage political scientists to expand their focus to the treatment of interests in the dynamics of a democratic system as a whole, and to the institutional arrangements that yield predictable inequities, rather than focusing primarily on policy congruence or on the power of agenda-setters in determining legislative outcomes.

To be sure, political scientists have sometimes turned to political theory as a source of motivation for their research agendas, but have often expressed frustration at the level of remove or abstraction from which political theorists working on questions of democracy tend to operate. Although there are often benefits from working at a high level of abstraction, one advantage of our approach is that in focusing on smaller-bore institutional questions and power dynamics, we hope to provide a more obvious point of departure. Political scientists have key insights into how legislatures, courts, and bureaucracies operate on the ground, and we hope this approach will foster fruitful collaborations across fields about the normative implications of such institutions from the perspective of competing societal interests.

Legal scholars have tended to focus on the substance of laws in their analyses of statutory and constitutional interpretation. By contrast, we argue that the equitable treatment of interests standard recommends a particular role for the judiciary, requiring them to analyze whether the legislative process was undermined by asymmetrical bargaining power. This recommends a structural due process approach to statutory interpretation. Rather than making a determination of whether the substantive content of the law accurately reflects the interests of citizens, the court can focus on whether all relevant interests had an opportunity for real consideration in the legislative process. This would involve an analysis of the rules and procedures that governed the process as well as an assessment of the extent to which asymmetries in power had a disproportionate influence over the legislative bargaining outcome.

We contend that this structural due process approach can provide a fairly clear method for courts to assess whether the legislature satisfied the democratic baseline. This alternative approach requires the court to answer certain empirical questions about the process, but it relieves it of the burden of determining the relevant content and distribution of interests in every case. For the primary focus would be on the question of whether the appropriate legislative process was undermined by the influence of asymmetric bargaining power. The court's analysis would rest on the notion that the greater the bargaining asymmetries, the greater the likelihood of an inequitable treatment of interests. If the court identified the influence of substantial power asymmetries, it would be required to investigate the source of those asymmetries to further determine if they are deemed justifiable or unjustifiable by the criterion of democracy. If the court, after reviewing the procedural history of a statute, determined that the procedural prerequisites of a democratically legitimate statute were satisfied, that would be enough for it to conclude that the legislation satisfied the democratic baseline.

In response to the claim of some critics that the structural due process approach would further complicate the task of statutory interpretation and would further involve the judiciary in the democratic decision-making process, we would counter that this approach actually limits the role of the judiciary by absolving the courts of the responsibility for determining the substantive legitimacy of the statute. As we have argued, the task of determining the appropriate balance of substantive interests in a statute is not a question that the judiciary is best prepared to answer. That substantive question should be left to the legislature. But the assessment of the process by which the statute was enacted is another matter.

Institutional Reforms

With these general tenets in mind, we have a few specific recommendations for institutional reform; we invite others to join the effort to develop a bargaining theory of democracy and to add to the list of potential reforms. We are guided by the notion that institutional design and reform is inherently a context-specific endeavor. What would diminish inequalities of bargaining power in one democracy may exacerbate them elsewhere, and so ultimately, an effective system will be grounded in the details of a specific social and political context. Some of the recommendations we have proposed, such as curbing gerrymandering and revising campaign finance laws, would be shared by most other theories of democracy, though their justifications might be different. Here we identify a few reforms that other accounts might resist or neglect: (1) support for earmarking, (2) an expansion of standing requirements for legal changes, (3) an expanded role for citizens in administrative rule-making, and (4) a comprehensive tool to enable courts to assess public bargains more effectively via what we term "political antitrust."

Earmarks

Earmarks are controversial insofar as they seem to promote particularistic spending, rather than spending in which the gains are more broadly distributed. House and Senate rules now characterize earmarks as congressionally directed spending, tax benefit, or tariff benefit that targets an entity or a specific state, locality, or district, and if such benefits were conferred other than through a statutory or administrative formula or a competitive award process (Lynch 2020). Congress imposed an earmark moratorium in the 112th Congress (2011–2012) in the wake of notable corruption scandals; the ban was lifted in 2021, though subject to new conditions. Broadly speaking, earmarking both helps to facilitate legislative bargaining and serves as a means of maintaining legislative supremacy over policymaking. As discussed in Chapter 3, earmarks can serve as a valuable tool of party cohesion—and bipartisan decision-making—as an inducement for recalcitrant legislators. Its absence may have tempted leaders to use threats rather than offers, and some of these threats may run afoul of the conditions discussed in Chapter 3. Moreover, earmarking serves as a means of expanding the distributive gains associated with lawmaking; it is a form of "greasing the wheels" in order to build broader coalitions for legislation (Evans 2004; Frisch and Kelly 2011), promoting bipartisan decision-making.

Earmarking also serves as a means of ensuring legislative supremacy: the earmark ban did not curb particularistic spending, but transferred it primarily to the executive branch. Whereas some would argue that earmarking constrains legislators to focus on the common good, rather than their local interests, in fact it generated a shift from earmarking to "lettermarking." Lettermarking is a mechanism by which members of Congress contact executive agency personnel to request targeted appropriations to their home districts, a mechanism that is far less transparent than earmarking (Dawson and Kleiner 2015). Congressional earmarking today requires the satisfaction of further conditions of transparency: the House requires lawmakers to provide evidence that communities support a proposed earmark; members must certify that neither they nor their families have any financial interest in the projects they request; and when members submit their proposal to the House Appropriations Committee, they must also post it online. The House Appropriations Committee[1] and the Senate Appropriations Committee[2] provide links to these requests. Such norms help citizens assess whether their representatives are in fact seeking to advance their interests, or whether they are merely paying lip service to their needs while focusing attention on other constituents.

Standing

Our justification of democratic bargaining hinges on the ability of citizens to pursue their interests in an open and transparent system. While voting and participating in the electoral process more generally are the primary mechanisms available to citizens, we also argue that the system is made more effective through citizen participation in other aspects of governance. The value of citizen participation supports our recommendation for the loosening of standing requirements for lawsuits to enable citizens to challenge the democratic pedigree of legislative bargains. In the United States, per contemporary standing requirements, the capacity of citizens to challenge the overall legitimacy of a statute is limited to those cases in which they have been able to demonstrate that the statute violated one of their constitutionally protected rights. As we noted in Chapter 4, some states have recognized a constitutional right to democracy in their state constitutions. And some scholars have argued for an interpretation of the US Constitution that would ground a right to democracy in its provisions. Although we believe that there is considerable merit in the argument advocating for a constitutional right to an effective democracy, we think that the availability of this kind of standing would be beneficial even if it is merely acknowledged as a statutory right that follows directly from a commitment to democracy. All citizens have a fundamental interest in making sure that democratic procedures are satisfied. Broader standing rules would enhance the agency of individual citizens to influence the democratic process. If such rules could be established, it would open up the possibility that citizens could challenge the statutory process and use the courts to call attention to problems of unjustifiable democratic bargaining.

Citizen Participation in Agency Rule-Making

A similar argument can be offered in support of the primary administrative reform that we recommend: greater public participation in implementation decisions. The basic idea is the creation of public bodies within administrative agencies to advise bureaucrats about issues of implementation and enforcement. The goal would be to diversify and expand the range of citizen input in the implementation process and to offset the influence of special interests in that process. In Chapter 4, we noted the example of the Federal Advisory Committee Act in the United States. This act authorizes the creation of committees to gather opinions from a wide range of citizens and to advise agencies in the executive branch on policy questions. This is just one example of efforts to do what we are recommending here.

Political Antitrust Regulation

This proposed reform highlights the oft-cited comparison between markets and democratic decision-making but reaches a somewhat different recommendation than the comparison often yields. As we noted in Chapter 1, courts have invoked antitrust laws as a way of addressing issues of unequal bargaining power in contract enforcement cases. They have tended to use it only in the most egregious cases, the threat of monopoly power, but it does serve as an explicit constraint on the effects of unequal bargaining power on private bargains. While antitrust laws have been justified as a means of protecting contracting parties from the unfair features of their individual transactions, we recommend an alternative justification that is more relevant for our purposes (Knight and Johnson 2011). Rather than conceiving of antitrust constraints as a protection against unfairness in individual exchanges, we argue that they can be seen as a mechanism for guaranteeing the effectiveness of market institutions.

When antitrust issues are conceived of in this alternative way, we can highlight the conditions that are necessary to achieve the collective benefits that derive from socially efficient markets. Most important of these conditions is the equality of bargaining power that characterizes perfectly competitive markets. The greater the disparities in bargaining power in a market, the less effective the market will be in producing socially beneficial outcomes. Thus, the justification for constraining private bargains generated by asymmetries in bargaining power follows from our collective interest in the institutional effectiveness of markets. In applying economic antitrust laws, courts have focused primarily on the ways by which market power is acquired and maintained. This puts the focus not so much on the exercise of the power advantage in the specific bargain but rather on the relative power asymmetries in the market as a whole. Thought about in this way, when applying antitrust law to private bargains, judges will seek market effectiveness and will look to determine those sources of bargaining power that undermine it.

We believe there is a strong analogy between market effectiveness and democratic efficacy. As we have argued throughout this book, theoretical claims about the benefits of democratic institutions commonly rest on the assumption about the equality of political actors. Whatever the specific justification for democratic political institutions, it is easy to demonstrate that those institutions will not achieve the desired relationships or benefits if they are characterized by significant inequalities among citizens. And this would recommend that a general rule against the exercise and use of too much bargaining power, similar to private monopolies, could serve as a standard for assessing democratic electoral laws and institutions. Such a reform could place under one institutional umbrella an array of rules governing election procedures, campaign strategies, lobbying efforts, and political financing regulations. It would have the primary effect of diminishing inequalities in political bargaining. Just as the concern with effectiveness can serve as the basis for constraints on private bargains, it can serve as a similar basis for public ones. Combined with a statute that authorizes standing to legally challenge unjustifiable political bargains, it would represent an all-encompassing commitment to an effective democratic system, controlling for the factors that undermine justifiable political bargains.[3]

In the Introduction to this book we compared two cases in which minority interests pertaining to water rights were imperiled: the vulnerable Whanganui Iwi of New Zealand and the wealthy homeowners of the Hamptons. A main challenge for democratic institutional design is how to protect minority rights without allowing powerful groups a blanket veto over majority decisions. As we have discussed, many normative theorists resist bargaining as a mechanism because of this concern; they suggest that only norms that could be justified to all members, or only those norms that could freely emerge as a consensus under deliberation, can justly bind us. We have argued that bargaining itself can constitute a means by which the claims of minorities can be satisfied subject to conditions. But it requires that we design a bargaining process and constrain its outcomes so as to ensure that vulnerable parties are not subject to predation, and that democracy specifically requires us to attend to the prospective ability of minority groups to participate on equal terms.

In the case of the Māori, the bargaining perspective focuses our attention on the competing claims of the New Zealand majority to decision-making over the Whanganui River, and the specific interests of the Whanganui Iwi over control. A standard institutional option would be to carve out of majority decision-making constitutional rights over river access, secured by a targeted veto on the part of the minority enabling them to prevent unjust deprivations. The bargaining approach we defend is both more sensitive and more flexible. It insists on actual negotiation among the parties, underpinned by a good-faith commitment both on the part of the majority to accommodate the fundamental interests of the minority and on the part of the minority to acknowledge the interests of the majority. As we have argued, we take fundamental interests to be those in ongoing democratic participation. The bargaining perspective insists that the communal organizational needs of the Whanganui River Māori can take precedence over the economic interests of the majority or other groups. But the majority can nonetheless prevail in terms of securing its own access to the water and to forms of activity that do not impede the self-determination interests of the minority. Although typically democratic theory has conceptualized minority rights as "trumps," designed to block majoritarian impositions, our approach enables greater flexibility on the part of minority groups to extract concessions, subject to limits on the set of bargaining strategies and the permissible asymmetries. Again, the aim is an equitable bargain under conditions of asymmetrical power, one that acknowledges competing considerations without treating all interests as if they are of equal significance. The paired case of the Hamptonites who seek to block a wind farm that impedes their view of the horizon demonstrates why equity considerations must be foregrounded. A contractarian approach that equates property rights with human rights—and treats harm to property values as tantamount to bodily injury—enables a powerful minority to veto bargains that produce significant social-welfare gains and pose no threat to the minority's fundamental interests in political agency. This is in part why we argue that our approach to contractual bargaining is preferable: it takes seriously common-law defenses to contract formation while narrowly tailoring them.

Throughout the book, we have argued that the primary challenge is to design democratic institutions that secure the conditions of democratic bargaining. One challenge is that of regress, as we saw in Chapter 2; constraints on political bargaining must themselves arise from a bargaining process. In part, we solve this problem by constraining our scope to democratic forms of bargaining. We have argued that the substantive and procedural limits to bargaining may be supported through the prospect of alternation in power; a majority that anticipates that it will lose power and find itself in the minority should be more likely to accept such limits. This is why we have attended specifically to the concerns raised by gerrymandering and other forms by which majoritarian power may be entrenched. To be sure, some short-term bargains, as we conceptualize them, will make key actors worse off than at their initial starting point. However, citizens must also have good reason to believe that their long-term, fundamental interests will be protected by political bargains, and that they are more likely to remain protected prospectively under democracy than under an alternative, feasible regime. A core challenge for contemporary democratic life is to assure minorities, particularly members of racial minorities and Indigenous groups, that their interests can be protected against majoritarian impulses. Although no mechanism can guarantee that a determined majority will not undermine the interests of a vulnerable minority, if bargaining could be shown to hamper their interests relative to other types of mechanisms, this would be a significant strike against it. We hope to have demonstrated that a deliberative approach cannot constitute any more reliable a means of securing the interests of minorities than our bargaining approach, and that mechanisms designed to produce compromise merely produce less institutionally robust forms of bargains.

We also hope to have vindicated the value of a normative inquiry into bargaining as the central mechanism of political life. Of course, given the range of sites of decision-making, there is much more work to be done. Research into the forms and locations of deliberation has occupied decades of scholarship; within political theory, the study of bargaining has remained a residual and unexamined category. Scholars of "realist" political theory have called for a reintegration of political theory within political science. If this ambition is to be realized, the study of bargaining is an excellent place to begin.

Introduction

1. https://www.politico.com/story/2009/05/senators-cut-deal-on-credit-card-bill-022360

2. https://www.nytimes.com/2009/05/20/us/politics/20cong.html?em

3. https://www.congress.gov/congressional-record/2009/05/20/house-section/article/H5823-2 [page H5937]

4. https://www.rollcall.com/2009/05/12/coburn-gun-amendment-tacked-on-to-credit-card-bill/

5. Rawls went on to argue that in fact "many, if not most" political questions do not concern fundamental matters; he cites "tax legislation and many laws regulating property" as among the norms that do not require public reasoning.

6. Thomas Christiano argues, though from a somewhat different theoretical perspective, that "each citizen has fundamental interests *in being able to see* that he is being treated as an equal in a society where there is significant diversity among persons in the conditions of well-being and where there is disagreement about justice and wherein each citizen can acknowledge fallibility and cognitive bias in their capacities for thinking about their interests and about justice" (Christiano 2008, 56). We concur with Christiano that members of democratic communities have a fundamental interest in publicly equal standing that helps to justify democratic decision-making, although our focus on bargaining yields a different theoretical frame than Christiano's. Further, although we share Christiano's characterization of democratic institutions as a means of advancing interests—and specifically on the necessity of an "equal say" in voting as a means of publicly signaling the equal importance of judgments of interests—our broader project departs from his in significant ways, including his priority on the value of public deliberation (Christiano 2008).

7. We admit this is a challenge. In his treatment of a similar worry in *Political Equality*, Charles Beitz characterizes the problem as one of democratic legitimacy: "The basic idea is that citizens might reasonably refuse to accept institutions under which it was predictable that their actual interests—that is, the satisfaction of their

needs and the success of their projects—would be unfairly placed in jeopardy" (Beitz 1989, 110). But Beitz also suggests that "the idea of equitable treatment is difficult to render more precisely, primarily because it is uncertain how the notion of an interest's 'being unfairly placed in jeopardy' should be interpreted" (Beitz 1989, 111). To mitigate these concerns, Beitz invokes a broadly constitutional approach, defending constraints such as a bill of rights, judicial review, and so forth. But he also argues that we require a more substantive account of social justice to determine whether the interest in equitable treatment has been satisfied over time (Beitz 1989, 112). Our approach departs from Beitz's in a few respects, notably that rather than relying on substantive views concerning social justice, we adopt a democratic approach.

8. Sophia Moreau argues more generally that wrongful discrimination, even sometimes in the form of "direct discrimination," does not necessarily "involve a causal claim that extends back to any objectionable mental states or processes in the discriminator" (Moreau 2020, 20).

9. Though he himself uses the language of "equal concern," T. M. Scanlon acknowledges that the term might mislead readers to believe that what is required is a certain attitude on the part of agents. He denies that this is correct, instead holding that the question of whether a policy satisfies the requirement of equal concern depends upon the *reasons* supporting it, "whether it can be justified taking the interests of all affected parties into account in the right way." Specifically, Scanlon argues that agents (for example, representatives) are obliged to give the interests of those affected by a policy "*appropriate* weight," that is, either "*sufficient* weight in relation to other values" or "*the same* weight as the interests of (certain) other individuals" (Scanlon 2018). Although in certain respects our conception of the equitable treatment of interests is close to Scanlon's, we depart from his account both in emphasizing the role of institutional design in promoting these aims (rather than focusing on the obligations of agents) and in highlighting the importance of democratic procedures to justify outcomes, rather than through scrutiny of the reasons that agents had for choosing them.

10. We take Peter Singer's principle of "equal consideration of interests" to be, in effect, a principle of equitable treatment of interests. In Singer's words, "The principle of equal consideration of interest acts like a pair of scales, weighing interests impartially. The scales favour the side where the interest is stronger or where several interests combine to outweigh a smaller number of similar interests" (Singer 2011, 20–21). So although we share Singer's view about variation in the importance of interests, and his view that a majority of ordinary interests may be outweighed by the fundamental interests of a vulnerable minority, we find the language of treatment and of "equitable" to be more intuitive.

11. Although we stipulate that citizens are the best judges of their *own* interests, we also do not assume that they are the best judges of *others'* interests. As

countless studies have demonstrated, ordinary citizens are typically not especially well-informed about conditions that do not immediately affect them. So we do not rest our argument on any assumptions about citizens' ability, either individually or collectively, to correctly answer questions about the optimal decisions for a community; nor, for that matter, do we assume the existence of such a right answer to such questions. We just assume that, when they vote, they reliably identify what they take to be their own interests, however they characterize them.

12. Avishai Margalit (2010) characterizes a "rotten compromise" as one that promotes cruelty and humiliation. Although we depart from Margalit's conception in a variety of respects, here it is helpful in identifying why we treat equal voting rights as effectively sacrosanct. Unequal voting rights do not necessarily produce cruelty, but in a democratic domain, the designation of some agents' interests as more important than others publicly renders some citizens inferior, which we take to be a source of humiliation and subordination.

13. Beginning with the design of the Senate, the United States Constitution itself runs afoul of these conditions immediately, and First Amendment jurisprudence in cases such as *Citizens United* exacerbates such inequalities. Although we focus attention on microlevel details of legislative behavior because of our interest in the bargaining process, this should not be taken to imply that we believe the background conditions in the United States today satisfy the fundamental conditions of equitable treatment of interests.

14. Our aim is not to develop a full-blown account of political authority, understood as the conditions under which citizens have moral reason to obey the laws created by some legislative body. We assume that such an account is available for a representative democracy, but we are largely agnostic about the form it takes.

15. This formulation is reminiscent of Joseph Raz's "normal justification thesis," in which a person should be acknowledged to have authority over a subject if the alleged subject is likely better to comply with reasons that apply to him if he accepts the directives of the alleged authority as binding, rather than trying to follow the reasons that apply to him directly. We obviously depart from Raz in many other respects, not least in our focus on interests rather than reasons, but we acknowledge the parallelism in structure (Raz 1986).

16. In many respects, this view is characteristic of what Melissa Williams described (and criticized) as the interest-group pluralist's approach to liberal representation, which she associates with Dahl: responsiveness depends on the electoral sanction, rather than on shared identities or affinities. Williams writes, "The representative fulfills his or her obligation to act in the interests of the represented by *bargaining for* those interests, not by *sharing* them" (Williams 1998, 80). In our treatment of permanent minorities and Indigenous peoples, however, we hope to vindicate the capacity of this general model to satisfy the distinctive claims of historically marginalized groups.

17. Sean Ingham has recently argued that any democratic system will feature multiple majorities; where a vulnerable minority's preferences can align with another, comprising a majority, and so long as the majority coalition feels sufficiently strongly about the matter, they are likely to be able to defeat their least preferred option (Ingham 2019, 163–68). Social-choice theory further specifies the cycles that will result through the logic of the uncovered set (Miller 1983; McKelvey 1986; McGann 2006). A "covered" alternative, x, is that which is beaten by another alternative under majority rule, and which also beat all those alternatives that x beats. An uncovered set includes all those alternatives that are not covered. Bianco, Jeliazkov, and Sened (2004) demonstrate, based on NOMINATE scores for the US House of Representatives, that the uncovered set can be relatively large, giving considerable range for strategic interactions among sophisticated actors and agenda-setting by party leaders.

18. In 2014, the Ruruku Whakatupua, a settlement deed, recognized the Whanganui River as a legal entity with legal personhood rights; legislation formalizing this legal entity, Te Awa Tupua Act, was formalized in 2017.

19. https://www.nytimes.com/2019/09/14/nyregion/hamptons-wind-farm.html

20. For an illuminating analysis of Habermas's overall approach to deliberation, see Johnson (1991, 1998).

21. Ian Shapiro also raises a set of concerns about deliberation as a means of enabling the powerful to "prevaricate and procrastinate," and he notes that the institutional means to promote deliberation might collapse into bargaining (Shapiro 2003, 36). Rather than abandoning deliberation, however, he argues for a "stripped-down" conception, though at points the distinction between deliberation and bargaining is somewhat blurry: "In [some] settings, such as those covered by the NLRA, government seeks to mandate deliberation through an affirmative duty to bargain. . . . As a normative matter we can say that the more one's basic interests are threatened, the strong one's claim is to insist upon deliberation, but that beyond some threat threshold even this is insufficient" (Shapiro 2003, 46). Although we believe that the spirit of our argument is compatible with Shapiro's main claims, we distinguish more sharply between deliberation and bargaining, and we treat deliberation as an intermediate mechanism by which interests can be identified, rather than a decision mechanism.

22. Note that this is even the case for courts, where the signal and distinctive feature is the obligation to give reasons for judgments. For courts, the reason-giving requirement primarily serves the aim of stabilizing expectations, and of providing explanations for decisions that are congruent with community norms. Rather than transforming preferences or demonstrating respect for persons in their capacity as reasoners, reason-giving in this context mostly serves to coordinate behavior.

23. Avishai Margalit specifically refers to game-theoretic accounts of bargaining as an "anemic" sense of compromise, and identifies any agreement that lies in the bargaining range as a compromise. A sanguine account of compromise, which is

the one that interests Margalit, is an "anemic compromise" plus recognition—bargaining, plus recognizing the other party as a legitimate partner. It is what other scholars typically term "negotiation" (Margalit 2010, 39–42).

24. Walton and McKersie (1965) develop this integrative approach, acknowledging their debt to Follett, though Fisher and Ury (2011), in *Getting to Yes*, did not do so adequately. See also Jane Mansbridge's helpful introduction to Follett (1998), and also Cohen (2020). We are grateful to Mansbridge for calling our attention to Follett's unduly neglected work, including on power.

25. Other scholars have responded skeptically to these arguments. For instance, in a critique of Warren and Mansbridge et al.'s view that "not revealing one's reservation price . . . border[s] on the unethical," Eric Beerbohm argued that bluffing and threats may be essential to the practice of compromise, and he rightly suggested that "in any legislature, information will be unevenly distributed" (Beerbohm 2018, 18). He recognized that virtually any legislative setting will be competitive, and each side may seek a "better deal," marked by "some inequalities in bargaining power." Yet in seeking to justify outcomes generated by threats and inequality, Beerbohm identified the goal of ensuring that legislation constitutes a "jointly performed" activity (19), holding that we can realize democracy's value through "equal sharing in authority over our political institutions," despite unequal power (30). Yet one might worry that a joint-intention account, like Beerbohm's, simply pushes the motivational question back a stage. After all, how could we ensure that any bargained-for outcome realizes a jointly intended plan for legislation, given that joint intentions constitute an especially thick account of shared motivations?

26. The focus of our book is on domestic politics, not the international realm, although much prior work on bargaining and its normative constraints has developed in the latter context. We do recognize the value of the assumption that domestic institutional bargains are liable to external disruption, and that politics "is dominated by struggles between collective actors who favor the institutional status quo and those who wish to overturn it," although they will have differential access to transnational forums and unequal bargaining power within such forums (Farrell and Newman 2019, 31). But this is beyond the scope of the current project.

1. The Enforcement of Private Bargains

1. While there is significant variation within the law and economics community on both methodological and conceptual questions, there is little variation on the reliance on efficiency to explain and justify the law of contracts.

2. Similarly, the *Restatement (Second) of Contracts* (§205 Comments [1981]) establishes that good faith "excludes a variety of types of conduct characterized as involving 'bad faith' because they violate community standards of decency, fairness or reasonableness."

3. See also Shiffrin (2000, 205–6).

4. Substantial support for this claim can be found in the comparative law literature. See, for example, Angelo and Ellinger (1992) and Rodriguez-Yong (2011).

5. See Knight and Johnson (2011) for a general argument about the necessary conditions for the optimal effectiveness of both market and democratic political institutions.

2. Constitutionalism and Democratic Bargaining

1. https://www.opendemocracy.net/en/can-europe-make-it/democracy-on-ice-post-mortem-of-icelandic-constitution/. In defending the value of the Icelandic project, Hélène Landemore (2020) cites these arguments, though she suggests that these failures should not discourage us from drawing positive inferences from the possibility of participatory constitutionalism.

2. A recent study of women's participation in Tunisia is illustrative. A highly mobilized women's movement helped women to garner 30 percent of the seats on the committee of experts, and some seats on the political council, drafting the rules of the October 2011 election of the national constituent assemblies. Crucially, this "higher authority" drafted a rule of "vertical parity" or a "vertical zipper," requiring the names on every party list to alternate between male and female candidates, avoiding party lists that relegated women to the bottom. Women ultimately won 31 percent of the seats in the constituent assembly (although they were underrepresented in leadership positions); however, because they occupied more than a third of the seats on the consensus committee, designed to resolve controversial issues, they were especially influential. When a provision identifying women as "complementary" rather than "equal" to men appeared in the first draft, protestors and civil society groups helped to press the constituent assembly to abandon the language of complementarity in the second draft. https://www.inclusivesecurity.org/wp-content/uploads/2018/02/How-Women-Influence-Constitution-Making.pdf

3. The negotiations would be marked by standard sources of asymmetry, including impatience and, potentially, duress; as Hampton suggests, this gives us little reason to expect that the resulting agreement would be on the two principles (Hampton 1980). Yet even a contractarian account that builds in bargaining may be doomed if it seeks to justify norms purely by appeal to hypothetical consent. For instance, David Gauthier seeks to justify norms that such persons would rationally choose in an initial bargaining position; his bargaining solution is "minimax relative concession," the point at which the greatest concession made by any of the bargainers is smallest (Gauthier 1987). In extending his contractarianism from morality to politics, however, Gauthier reveals the limitations of the approach. Gauthier characterizes the "core" of political contractarianism as a doctrine of justification. The aim is mutual advantage, and so the specific contractarian test that Gauthier defends, generates the following constraint: "No one can be rationally

accepted into society who chooses a life-plan which would impose net overall costs on his fellows, and so make him a malefactor instead of a benefactor" (Gauthier 1997). To illuminate the approach, Gauthier suggests that a woman on welfare who chose to bear a child rather than have an abortion would violate the condition of a "cooperative venture for mutual advantage," and that society "does not thereby license persons to choose to be a net cost to their fellows, or to choose to bring into existence those who would be a net cost." In our view, this merely highlights the problems of the hypothetical consent approach to political justification. A familiar worry about such justifications is that the hypothetical agents' own limitations, their own situated perspective (as imbued by their author), may lead them to mistake the partial or unreasonable for the impartial or reasonable. Anyone who appreciates the range of circumstances under which women may become pregnant, and the ex ante difficulty of specifying conditions under which they might be willing to terminate a pregnancy, would be unlikely to accept the claim that a contract provision that provided material support in these circumstances automatically falls beyond the bounds of deliberative rationality. In short, one theorist's deliberative rationality is another theorist's procedural unconscionability, and we take this to be a main deficiency of the hypothetical consent model.

4. We think there are good reasons to believe that a democracy is the only fully justifiable form of regime in terms of generating relations of authority, but we do not provide such an argument here.

5. The difference between ordinary and constitutional politics runs deep in normative political theory, including through the work of Ronald Dworkin, who distinguished "choice-sensitive" from "choice-insensitive matters" (Dworkin 2002). The first category, matters of policy that can be resolved by reference to the distribution of preferences in the political community, includes questions such as whether to build a new road system; the latter category, which includes questions such as the permissibility of capital punishment, should be assigned to the body most likely to answer these questions correctly, which Dworkin took to be the US Supreme Court. One obvious problem is that matters of policy very quickly bleed into matters of principle, and so it is difficult to draw a line between those matters that should be considered "choice-sensitive," open to majoritarian politics and (in principle) bargaining, and those that are "choice-insensitive" and immune from the contest of politics. To adopt the example of a road system, Robert Moses's construction of the Cross Bronx Expressway displaced 1,500 families, largely of color, and destroyed the community of East Tremont. Is this merely a matter of "policy," immune from questions of principle? Insofar as public reason is required to justify matters of principle, it is difficult to explain why matters of policy must be relegated to mere preference aggregation. But similarly, if matters of principle ought to be assigned primarily to judges, so that they can discern the right answer, one might reasonably ask which questions would be left for legislatures, or for representative democracy more generally.

6. Yet, as Elster himself later argued, precommitment cannot accurately characterize constitution-making, in part because constitutional assemblies rarely are marked only by calm, rational deliberation; rather, their members are gripped by passions and interests, engaged in bargaining as well as arguing (Elster 2000b). Moreover, the framers of constitutions primarily seek to bind others, rather than themselves.

7. Here we adapt John Searle's famous distinction between "constitutive" and "regulative" rules. Constitutive rules make a practice or an action possible, defining and creating institutions, whereas a regulative rule governs preexisting or independently existing institutions (Searle 1969).

8. *Reference re Secession of Quebec*, 2 SCR 217 [1998].

9. Admittedly, secession is not always available as a source of bargaining power; the Quebec example is atypical insofar as the Quebecers are geographically concentrated. We thank Eric MacGilvray and David Wiens for helpful discussions of this matter.

10. Drawing a parallel to family law, Sunstein argues that treating the unit as an indivisible exception in extraordinary circumstances "can serve to promote compromise, to encourage people to live together, to lower the stakes during disagreements, and to prevent any person from achieving an excessively strong bargaining position." Stigmatizing divorce "may lead to happier as well as more stable marriages" by "providing an incentive for spouses to adapt their behavior" (Sunstein 1991, 649).

11. In his earlier work, however, Buchanan advocates that we consider how to "domesticate" the right to secede, in a vein similar to Weinstock and Norman (Buchanan 1991).

12. In arguing against his prior views of constitutional precommitment, Jon Elster makes a similar observation (Elster 2000b), as we discuss further in the penultimate section of this chapter. Brendan O'Leary argues similarly, on the basis of his experience in Ireland/Northern Ireland:

> Makers of constitutions are not narrowly rational future-oriented agents, maximizers of benefits net of costs, willing to write off the past. Some want complete vindication of their readings of the past. Seated with their former, and likely recurrent, adversaries, they will not calmly select from among the infinite array of institutional options those that will maximize their future joint net expected utilities.... They know their pasts, and their presents, and have decided views about them.... Not all are dishonest demagogues (some will be), but all are opportunistic, and error-prone, negotiators in bargaining processes. (O'Leary 2019, 191)

13. Wayne Norman offered a similar agreement (Norman 1998, 53).

14. This synopsis draws on the much more detailed account of Indigenous participation in Canadian constitutional bargaining provided in Borrows (2016).

15. We recognize that language concerning Indigenous peoples and Aboriginal rights is in flux. We use "Indigenous" to refer to peoples, and "Aboriginal" to refer to Canadian Constitutional law that impacts Indigenous peoples. We try to avoid offensive failures to capitalize "Aboriginal," and formulations such as "Aboriginal peoples of Canada," preferring "Indigenous peoples in Canada," but occasionally choose to quote the language of the Supreme Court directly. We thank Yasmin Dawood for helpful discussion of these important issues.

16. Section 35 was subsequently amended. It now includes these statements:

> (3) For greater certainty, in subsection (1) "treaty rights" includes rights that now exist by way of land claims agreements or may be so acquired.
> (4) Notwithstanding any other provision of this Act, the aboriginal and treaty rights referred to in subsection (1) are guaranteed equally to male and female persons.

17. See Lenowitz (2022) for a discussion of the circumstances under which constitutional ratification referendums fail, sometimes undermining carefully wrought bargains.

18. According to Dwight G. Newman's analysis of the duty to consult from *Haida Nation*, "The structuring of negotiation will be dependent on the circumstances that give rise to claims for greater or lesser bargaining power by the different parties. It is appropriate that Aboriginal communities with relatively stronger *prima facie* claims, or whose claims are more seriously affected, have greater power in the relevant negotiation processes. . . . An Aboriginal rights claim of little *prima facie* strength in the context of a near-trivial impact on the community would arguably not give rise to a moral reason to create any bargaining power at all for the Aboriginal community, yet the duty to consult doctrine would nonetheless create some rights" (Newman 2019, 30).

19. Borrows, for instance, argues that "Indigenous self-determination does not animate Canadian legislation in any meaningful way," and that in fact provincial autonomy has come at the expense of Indigenous agency (Borrows 2016, 165.

20. Although the fiduciary account of the Crown's duty suggests that the Crown has a special responsibility to attend to the interests of its beneficiaries, this has not always been clear: courts have sometimes held that the "fiduciary duty to consult is a two-way street," reflecting a certain discomfort with characterizing the relationship as a fiduciary one rather than one of mutual negotiation (Henderson 2006, 909).

21. By contrast, see Roberto Gargarella's critical assessment of Latin American constitutionalism's treatment of Indigenous groups' rights under a "mixed constitution" approach: "One has reasons to resist . . . bargaining, taking into account

that we are dealing with some fundamental interests that require unconditional respect, rather than mere haggling" (Gargarella 2013, 185).

22. The court cannot dictate the settlement position—and as such, the court declined to direct the Minister to "consider all possible options including the acquisition of third-party interests in the Culbertson Tract [relevant land] and returning the land to the applicant." Yet though the court denied there was sufficient evidentiary foundation to find a breach of the duty of good faith, the court did indicate that the applicant may wish to "return to this court advance the argument that the settlement negotiations should be examined and that they would, in turn, establish the breach of the duty."

23. Constitutional boilerplate may also constitute signaling to the international community the intention to uphold human rights norms (Farber 2002; Ginsburg 2013). Law and Versteeg argue that constitutional conformity to a template is a "rational strategy for weaker states . . . as a means of currying favor with dominant states and securing recognition from the international community" (Law and Versteeg 2011, 1178). Of course, this is self-defeating. If this language became mandatory for states to receive international recognition, the value of these provisions as genuine signals of the commitment of the regime to abide by them (and to treat fundamental interests as such) would be weakened. Moreover, if powerful states insisted that weaker ones include certain provisions as a condition of aid or recognition, one might worry that the constitution-making process would be tainted by duress. That said, the extent to which this imposition constitutes a defeat to constitutional enforcement is likely to be a function of the substantive content of these norms. If they help a fledgling state achieve the equitable treatment of interests standard, concerns about duress may be obviated by the prospective benefits for democratic bargaining.

24. However, Arato also holds that fair bargaining does require an "interactive framework," unavailable except by persuasion.

25. Elster's example of the vote on bicameralism during the French Revolution clarifies how duress may operate in a constitution-making process. The Monarchiens sought to create a constitutional monarchy, providing the King an absolute veto and creating a bicameral legislature. Large majorities defeated these proposals: the left because of the worry that the aristocracy would control the upper house, and the right because of the hope that a unicameral legislature would devolve into anarchy, generating calls for restoration of the ancien régime (Elster 2012, 32). By demanding a roll-call vote, the left also threatened to expose supporters of bicameralism to popular violence. Elster cites the following passage:

> Some deputies from the third estate have told me, I do not want my wife and children to have their throats cut. The bicameralist proposal had yet another kind of adversary, those who regret the ancien régime and want the new one

to be so bad that it cannot subsist. I have received on this topic confidential communications that I met with neither gratitude nor politeness. These are two strange bases for a constitution, the fear of being assassinated and the desire to make it collapse. (Lally-Tollendal 179c, 141, cited in Elster 2012)

The main question here is whether visceral fear, in this case the fear of assassination, means that the resulting constitution derives from duress; the second desire, the "desire to make it collapse," is what we have characterized as a violation of good faith.

3. The Scope and Limits of Legislative Bargaining

1. See Rawls (1993; 1995) and Habermas (1995); see also Knight and Schwartzberg (2020) and this book's Introduction and Chapter 1 for discussion.

2. In a large literature, see Baron and Ferejohn (1989), Laver and Schofield (1990), Laver and Shepsle (1990), and Austen-Smith and Banks (2005).

3. In a large literature, see Stone (2011), Guerrero (2014), Gastil and Wright (2018), Landemore (2020), and Abizadeh (2021).

4. In part for this reason, Landa and Pevnick (2021) identify random selection as especially prone to capture.

5. In defending partisanship, Jonathan White and Lea Ypi specifically bracket the organizational form that parties should take: rather, they support "a practice that involves citizens acting to promote certain shared normative commitments according to a distinctive interpretation of the common good" (White and Ypi 2011, 382). Although this is an unobjectionable vision of partisanship, few parties would characterize their agendas as failing to promote the common good or as promoting merely factional advantage against others; even neo-Nazi parties typically characterize their ambition as promoting the common good of the nation against the putative distortions of Jewish elites.

6. Shortly after this book went to press, Rep. Matt Gaetz (R-FL) used the "motion to vacate" to oust House Speaker Kevin McCarthy (R-CA); after three weeks of failed nominations, the House elected Rep. Mike Johnson (R-LA). It is still too soon to know whether the change in the motion to vacate will produce a structural change in the distribution of power in the House.

7. For instance, the 456 pages of the 2008 *House Ethics Manual* allude only once to the use of threats "to retaliate against a fellow Member because of the Member's vote on particular legislation," and there only in a subclause of a long list of the circumstances in which Rule 23, Clause 1 (requiring that a member, officers, or employees of the House "shall conduct himself at all times in a manner that shall reflect creditably on the House") has been invoked. We return to this rule in the conclusion to this chapter.

8. There is a substantial literature on the obligatory force of "coerced" and "forced" promises. We are less interested in the moral quality of the obligations that capitulation to threats and acceptance of offers generate on the part of the recipient, and more interested in the characteristics of the threats and offers themselves: both the action that the threat or offer seeks to elicit, and the form that the threat or offer takes.

9. Nozick (1969) disagrees; coercion must be successful to be identified as such.

10. Wertheimer (1987) describes this as a "phenomenological" baseline—in essence, what the member believes should happen.

11. From a "moralized" baseline perspective, of course, it is possible that Murkowski and the Alaskans have no justified claim to Republican support. If such drilling would cause environmental harm and such harm was not outweighed by other benefits, it is possible that they should not consider Republican support to be part of their baseline, even if on a "phenomenological" account of the baseline they would. We bracket this consideration just for the sake of clarity.

12. We thank Daniel Viehoff for this example.

13. For this reason, some people call for the authorization of a new Defense Base Closure and Realignment Commission, which presents prospective closures as a "take it or leave it" package to Congress and the president. We disagree: although a BRAC (Base Realignment and Closure) Commission could make recommendations, we believe this is a matter for a legislature to determine, and a commission would restrict the ability of legislators to bargain on behalf of the interests of their constituents.

14. One question is whether particularly poor districts might be especially vulnerable to such coercive offers; we accept that differently situated districts might experience offers and threats more acutely.

15. The classic characterization of "dirty hands" is offered by Walzer (1973); see also Williams (1978), Parrish (2009), Beerbohm (2018), and Hall and Sabl (2022).

16. We are grateful to Kevin Elliott for pressing us on this point.

17. Although we cannot take this issue at length, note that this is a reason to resist supermajority rules such as the cloture rule governing the Senate filibuster (Schwartzberg 2014; 2018).

18. "MILESTONE: Most Closed Congress in US History," https://democrats-rules.house.gov/press-release/milestone-most-closed-congress-us-history.

19. We are grateful to Senator Merkley and his long-time chief of staff, Mike Zamore, for sharing this anecdote with us, which is scheduled to appear just prior to the publication of this work in their own book, *Filibustered! How to Fix the Broken Senate and Save America* (Merkley and Zamore 2024). Of course, this anecdote also suggests that whereas information-restricting rules preclude representatives from engaging in further exchanges that could satisfy the interests of competing groups, potentially distributing benefits more equitably, certain beneficial bargains also might not emerge if subject to an open rule.

20. Eric Lipton, "With No Warning, House Republicans Vote to Hobble Independent Ethics Office," *New York Times*, January 2, 2017, https://www.nytimes.com/2017/01/02/us/politics/with-no-warning-house-republicans-vote-to-hobble-independent-ethics-office.html; Susan David, "House GOP Votes to Strip Independence from Congressional Ethics Office," *NPR*, January 2, 2017, https://www.npr.org/2017/01/02/507955013/house-gop-votes-to-strip-independence-from-congressional-ethics-office.

4. Interpretation, Implementation, and Enforcement

1. Nothing in our analysis hinges on this choice of the US system. We employ it because of its familiarity as well as the fact that it explicitly distinguishes the different tasks of governance and how they are distributed among government officials. In the course of our analysis, we will demonstrate how the institutional distribution of the US system implicates questions of independence and accountability among these officials. As we will argue, this distribution significantly influences the relative bargaining power of the relevant officials. We could make a similar assessment of any other democracy's system of distribution. The nature of the analysis would be the same, but we expect that the conclusions about the relative distribution of bargaining power might be different.

2. See Biskupic (2019) for a detailed account of the bargaining that took place among the justices in this case.

3. Justifications of constitutional review that appeal to the moral deliberations of justices include Dworkin (1986; 1996) and Rawls (1993). Gutmann and Thompson (1996) specifically argue that the deliberative quality of judicial decision-making should extend to legislatures. For an argument drawing on the judicial bargaining literature to demonstrate that deliberative democrats tend to romanticize the courts, see Sen (2013).

4. For a review of the literature, see Beim, Cameron, and Kornhauser (2010); Bonneau et al. (2007); Carrubba et al. (2012); and Clark and Lauderdale (2010).

5. These may be concurrences in judgment, regular concurrences, concurrences in part and dissents in part, dissents, or memoranda opinions.

6. The importance of strategic threats for judicial bargaining was further demonstrated in the recent US Supreme Court case *Dobbs v. Jackson Women's Health Organization* (No. 19-1392, 597 U.S. ___ [2022]). During the course of the court's collegial deliberations on this case, someone released a preliminary draft opinion to the public. The question of who released the draft has not been answered. But a strong argument can be made that it was strategically released by a justice (or one of their representatives) on either side of the debate as a means of influencing justices who were not yet set on their position on the merits. We can hardly imagine a more obvious instance of strategic behavior on a collegial court than this.

7. See Lax and Rader (2015) for an excellent review of these findings.

8. What these differing approaches do suggest is that any legislature interested in the future implications of judicial interpretations of its statutes should be as explicit as possible about the purposes and goals of its enactments. A commitment to legislative supremacy would seem to entail a commitment to clarity and precision in statutory draftsmanship.

9. See, for example, Gely and Spiller (1990), Ferejohn and Weingast (1992), and Eskridge and Ferejohn (1992).

10. By contrast, Seana Shiffrin (2021) argues that if state laws manifest new discretionary interests (departing from the status quo), and if state actors cannot demonstrate the consistency of such interests throughout the fabric of their law to the satisfaction of courts, they ought to enjoy little weight in constitutional balancing tests. Evidence of the "strength and sincerity" of the state's interest must be provided, potentially requiring a showing that a state has adopted a serious approach to securing the interest over time. Although we accept the possibility of pretextual claims of state interests, we do not think courts are capable of determining the sincerity of state actors' motivations to realize certain interests over time, and so instead would focus on a narrower set of procedural questions for review.

11. It is also similar to the "due process of lawmaking" approach proposed by Linde (1976).

12. Our support of a structural due process approach also shares an intuition with John Hart Ely's (1980) work on judicial review in a democracy. Both put the emphasis on the procedural analysis of the legislative process. But, while Ely focused primarily on the protection of individual rights and the facilitation of representation of minorities, we propose a broader scope of analysis that highlights the overall structure of political bargaining and its influence on the effectiveness of democratic decision-making institutions.

13. The literature on the complexity of the role of experts in a democratic society is voluminous. We do not have the space to sort out all these issues here. But we do recommend two recent attempts to assess the role of experts that share our concern with the institutional framework necessary to legitimize their participation in democratic decision-making: Moore (2017) and Pamuk (2021).

14. See Cameron (2000) for a good overview of this literature.

15. It is, of course, possible that these groups might also be subject to capture, and—as in our discussion of inclusive constitutionalism—we do not recommend that they have a direct say, because of the risk that they will themselves be subject to the disproportionate influence of those able to participate. Nonetheless, we do think that such bodies have a role to play in identifying interests and potentially increasing the costs on those who would seek to undermine the equitable treatment of interests. For a discussion of the various ways in which power can be dispersed and the role of deliberation in administrative decision-making, see Bagg (2021) and Bagg (forthcoming).

16. In Chapter 5 we consider just such a question, when we assess whether there is a value underlying plea-bargaining that overweighs the normative problems associated with the practice.

5. Bargaining "On the Ground"

1. The *U.S. Federal Sentencing Guidelines* explicitly allows for such reductions in the case of federal crimes (Federal Rules of Criminal Procedure 11[c][1], 2017).

2. This type of bargain is especially relevant to systems like the US federal system in which many crimes are associated with mandatory minimum sentences (Federal Rules of Criminal Procedure 11[c][1][A], 2017).

Conclusion

1. For House Appropriations Committee funding requests for Fiscal Year 2022, see https://democrats-appropriations.house.gov/transparency/fiscal-year-2022.

2. For Congressionally Directed Spending Requests in 2023, see https://www.appropriations.senate.gov/congressionally-directed-spending-requests.

3. There has been a recent revival of interest in research on the implications of economic antitrust enforcement for democracy. See, for example, "Antitrust in the Age of Concentrated Power," a special issue of *Politics and Society* (2023). This research raises important questions about how antitrust enforcement against market actors can indirectly influence the accumulation of political power in a democratic society. This research is related in important ways to our arguments about political bargaining. However, our analysis is somewhat different in that we are arguing that a commitment to democracy supports the creation and maintenance of explicitly *political* antitrust enforcement, entailing an analysis of the direct effects of power asymmetries (not limited to economic power) on the effectiveness of democratic institutions.

REFERENCES

Abizadeh, Arash. 2021. "Representation, Bicameralism, Political Equality, and Sortition: Reconstituting the Second Chamber as a Randomly Selected Assembly." *Perspectives on Politics* 19, no. 3: 791–806.

Ackerman, Bruce. 1993. *We the People.* Vol 1, *Foundations.* Cambridge, MA: Harvard University Press.

Alschuler, Albert. 1968. "The Prosecutor's Role in Plea Bargaining." *The University of Chicago Law Review* 36, no. 1: 50–112.

———. 1981. "The Changing Plea Bargaining Debate." *California Law Review* 69, no. 3: 652–731.

Anderson, Elizabeth. 1999. "What Is the Point of Equality?" *Ethics* 109: 287–337.

Angelo, A. H., and E. P. Ellinger. 1992. "Unconscionable Contracts: A Comparative Study of the Approaches in England, France, Germany, and the United States." *Loyola of Los Angeles International and Comparative Law Review* 14, no. 3: 455–506.

Arato, Andrew. 2009. *Constitution Making Under Occupation.* New York: Columbia University Press. https://doi.org/10.7312/arat14302.

Austen-Smith, David, and Jeffrey S. Banks. 2005. "Legislative Bargaining." In *Positive Political Theory II,* 193–252. Strategy and Structure. Ann Arbor: University of Michigan Press.

Bagenstos, Samuel R. 2006. "The Structural Turn and the Limits of Antidiscrimination Law." *California Law Review* 94, no. 1: 1–48.

Bagg, Samuel. 2021. "Fighting Power with Power: The Administrative State as a Weapon Against Concentrated Private Power." *Social Philosophy and Policy* 38, no. 1: 220–43.

———. Forthcoming. *The Dispersion of Power: A Critical Realist Theory of Democracy.* New York: Oxford University Press.

Baldwin, John, and Michael McConville. 1979. "Plea Bargaining and Plea Negotiation in England." *Law and Society Review* 13, no. 2: 287–307.

Baranski, Andrzej, Nicholas Haas, and Rebecca Morton. 2023. "Pork versus Policy: Experimental Evidence on Majoritarian Bargaining with Real-World Consequences." *The Journal of Politics* 85, no. 2: 537–52.

Barnhizer, Daniel D. 2005. "Inequality of Bargaining Power." *University of Colorado Law Review* 76, no. 1: 139–241.

Baron, David P., and John A. Ferejohn. 1989. "Bargaining in Legislatures." *The American Political Science Review* 83, no. 4: 1181–1206. https://doi.org /10.2307/1961664.

Barry, Brian. 1991. *Theories of Justice*. Berkeley: University of California Press.

Bar-Siman-Tov, Ittai. 2011. "The Puzzling Resistance to Judicial Review of the Legislative Process." *Boston University Law Review* 91, no. 6: 1915–74.

Bartels, Brandon, and Christopher Johnston. 2020. *Curbing the Court: Why the Public Constrains Judicial Independence*. New York: Cambridge University Press.

Beerbohm, Eric. 2018. "The Problem of Clean Hands: Negotiated Compromise in Lawmaking." In *Compromise*, edited by Jack Knight. NOMOS, LIX. New York: NYU Press.

Beim, Deborah, Charles Cameron, and Lewis Kornhauser. 2010. "Policy and Disposition Coalitions on the Supreme Court of the United States." Paper presented at the 5th Annual Conference on Empirical Legal Studies, October 23, 2010. http://dx.doi.org/10.2139/ssrn.1641542.

Beitz, Charles. 1989. *Political Equality: An Essay in Democratic Theory*. Princeton, NJ: Princeton University Press.

Bianco, William T., Ivan Jeliazkov, and Itai Sened. 2004. "The Uncovered Set and the Limits of Legislative Action." *Political Analysis* 12, no. 3: 256–76. https://doi.org/10.1093/pan/mph018.

Binder, Sarah A. 2010. "A Primer on Self-Executing Rules." *Brookings Institution* (blog). March 17, 2010. https://www.brookings.edu/blog/up -front/2010/03/17/a-primer-on-self-executing-rules/.

Biskupic, Joan. 2019. *The Chief: The Life and Turbulent Times of Chief Justice John Roberts*. New York: Basic Books.

Blake, Aaron. 2019. "Thom Tillis's Remarkable Flip-Flop on Trump's National Emergency and 4 Others Who Also Backed off." *Washington Post*, March 14, 2019. https://www.washingtonpost.com/politics/2019/03/14/thom-tilliss-re markable-flip-flop-trumps-national-emergency-others-who-also-backed-off/.

Bohman, James, and William Rehg. 1997. *Deliberative Democracy: Essays on Reason and Politics*. Cambridge, MA.: MIT Press.

Bonneau, Chris W., Thomas H. Hammond, Forrest Maltzman, and Paul J. Wahlbeck. 2007. "Agenda Control, the Median Justice, and the Majority Opinion on the U.S. Supreme Court." *American Journal of Political Science* 51, no.4: 890–905.

Borrows, John. 2016. *Freedom and Indigenous Constitutionalism*. Toronto: University of Toronto Press.

Bowers, Josh. 2016. "Plea Bargaining's Baselines." *William and Mary Law Review* 57, no. 4: 1083–1146.

Bowler, Shaun, David M. Farrell, and Richard S. Katz. 1999. "Party Cohesion, Party Discipline, and Parliaments." In *Party Discipline and Parliamentary Government*, edited by Shaun Bowler, David M. Farrell, and Richard S. Katz, 3–22. Columbus: Ohio State University Press.

Buchanan, Allen E. 1991. *Secession: The Morality of Political Divorce from Fort Sumter to Lithuania and Quebec*. Boulder, CO: Westview Press.

———. 1998. "Democracy and Secession." In *National Self-Determination and Secession*, edited by Margaret Moore, 14–33. Oxford: Oxford University Press.

Buchanan, James, and Geoffrey Brennan. 1985. *The Collected Works of James M. Buchanan*. Vol. 10, *The Reason of Rules*. Indianapolis: Liberty Fund.

Buchanan, James, and Gordon Tullock. 1962. *The Calculus of Consent: Logical Foundations of Constitutional Democracy*. Ann Arbor: University of Michigan Press.

Bulman-Pozen, Jessica, and Miriam Seifter. 2021. "The Democracy Principle in State Constitutions." *Michigan Law Review* 119 (January): 859.

Cameron, Charles M. 2000. *Veto Bargaining: Presidents and the Politics of Negative Power*. Political Economy of Institutions and Decisions. Cambridge: Cambridge University Press.

Cameron, Charles, and Nolan McCarty. 2004. "Models of Vetoes and Veto Bargaining." *Annual Review of Political Science* 7, no. 1: 409–35.

Carey, John M, and Matthew Soberg Shugart. 1995. "Incentives to Cultivate a Personal Vote: A Rank Ordering of Electoral Formulas." *Electoral Studies* 14, no. 4: 417–39.

Caro, Robert. (2013). *The Years of Lyndon Johnson*. 3 vols. New York: Knopf.

Carroll, Royce, and Henry A. Kim. 2010. "Party Government and the 'Cohesive Power of Public Plunder.'" *American Journal of Political Science* 54, no. 1: 34–44.

Carroll, Royce, and Monika Nalepa. 2020. "The Personal Vote and Party Cohesion: Modeling the Effects of Electoral Rules on Intraparty Politics." *Journal of Theoretical Politics* 32, no. 1: 36–69.

———. 2021. "When Does the Personal Vote Matter for Party Loyalty? The Conditional Effects of Candidate-Centred Electoral Systems." *Parliamentary Affairs* 74, no. 1: 102–20.

Carrubba, Cliff, Barry Friedman, Andrew D. Martin, and Georg Vanberg. 2012. "Who Controls the Content of Supreme Court Opinions?" *American Journal of Political Science* 56, no. 2: 400–412.

Chapman, Emilee Booth. 2020. "New Challenges for a Normative Theory of Parties and Partisanship." *Representation* 57, no. 3: 1–16. https://doi.org/10.1080/00344893.2020.1738539.

Christiano, Thomas. 2008. *The Constitution of Equality*. Oxford: Oxford University Press.

Clark, Tom, and Benjamin Lauderdale. 2010. "Locating Supreme Court Opinions in Doctrine Space." *American Journal of Political Science* 54, no. 10: 871–90.

Cohen, Amy J. 2020. "A Labor Theory of Negotiation: From Integration to Value Creation." *Journal of Law and Political Economy* 1, no. 1: 147–84. https://doi.org/10.5070/LP61150260.

Cohen, Joshua. 1989. "Deliberation and Democratic Legitimacy." In *The Good Polity*, edited by Alan Hamlin and Philip Pettit, 17–34. Oxford: Blackwell.

Committee on Standards of Official Conduct. 2004. "Investigation of Certain Allegations Related to Voting on the Medicare Prescription Drug, Improvement, and Modernization Act of 2003." House of Representatives. https://www.congress.gov/108/crpt/hrpt722/CRPT-108hrpt722.pdf.

———. 2008. *House Ethics Manual*. Washington, DC: Committee on Ethics.

Cox, Gary W., and Mathew D. McCubbins. 2005. *Setting the Agenda: Responsible Party Government in the U.S. House of Representatives*. Cambridge: Cambridge University Press.

"CQ Press Supreme Court Collection." 2022. https://library.cqpress.com/scc/.

Crenshaw, Kimberle. 1989. "Demarginalizing the Intersection of Race and Sex: A Black Feminist Critique of Antidiscrimination Doctrine, Feminist Theory and Antiracist Politics." *University of Chicago Legal Forum* 1989, no. 1: 139–67.

Crespo, Andrew Manuel. 2018. "The Hidden Law of Plea Bargaining." *Columbia Law Review* 118, no. 5: 1303–1424.

Curry, James M. 2015. *Legislating in the Dark: Information and Power in the House of Representatives*. Chicago: The University of Chicago Press.

Dagan, Hanoch, and Michael Heller. 2017. *The Choice Theory of Contracts*. Cambridge: Cambridge University Press.

Dahl, Robert. 2006. *A Preface to Democratic Theory*. Expanded Edition. Chicago: The University of Chicago Press.

Daughety, Andrew, and Jennifer Reinganum. 2020. "Reducing Unjust Convictions: Plea Bargaining, Trial, and Evidence Disclosure." *Journal of Law, Economics and Organization* 36, no. 2: 378–414.

David, Susan. 2017. "House GOP Votes to Strip Independence from Congressional Ethics Office." *NPR*. https://www.npr.org/2017/01/02/507955013/house-gop-votes-to-strip-independence-from-congressional-ethics-office.

Dawson, James, and Sam Kleiner. 2015. "Curbing Lettermarks." *Yale Journal on Regulation* 32, no. 1: 201–10.

DeCell, Carrie. 2011. "Deweyan Democracy and the Administrative State." *Harvard Law Review* 125, no. 2.

Dervan, Lucian R. 2019. "Bargained Justice: The History and Psychology of Plea Bargaining and the Trial Penalty." *Federal Sentencing Reporter* 31, no. 4–5: 239–47.

Dewey, John. 1954. *The Public and Its Problems*. Athens, OH: Swallow Press.

Dickson, Jamie D. 2019. *The Honour and Dishonour of the Crown: Making Sense of Aboriginal Law in Canada*. Vancouver: UBC Press.

Diermeier, Daniel, and Timothy J. Feddersen. 1998. "Cohesion in Legislatures and the Vote of Confidence Procedure." *The American Political Science Review* 92, no. 3: 611–21.

Doran, Michael. 2010. "The Closed Rule." *Emory Law Journal* 59, no. 6: 1363–1454.

Drutman, Lee. 2016. "The Freedom Caucus Is (Sort of) Right." *Washington Monthly* (blog). January 10, 2016. http://washingtonmonthly.com/2016/01/10/the-freedom-caucus-is-sort-of-right/.

Du Bois, W. E. B. 1999. *Darkwater: Voices from Within the Veil*. New York: Dover.

Dworkin, Ronald. 1986. *Law's Empire*. Cambridge, MA: The Belknap Press of Harvard University Press.

———. 1996. *Freedom's Law: The Moral Reading of the American Constitution*. Cambridge, MA: Harvard University Press.

———. 2002. *Sovereign Virtue*. Cambridge, MA: Harvard University Press.

Edkins, Vanessa A., and Allison D. Redlich. 2019. "Introduction: A System of Pleas." In *A System of Pleas*, edited by Vanessa Edkins and Allison Redlich, 1–10. Oxford: Oxford University Press.

Eisenberg, Melvin. 2009. "The Role of Fault in Contract Law: Unconscionability, Unexpected Circumstances, Interpretation, Mistake and Nonperformance." *Michigan Law Review* 107, no. 8: 1413–30.

Elliott, Kevin J. 2023. *Democracy for Busy People*. Chicago: The University of Chicago Press.

Elster, Jon. 1979. *Ulysses and the Sirens: Studies in Rationality and Irrationality*. Cambridge: Cambridge University Press.

———. 2000a. "Arguing and Bargaining in Two Constituent Assemblies." *University of Pennsylvania Journal of Constitutional Law* 2: 345–421.

———. 2000b. *Ulysses Unbound*. New York: Cambridge University Press.

———. 2012. "Constitution-Making and Violence." *Journal of Legal Analysis* 4, no. 1: 7–39.

Elster, Jon, Claus Offe, and Ulrich K. Preuss. 1998. *Institutional Design in Post-Communist Societies: Rebuilding the Ship at Sea*. Cambridge: Cambridge University Press.

Ely, John Hart. 1980. *Democracy and Distrust: A Theory of Judicial Review.* Cambridge, MA: Harvard University Press.

Epstein, Lee, and Jack Knight. 1998. *The Choices Justices Make.* Washington, DC: CQ Press.

Eskridge, William, and John Ferejohn. 1992. "Making the Deal Stick: Enforcing the Original Constitutional Structure of Lawmaking in the Modern Regulatory State." *Journal of Law, Economics, & Organization* 8, no. 1: 165–89.

Eskridge, William, and Philip Frickey. 2012. *Cases and Materials on Statutory Interpretation.* St. Paul, MN: West Academic Publishing.

Evans, Diana. 2004. *Greasing the Wheels: Using Pork Barrel Projects to Build Majority Coalitions in Congress.* Cambridge: Cambridge University Press.

Farber, Daniel A. 2002. "Rights as Signals." *The Journal of Legal Studies* 31, no. 1: 83–98.

Farnsworth, Alan. 2004. *Contracts.* New York: Wolters Kluwer.

Farrell, Henry, and Abraham L. Newman. 2019. *Of Privacy and Power: The Transatlantic Struggle over Freedom and Security.* Princeton, NJ: Princeton University Press.

Feeley, Malcolm M. 1979. "Perspectives on Plea Bargaining." *Law and Society Review* 13, no. 2: 199–209.

Ferejohn, John, and Barry R. Weingast. 1992. "A Positive Theory of Statutory Interpretation." *International Review of Law and Economics* 12, no. 2: 263–79.

Fisher, Roger, and William S. Ury. 2011. *Getting to Yes: Negotiating Agreement without Giving In.* 3rd ed. New York: Penguin Books.

Fishkin, James S. 2009. *When the People Speak: Deliberative Democracy and Public Consultation.* Oxford: Oxford University Press.

Follett, Mary Parker. 1998. *New State: Group Organization the Solution of Popular Government.* University Park: Pennsylvania State University Press.

Fréchette, Guillaume R., John H. Kagel, and Steven F. Lehrer. 2003. "Bargaining in Legislatures: An Experimental Investigation of Open versus Closed Amendment Rules." *The American Political Science Review* 97, no. 2: 221–32.

Frickey, Philip, and Steven S. Smith. 2001. "Judicial Review and the Legislative Process: Some Empirical and Normative Aspects of Due Process of Lawmaking." SSRN. https://doi.org/10.2139/ssrn.279433.

———. 2002. "Judicial Review, the Congressional Process, and the Federalism Cases: An Interdisciplinary Critique." *The Yale Law Journal* 111, no. 7: 1707–56.

Fried, Charles. 2015. *Contract as Promise.* New York: Oxford University Press.

Friedman, Lawrence. 1979. "Plea Bargaining in Historical Perspective." *Law and Society Review* 13, no. 2: 247–59.

Frisch, Scott A., and Sean Q. Kelly. 2011. *Cheese Factories on the Moon: Why Earmarks Are Good for American Democracy*. London: Routledge/Taylor & Francis.

Gailmard, Sean, and Jeffery A. Jenkins. 2007. "Negative Agenda Control in the Senate and House: Fingerprints of Majority Party Power." *The Journal of Politics* 69, no. 3: 689–700. https://doi.org/10.1111/j.1468-2508.2007.00568.x.

Gargarella, Roberto. 2013. *Latin American Constitutionalism, 1810–2010: The Engine Room of the Constitution*. New York: Oxford University Press.

Gastil, John, and Erik Olin Wright. 2018. "Legislature by Lot: Envisioning Sortition within a Bicameral System." *Politics & Society* 46, no. 3: 303–30. https://doi.org/10.1177/0032329218789886.

Gaus, Gerald F. 1996. *Justificatory Liberalism: An Essay on Epistemology and Political Theory*. Oxford: Oxford University Press.

Gauthier, David. 1987. *Morals by Agreement*. Oxford: Oxford University Press.

———. 1997. "Political Contractarianism." *Journal of Political Philosophy* 5, no. 2: 132–48. https://doi.org/10.1111/1467-9760.00027.

Gely, Rafael, and Pablo T. Spiller. 1990. "A Rational Choice Theory of Supreme Court Statutory Decisions with Applications to the 'State Farm' and 'Grove City Cases.'" *Journal of Law, Economics, & Organization* 6, no. 2: 263–300.

Ginsburg, Tom. 2013. "Constitutions as Contract, Constitutions as Charters." In *Social and Political Foundations of Constitutions*, edited by Denis J. Galligan and Mila Versteeg, 182–204. Comparative Constitutional Law and Policy. Cambridge: Cambridge University Press. https://doi.org/10.1017/CBO9781139507509.010.

Gluck, Abbe R., Mark Regan, and Erica Turret. 2020. "The Affordable Care Act's Litigation Decade." *Georgetown Law Journal* 108, no. 6: 1472–1534.

Guerrero, Alexander. 2014. "Against Elections: The Lottocratic Alternative." *Philosophy and Public Affairs* 42, no. 2: 135–78.

Gutmann, Amy, and Dennis Thompson. 1990. "Moral Conflict and Political Consensus." *Ethics* 101, no. 1: 64–88.

———. 1996. *Democracy and Disagreement*. Cambridge, MA: Belknap Press.

———. 2014. *The Spirit of Compromise*. Princeton, NJ: Princeton University Press.

Habermas, Jürgen. 1989. *The Structural Transformation of the Public Sphere*. Cambridge, MA: MIT Press.

———. 1995. "Reconciliation Through the Public Use of Reason: Remarks on John Rawls's Political Liberalism." *The Journal of Philosophy* 92, no. 3: 109–31. https://doi.org/10.2307/2940842.

Hadfield, Gillian K., and Barry R. Weingast. 2012. "What Is Law? A Coordination Model of the Characteristics of Legal Order." *Journal of Legal Analysis* 4, no. 2: 471–514. https://doi.org/10.1093/jla/las008.

Hahm, Chaihark, and Sung Ho Kim. 2010. "To Make 'We the People': Constitutional Founding in Postwar Japan and South Korea." *International Journal of Constitutional Law* 8, no. 4: 800–848. https://doi.org/10.1093/icon/mor007.

Haljan, David P. 1999. "A Constitutional Duty to Negotiate Amendments: Reference Re Secession of Quebec." *The International and Comparative Law Quarterly* 48, no. 2: 447–57.

Hall, Edward, and Andrew Sabl. 2022. "Introduction: Dirty Hands and Beyond." In *Political Ethics: A Handbook*, edited by Edward Hall and Andrew Sabl, 1–20. Princeton, NJ: Princeton University Press.

Hampton, Jean. 1980. "Contracts and Choices: Does Rawls Have a Social Contract Theory?" *The Journal of Philosophy* 77, no. 6: 315–38. https://doi.org/10.2307/2025640.

Hardin, Russell. 1989. "Why a Constitution?" In *The Federalist Papers and the New Institutionalism*, edited by Bernard Grofman and Donald Wittman, 100–20. New York: Agathon Press.

———. 1999. *Liberalism, Constitutionalism, and Democracy*. New York: Oxford University Press.

Hart, Vivienne. 2003. "Democratic Constitution Making." *United States Institute of Peace Special Report 107* (July). Washington, DC: USIP.org.

Henderson, James Youngblood. 2006. *First Nations Jurisprudence and Aboriginal Rights: Defining the Just Society / James Youngblood Henderson*. Saskatoon: Native Law Centre, University of Saskatchewan.

Herzog, Donald J. 2000. "'Externalities and Other Parasites.' Review of The Strategic Constitution, by R. D. Cooter, and Constitutional Democracy, by D. C. Mueller." *University of Chicago Law Review* 67, no. 3: 895–924.

Hirschman, Albert. 1972. *Exit, Voice and Loyalty*. Cambridge, MA: Harvard University Press.

Hoehn, Felix. 2020. "The Duty to Negotiate and the Ethos of Reconciliation." *Saskatchewan Law Review* 83, no. 1: 1–44.

Holmes, Stephen. 1997. *Passions and Constraint: On the Theory of Liberal Democracy*. Chicago: The University of Chicago Press.

Huber, John D. 1996. "The Vote of Confidence in Parliamentary Democracies." *The American Political Science Review* 90, no. 2: 269–82. https://doi.org/10.2307/2082884.

Ingham, Sean. 2019. *Rule by Multiple Majorities*. New York: Cambridge University Press.

Johnson, James. 1991. "Habermas on Strategic and Communicative Action." *Political Theory* 19, no. 2: 181–201. https://doi.org/10.1177/0090591791019002003.

Kam, Christopher. 2011. *Party Discipline and Parliamentary Politics*. Cambridge: Cambridge University Press.

———. 2014. "Party Discipline." In *Oxford Handbook of Legislative Studies*, edited by Shane Martin, Thomas Saafeld, and Kaare Strom, 399–417. Oxford: Oxford University Press. http://www.oxfordhandbooks.com /view/10.1093/oxfordhb/9780199653010.001.0001/oxfordhb-978019 9653010-e-020.

Kim, Seung Min, and Erica Werner. 2019. "Trump Administration Seeks GOP Support on Border Wall as Senators Confront Hard Choices." *Washington Post*, March 5, 2019. https://www.washingtonpost.com/politics/trump-ad ministration-seeks-gop-support-on-border-wall-as-senators-confront-hard -choices/2019/03/05/2d4e1b4a-3f81-11e9-9361-301ffb5bd5e6_story.html.

Kingsbury, Benedict. 2002. "Competing Conceptual Approaches to Indigenous Group Issues in New Zealand Law." *The University of Toronto Law Journal* 52, no. 1: 101–34.

Kipnis, Kenneth. 1976. "Criminal Justice and the Negotiated Plea." *Ethics* 86, no. 2: 93–106.

Knight, Jack, and Lee Epstein. 1996. "On the Struggle for Judicial Supremacy." *Law and Society Review* 30, no. 1: 87–130.

Knight, Jack, and James Johnson. 1994. "Aggregation and Deliberation: On the Possibility of Democratic Legitimacy." *Political Theory* 22, no. 2: 277–96.

———. 2011. *The Priority of Democracy: Political Consequences of Pragmatism*. Princeton, NJ: Princeton University Press.

Knight, Jack, and Melissa Schwartzberg. 2020. "Institutional Bargaining for Democratic Theorists (or How We Learned to Stop Worrying and Love Haggling)." *Annual Review of Political Science* 23, no. 1: 259–76.

Kolodny, Niko. 2014. "Rule over None II: Social Equality and the Justification of Democracy." *Philosophy and Public Affairs* 42, no. 4: 287–336.

Krehbiel, Keith. 1992. *Information and Legislative Organization*. Ann Arbor: University of Michigan Press.

———. 1993. "Where's the Party?" *British Journal of Political Science* 23, no. 2: 235–66.

Kymlicka, Will. 1998. "Multinational Federalism in Canada: Rethinking the Partnership." In *Beyond the Impasse*, edited by Roger Gibbons and Guy LaForest, 15–50. Montreal: Institute for Research on Public Policy.

Landa, Dimitri, and Ryan Pevnick. 2020. "Representative Democracy as Defensible Epistocracy." *American Political Science Review* 114, no. 1: 1–13. https://doi.org/10.1017/S0003055419000509.

Landemore, Hélène. 2020. *Open Democracy: Reinventing Popular Rule for the Twenty-First Century*. Princeton, NJ: Princeton University Press.

Laver, Michael, and Norman Schofield. 1990. *Multiparty Government: The Politics of Coalition in Europe*. Oxford: Oxford University Press.

Laver, Michael, and Kenneth A. Shepsle. 1990. "Coalitions and Cabinet Government." *The American Political Science Review* 84, no. 3: 873–90. https://doi.org/10.2307/1962770.

Law, David S. 2013. "The Myth of the Imposed Constitution." In *Social and Political Foundations of Constitutions*, edited by Denis J. Galligan and Mila Versteeg, 239–68. Comparative Constitutional Law and Policy. New York: Cambridge University Press. https://doi.org/10.1017/CBO9781139507509.013.

Law, David S., and Mila Versteeg. 2011. "The Evolution and Ideology of Global Constitutionalism." *California Law Review* 99, no. 5: 1163–1257.

Lax, Jeffrey, and Kelly Rader. 2015. "Bargaining Power in the Supreme Court: Evidence from Opinion Assignment and Vote Switching." *The Journal of Politics* 77, no. 3: 648–63.

Lazarus, Jeffrey. 2010. "Giving the People What They Want? The Distribution of Earmarks in the U.S. House of Representatives." *American Journal of Political Science* 54, no. 2: 338–53. https://doi.org/10.1111/j.1540-5907.2010.00434.x.

———. 2018. "Bringing Back Earmarks Could Grease the Wheels for Getting Bills Passed." *The Hill* (blog), April 18, 2018. https://thehill.com/blogs/congress-blog/economy-budget/383776-bringing-back-earmarks-could-grease-the-wheels-for-getting/.

Lee, Frances E. 2003. "Geographic Politics in the U.S. House of Representatives: Coalition Building and Distribution of Benefits." *American Journal of Political Science* 47, no. 4: 714–28. https://doi.org/10.2307/3186129.

Lenowitz, Jeffrey. 2022. *Constitutional Ratification without Reason*. New York: Oxford University Press.

Levinson, Daryl, and Richard Pildes. 2006. "Separation of Parties, Not Powers." *Harvard Law Review* 119, no. 8: 2311–86.

Li, Yuhui. 2019. *Dividing the Rulers: How Majority Cycling Saves Democracy*. Ann Arbor: University of Michigan Press.

Linde, Hans. 1976. "Due Process of Lawmaking." *Nebraska Law Review* 55, no. 2: 197–255.

Lipton, Eric. 2017. "With No Warning, House Republicans Vote to Hobble Independent Ethics Office." *New York Times*, January 2, 2017. https://www.nytimes.com/2017/01/02/us/politics/with-no-warning-house-republicans-vote-to-hobble-independent-ethics-office.html.

Lowi, Theodore J. 1979. *The End of Liberalism: The Second Republic of the United States*. 2nd ed. New York: Norton.

Lynch, Megan S. 2020. "Lifting the Earmark Moratorium: Frequently Asked Questions." CRS Report R45429. Washington, DC: Congressional Research Service.

Manin, Bernard. 1987. "On Legitimacy and Political Deliberation." *Political Theory* 15, no. 3: 338–68.

———. 1997. *The Principles of Representative Government*. Themes in the Social Sciences. Cambridge: Cambridge University Press.

Mansbridge, Jane. 2003. "Rethinking Representation." *American Political Science Review* 97, no. 4: 515–28. https://doi.org/10.1017/S0003055403000856.

———. 2011. "Clarifying the Concept of Representation." *American Political Science Review* 105, no. 3: 621–30. https://doi.org/10.1017/S0003055411000189.

Margalit, Avishai. 2010. *On Compromise and Rotten Compromises*. Princeton, NJ: Princeton University Press. http://www.jstor.org/stable/j.ctt7sxkv.

Markovits, Daniel. 2014. "Good Faith as Contract's Core Value." In *Philosophical Foundations of Contract Law*. Oxford: Oxford University Press. https://doi.org/10.1093/acprof:oso/9780198713012.003.0014.

Marks, Brian A. 1988. "A Model of Judicial Influence on Congressional Policymaking: *Grove City College v. Bell*." In *Working Papers in Political Science*. The Hoover Institution. Palo Alto, CA: Stanford University.

Martin, Lanny W., and Georg Vanberg. 2020. "Coalition Government, Legislative Institutions, and Public Policy in Parliamentary Democracies." *American Journal of Political Science* 64, no. 2: 325–40.

Martinson, Erica. 2017. "Trump Administration Threatens Retribution against Alaska over Murkowski Health Votes." *Anchorage Daily News*, July 27, 2017. https://www.adn.com/politics/2017/07/26/trump-administration-signals-that-murkowskis-health-care-vote-could-have-energy-repercussions-for-alaska/.

May, Kenneth O. 1952. "A Set of Independent Necessary and Sufficient Conditions for Simple Majority Decision." *Econometrica* 20, no. 4: 680–84.

Mayhew, David R. 1974. *Congress: The Electoral Connection*. New Haven, CT: Yale University Press.

McConnell, Michael W. 2010. "Michael W. McConnell: The Health Vote and the Constitution—II." *Wall Street Journal*, March 20, 2010. https://www.wsj.com/articles/SB10001424052748703580904575131460390057440.

McCubbins, Matthew D., Roger G. Noll, and Barry R. Weingast. 1987. "Administrative Procedures as Instruments of Political Control." *Journal of Law, Economics, & Organization* 3, no. 2: 243–77.

———. 1989. "Structure and Process, Politics and Policy: Administrative Arrangements and the Political Control of Agencies." *Virginia Law Review* 75, no. 2: 431–82. https://doi.org/10.2307/1073179.

McGann, Anthony J. 2006. *The Logic of Democracy: Reconciling Equality, Deliberation, and Minority Protection*. Ann Arbor: University of Michigan Press.

McKelvey, Richard D. 1986. "Covering, Dominance, and Institution-Free Properties of Social Choice." *American Journal of Political Science* 30, no. 2: 283–314. https://doi.org/10.2307/2111098.

Merkley, Jeff, and Mike Zamore. 2024. *Filibustered! How to Fix the Broken Senate and Save America*. New York: The New Press.

"MILESTONE: Most Closed Congress in US History." 2015. United States House of Representatives, Committee on Rules, Democrats. November 17, 2015. https://web.archive.org/web/20181227190455/https://democrats-rules.house.gov/press-release/milestone-most-closed-congress-us-history.

Miller, Nicholas R. 1983. "Pluralism and Social Choice." *The American Political Science Review* 77, no. 3: 734–47. https://doi.org/10.2307/1957271.

Mills, C. Wright. 1956. *The Power Elite*. New York: Oxford University Press.

Moe, Terry. 1985. "The Politicized Presidency." In *New Directions in American Politics*, edited by John E. Chubb and Paul E. Peterson, 235–71. Washington, DC: Brookings Institution.

Moore, Alfred. 2017. *Critical Elitism: Deliberation, Democracy, and the Problem of Expertise*. Cambridge: Cambridge University Press.

Moreau, Sophia Reibetanz. 2020. *Faces of Inequality: A Theory of Wrongful Discrimination*. New York: Oxford University Press.

Mueller, Dennis C. 1996. *Constitutional Democracy*. New York: Oxford University Press.

Newman, Dwight G. 2019. *Revising the Duty to Consult Aboriginal Peoples*. Saskatoon, SK: Purich Publishing.

Norman, Wayne. 1998. "The Ethics of Secession as the Regulation of Secessionist Politics." In *National Self-Determination and Secession*, edited by Margaret Moore, 34–61. Oxford: Oxford University Press. https://doi.org/10.1093/0198293844.003.0003.

Nozick, Robert. 1969. "Coercion." In *Philosophy, Science, and Method: Essays in Honor of Ernest Nagel*, edited by Sidney Morgenbesser, Patrick Suppes, and Morton White, 440–72. New York: St. Martin's Press.

Obama, Barack. 2020. *A Promised Land*. New York: Crown.

O'Leary, Brendan. 2019. "Making Constitutions in Deeply Divided Places." In *Comparative Constitution Making*, edited by David Landau and Hanna Lerner, 186–211. Cheltenham, UK: Edward Elgar Publishing.

Oman, Nathan B. 2016. *The Dignity of Commerce*. Chicago: The University of Chicago Press.

Ordeshook, Peter C. 1992. "Constitutional Stability." *Constitutional Political Economy* 3, no. 2: 137–75. https://doi.org/10.1007/BF02393118.

Osborne, Martin J., and Ariel Rubinstein. 1990. *Bargaining and Markets*. San Diego, CA: Academic Press.

Page, Scott E. 2010. *Diversity and Complexity*. Princeton, NJ: Princeton University Press.

Palmer, Matthew S. R. 2022. "Indigenous Rights: New Zealand." In *Constitutionalism in Context*, edited by David S. Law, 303–29. Comparative Constitutional Law and Policy. Cambridge: Cambridge University Press. https://doi.org/10.1017/9781108699068.015.

Pamuk, Zeynep. 2021. *Politics and Expertise*. Princeton, NJ: Princeton University Press. https://press.princeton.edu/books/hardcover/9780691218939/politics-and-expertise.

Parrish, John M. 2009. *Paradoxes of Political Ethics: From Dirty Hands to the Invisible Hand*. Cambridge: Cambridge University Press.

Pateman, Carole, and Charles W. Mills. 2007. *Contract and Domination*. Cambridge: Polity.

Pearson, Kathryn. 2015. *Party Discipline in the U.S. House of Representatives*. Ann Arbor: University of Michigan Press.

Pettit, Philip. 1997. *Republicanism: A Theory of Freedom and Government*. Oxford: Oxford University Press.

Posner, Eric. 2016. *Contract Law and Theory*. New York: Wolters Kluwer.

Przeworski, Adam. 1991. *Democracy and the Market*. New York: Cambridge University Press.

Rae, Douglas W. 1969. "Decision-Rules and Individual Values in Constitutional Choice." *The American Political Science Review* 63, no. 1: 40–56. https://doi.org/10.2307/1954283.

Rawls, John. 1971. *A Theory of Justice*. Cambridge, MA: Harvard University Press.

———. 1993. *Political Liberalism*. Cambridge, MA: Harvard University Press.

———. 1995. "Political Liberalism: Reply to Habermas." *The Journal of Philosophy* 92, no. 3: 132–80. https://doi.org/10.2307/2940843.

———. 2001. *Justice as Fairness: A Restatement*. Cambridge, MA: The Belknap Press of Harvard University Press.

Raz, Joseph. 1986. *The Morality of Freedom*. Oxford: Oxford University Press.

Reports of Cases Relating to Maritime Law. 1903. London: H. Cox.

Riker, William H. 1982. *Liberalism Against Populism*. Long Grove, IL: Waveland Press.

Rodriguez-Yong, Camilo A. 2011. "The Doctrines Of Unconscionability And Abusive Clauses: A Common Point Between Civil And Common Law Legal Traditions." *University of Oxford Comparative Law Forum* (blog). 2011. https://ouclf.law.ox.ac.uk/the-doctrines-of-unconscionability-and-abusive-clauses-a-common-point-between-civil-and-common-law-legal-traditions/.

Rosenblum, Nancy L. 2008. *On the Side of the Angels*. Princeton, NJ: Princeton University Press. https://doi.org/10.2307/j.ctt7stm2.

Sabl, Andrew. 2017. "Realist Liberalism: An Agenda." *Critical Review of International Social and Political Philosophy* 20, no. 3: 366–84. https://doi.org/10 .1080/13698230.2017.1293916.

Sanders, Lynn M. 1997. "Against Deliberation." *Political Theory* 25, no. 3: 347–76.

Satz, Debra. 2010. *Why Some Things Should Not Be for Sale: The Moral Limits of Markets*. Oxford: Oxford University Press.

Scanlon, T. M. 2018. *Why Does Inequality Matter?* New York: Oxford University Press.

Scheffler, Samuel. 2015. "The Practice of Equality." In *Social Equality: What It Means to Be Equals*, edited by Carina Fourie, Fabian Schuppert, and Ivo Wallimann-Helmer, 21–44. New York: Oxford University Press. https://doi .org/10.1093/acprof:oso/9780199331109.003.0002.

Schwartzberg, Melissa. 2007. *Democracy and Legal Change*. New York: Cambridge University Press.

———. 2014. *Counting the Many: The Origins and Limits of Supermajority Rule*. New York: Cambridge University Press.

———. 2018. "Uncompromising Democracy." In *Compromise*, edited by Jack Knight, 167–85. NOMOS, LIX. New York: NYU Press.

Scott, Robert E., and William J. Stuntz. 1992. "Plea Bargaining as Contract." *Yale Law Journal* 101, no. 8: 1909–68.

Searle, John R. 1969. *Speech Acts: An Essay in the Philosophy of Language*. London: Cambridge University Press.

Segal, Jeffrey A. 1997. "Separation-of-Powers Games in the Positive Theory of Congress and Courts." *The American Political Science Review* 91, no. 1: 28–44. https://doi.org/10.2307/2952257.

Segal, Jeffrey A., Chad Westerland, and Stefanie A. Lindquist. 2011. "Congress, the Supreme Court, and Judicial Review: Testing a Constitutional Separation of Powers Model." *American Journal of Political Science* 55, no. 1: 89–104.

Sen, Maya. 2013. "Courting Deliberation: The Role of Deliberative Democracy in the American Judicial System." *Notre Dame Journal of Law, Ethics and Public Policy* 27: 303–31.

Shapiro, Ian. 2003. *The State of Democratic Theory*. Princeton, NJ: Princeton University Press.

Shelby, Tommie. 2016. *Dark Ghettos*. Cambridge, MA: Harvard University Press.

Shiffrin, Seana Valentine. 2000. "Paternalism, Unconscionability Doctrine and Accommodation." *Philosophy and Public Affairs* 29, no. 3: 205–50.

———. 2007. "The Divergence of Contract and Promise." *Harvard Law Review* 120, no. 3: 708–53.

———. 2021. "Democratic Law." In *Democratic Law*, edited by Hannah Ginsborg, with commentaries by Niko Kolodny, Richard Rexford, Wayne Brooks, and Anna Stilz, 17–60. New York: Oxford University Press.

Sinclair, Barbara. 1997. *Unorthodox Lawmaking: New Legislative Processes in the U.S. Congress.* Washington, DC: CQ Press.

———. 2006. *Party Wars: Polarization and the Politics of National Policy Making.* Norman: University of Oklahoma Press.

Singer, Peter. 2011. *Practical Ethics.* Cambridge: Cambridge University Press.

Slattery, Brian. 2005. "Aboriginal Rights and the Honour of the Crown." *The Supreme Court Law Review: Osgoode's Annual Constitutional Cases Conference* 29.

Stears, Marc. 2007. "Liberalism and the Politics of Compulsion." *British Journal of Political Science* 37, no. 3: 533–53.

Stein, Michael B. 1997. "Improving the Process of Constitutional Reform in Canada: Lessons from the Meech Lake and Charlottetown Constitutional Rounds." *Canadian Journal of Political Science/Revue Canadienne de Science Politique* 30, no. 2: 307–38.

Stone, Peter. 2011. *The Luck of the Draw.* Oxford: Oxford University Press.

Sunstein, Cass R. 1985. "Interest Groups in American Public Law." *Stanford Law Review* 38, no. 1: 29–87.

———. 1991. "Constitutionalism and Secession." *University of Chicago Law Review* 58, no. 2: 633–70.

Thompson, Dennis F. 1995. *Ethics in Congress: From Individual to Institutional Corruption.* Washington, DC: Brookings Institution.

Tillis, Thom. 2019. "I Support Trump's Vision on Border Security. But I Would Vote against the Emergency." *Washington Post,* February 25, 2019. https://www.washingtonpost.com/opinions/2019/02/25/i-support-trumps-vision-border-security-i-would-vote-against-emergency/.

Tribe, Laurence H. 1975. "Structural Due Process." *Harvard Civil Rights-Civil Liberties Law Review* 10, no. 2: 269–321.

Tsebelis, George. 2002. *Veto Players.* Princeton, NJ: Princeton University Press. https://doi.org/10.2307/j.ctt7rvv7.

Tushnet, Mark. 2011. "Administrative Law in the 1930s: The Supreme Court's Accommodation of Progressive Legal Theory." *Duke Law Journal* 60, no. 7: 1565–1637.

United States Sentencing Commission. 2020. *Federal Sentencing: The Basics.* Washington, DC: U.S. Sentencing Commission.

Vogel, David. 2012. *The Politics of Precaution: Regulating Health, Safety, and Environmental Risks in Europe and the United States.* Princeton, NJ: Princeton University Press.

Waitangi Tribunal. 1999. "The Whanganui River Report." Wellington, New Zealand: GP Publications.

Waldron, Jeremy. 1999. *Law and Disagreement.* Oxford: Oxford University Press.

———. 2006. "The Core of the Case against Judicial Review." *The Yale Law Journal* 115, no. 6: 1346–1406. https://doi.org/10.2307/20455656.

Waldstein, Sophia. 2020. "Open-File Discovery: A Plea For Transparent Plea-Bargaining." *Temple Law Review* 92, no. 2: 517–49.

Walton, Richard E., and Robert B. McKersie. 1965. *A Behavioral Theory of Labor Negotiations*. New York: McGraw-Hill.

Walzer, Michael. 1973. "Political Action: The Problem of Dirty Hands." *Philosophy & Public Affairs* 2, no. 2: 160–80.

Warren, Mark E., and Jane Mansbridge. 2015. "Deliberative Negotiation." In *Political Negotiation: A Handbook*, edited by Jane Mansbridge and Cathie Jo Martin, 141–98. Washington, DC: Brookings Institution Press.

Weingast, Barry R. 1997. "The Political Foundations of Democracy and the Rule of Law." *The American Political Science Review* 91, no. 2: 245–63. https://doi.org/10.2307/2952354.

Weinstock, Daniel. 2001. "Constitutionalizing the Right to Secede." *Journal of Political Philosophy* 9, no. 2: 182–203. https://doi.org/10.1111/1467-9760.00124.

Werner, Erica, and John Wagner. 2019. "GOP Opposition to Emergency Declaration Grows as Trump Warns Lawmakers." *Washington Post*, February 28, 2019. https://www.washingtonpost.com/politics/trump-republicans-who-cross-him-on-national-emergency-are-at-great-jeopardy/2019/02/28/07d3d334-3b6a-11e9-a2cd-307b06d0257b_story.html.

Wertheimer, Alan. 1979. "Morality, Plea Bargaining and the Supreme Court." *Philosophy and Public Affairs* 8, no. 3: 203–34.

———. 1987. *Coercion*. Princeton, NJ: Princeton University Press.

———. 1992. "Unconscionability and Contracts." *Business Ethics Quarterly* 2, no. 4: 479–96. https://doi.org/10.2307/3857584.

White, Jonathan, and Lea Ypi. 2011. "On Partisan Political Justification." *American Political Science Review* 105, no. 2: 381–96.

Williams, Bernard. 1978. "Politics and Moral Character." In *Public and Private Morality*, edited by Stuart Hampshire, 55–74. Cambridge: Cambridge University Press.

Williams, Melissa S. 1998. *Voice, Trust, and Memory*. Princeton, NJ: Princeton University Press.

Wolin, Sheldon S. 1969. "Political Theory as a Vocation." *The American Political Science Review* 63, no. 4: 1062–82. https://doi.org/10.2307/1955072.

Wong, Scott, and Alexander Bolton. 2019. "GOP's Tillis Comes under Pressure for Taking on Trump." *The Hill* (blog). March 13, 2019. https://thehill.com/homenews/senate/433929-gops-tillis-comes-under-pressure-for-taking-on-trump/.

Young, Michael. 2013. "In Defense of Plea-Bargaining's Possible Morality." *Ohio Northern University Law Review* 40, no. 1: 251–77.

Zacka, Bernardo. 2017. *When the State Meets the Street: Public Service and Moral Agency*. Cambridge, MA: The Belknap Press of Harvard University Press.

ACKNOWLEDGMENTS

The idea for this book arose one day in the fall of 2014 in a contracts course, taught by Barry Adler, at the NYU School of Law, where Melissa Schwartzberg was studying under the auspices of an Andrew W. Mellon "New Directions" Fellowship. The bargaining theory of contracts seemed to explain at least some of the public bargains that political scientists usually study, and the defensive doctrines appeared to characterize the conditions under which they ought to be unenforceable. Melissa was tempted to begin writing immediately, but realized that practically everything she knew about institutional bargaining she had learned from Jack Knight, who had served as her senior thesis adviser at Washington University in St. Louis.

Melissa remains astonished that Jack agreed to coauthor the book.

In addition to the "New Directions" Fellowship, a Guggenheim Fellowship and NYU sabbatical funds provided leave for Melissa to write, for which she is very grateful. Jack gratefully acknowledges the support of Duke University sabbatical funds.

The first paper related to the book was presented at the inaugural Political Theory In/And/As Political Science conference at McGill University in the spring of 2018. The authors thank Jacob Levy, who served as the primary organizer of that conference, and as co-PI of the original PTPS project. Support from NYU and Duke enabled the development of a plan for the book while Jack served as a visiting scholar at NYU in 2018–2019, and allowed him to write an article version of the initial paper for the *Annual Review of Political Science*; the authors are grateful to Margaret Levy and Nancy Rosenblum for that invitation.

The University of Richmond generously hosted a book manuscript workshop in the fall of 2022: many thanks to the commentators, especially Claudio López-Guerra, for their advice and hospitality. The University of California San Diego also held a day-long event in spring 2022 in which three chapters received careful attention; thanks are due the graduate student commentators and faculty (including David Wiens, Sean Ingham, Zeynep Pamuk, and Sebastian Saiegh), who helped reframe some key arguments in the first half of the book. Participants in the Berkeley Law, Philosophy, and Political Theory Workshop, the King's College London Political Economy Seminar, and the Northwestern University Political Theory Workshop all offered helpful discussions of Chapter 3.

The authors are grateful for detailed comments on the manuscript from Lou Brown, Kevin Elliott, Henry Farrell, Jeffrey Lenowitz, Eric MacGilvray, Ryan Pevnick, and Daniel Viehoff, as well as from the two readers for Harvard University Press. Benjamin Brown Knight provided critical comments and editorial assistance at crucial stages. Many other colleagues and friends offered references, comments, and/or moral support, including Sam Bagg, Rick Brooks, J. Martin Daughtry, Yasmin Dawood, Patrick Egan, Jennifer Gandhi, Bryan Garsten, Sanford Gordon, Jonathan Gould, Catherine Hafer, Mark Hornung, Turkuler Isiksel, James Johnson, Kimuli Kasara, Alex Kirshner, Dimitri Landa, Jacob Levy, Jane Mansbridge, Karuna Mantena, Gwyneth McClendon, Samuel Moyn, Josiah Ober, Kim Phillips-Fein, Adam Przeworski, Arturas Rozenas, David Stasavage, and Anna Stilz.

The authors have had the great fortune to work with Sam Stark and Harvard University Press on this book. Sam has supported this project well beyond his duty as editor, providing substantive advice and even line edits, and the book would be poorer for his absence.

Melissa would like to thank her husband, David Jones, and her children, Isaiah and Leah Jones, for love and support throughout—even though writing this book has delayed a different one, with a dedication long ago promised to Izzy and Leah. Their patience has been noted. But this book exists instead, and does so in large part because Malka Schnaidman cared for Leah during COVID-19 school closures. The Schwartzberg-Jones family cannot adequately express its appreciation.

Melissa also thanks her extended family, Schwartzberg and Jones alike, for their love, especially through the challenging times of the past several years.

Melissa dedicates this book to her fathers: by birth, by marriage, and by scholarly engagement. Barry Schwartzberg's gimlet-eyed accounts of bargaining (which he describes instead as "begging") by his public-sector union, the New York State Public Employees Federation, surely played some role in this book's conception. In the later stages of writing, she engaged in imaginary conversations with her late father-in-law, Howard Jones, drawing on myriad discussions of bargaining in the Middle East, over rules in retirement communities, and with respect to the strategies of Chester County Democrats. Finally, even though this book is presentist and skeptical of deliberation, she hopes her *Doktorvater*, Bernard Manin, will not object to its dedication.

Jack would like to thank his wife, Margaret Louise Brown, and his son, Benjamin Brown Knight, for their love and support throughout the trying times in which this book was written. It would have been a very different book without them. He dedicates the book to Lou, who finally gets the dedication that she has deserved for many years.